P9-CEJ-728

Fiction is rooted in an act of faith: a presumption of an inherent significance in human activity, that makes daily life worth dramatizing and particularizing. There is even a shadowy cosmic presumption that the universe — the totality of what is, which includes our subjective impressions as well as objective data — composes a narrative and contains a poem, which our own stories and poems echo.

— John Updike

John Updike and Religion

The Sense of the Sacred and the Motions of Grace

Edited by

James Yerkes

William B. Eerdmans Publishing Company
Grand Rapids, Michigan / Cambridge, U.K.

255 Jefferson Ave. S.E., Grand Rapids, Michigan 49503 /
P.O. Box 163, Cambridge CB3 9PU U.K.

Printed in the United States of America

05 04 03 02 01 00 99 7 6 5 4 3 2 1

Library of Congress Cataloging-in-Publication Data

John Updike and religion: the sense of the sacred and the motions of grace /
edited by James Yerkes

p. cm.

Includes bibliographical references and index.

ISBN 0-8028-3873-1 (alk. paper)

1. Updike, John — Religion.
2. Christianity and literature — United States — History — 20th century.
3. Religion fiction, American — History and criticism.
4. Grace (Theology) in literature.
5. Holy, The, in literature.

I. Yerkes, James.

PS3571.P4.Z743 1999

813′.54 — dc21 99-04618

Grateful acknowledgment is made to Alfred A. Knopf, Inc., a Division of Random House, Inc., for permission to quote from the copyrighted works of John Updike.

To my students

at

Wheaton College
Earlham School of Religion
Mercer University Atlanta
Moravian College

who unfailingly have been

my teachers

Contents

Preface

This book of essays explores John Updike's understanding of religion in ordinary human experience, in the context of historic Christian witness, and in twentieth-century American culture. In his very first piece of autobiography, first published in 1962 and later titled "The Dogwood Tree: A Boyhood," Updike characterized religion as one of "the three great secret things" in human experience, the others being sex and art. Since then his literary production of more than fifty books in four main genres — novels, short stories, poetry, and critical essays — has consistently and insightfully explored a wide range of religious issues. The essays collected here evaluate the religious dimension of Updike's prodigious literary vision, what he calls "the sense of the sacred," and which, he observes, "certainly does play into one's art."

The three main sections of the book comprise fifteen original essays, five in each section, together with an introductory essay by John Updike, used with his special permission. The three sections explore this "sense of the sacred" as a pervasive dynamic in human experience, as what gives existential credibility to historic Christian witness, and as that which ultimately undergirds the peculiarly American religious understanding of cultural obligation and order. This study does not pretend to be exhaustive, but it is thoughtfully representative of the full range of Updike's literary production to date as it bears on issues of religion. Given the current interest in religious issues spawned by America's culture wars, it is our hope that this book will spark provocative and productive dialogue on those issues within the context of John Updike's unique literary vision, a widely honored authorial perspective that spans the last half of the twentieth century.

Especially noteworthy is the fact that a number of the essays focus on some of Updike's works considered by many establishment critics as among his worst: *S., Memories of the Ford Administration, Brazil,* and *Toward the End of Time.* Precisely because of this dismissal, a more careful consideration produces some very interesting insights. Balancing this emphasis on overlooked and avoided Updike writings is the emphasis on Updike's links to the classic texts of Hawthorne and Melville in the American Renaissance and on some of his most respected works, early and late: *The Poorhouse Fair,* the *Rabbit Angstrom* tetralogy, *Pigeon Feathers, The Centaur, The Music School, A Month of Sundays, The Witches of Eastwick,* and *In the Beauty of the Lilies.* Along the way, of course, many others of his works are also considered.

It should be noted that all references to Updike's works are paginated from the hardback first editions, dominantly Knopf, with the obvious exception of those paperback first editions which had no hardback precedents. The happy circumstance of Fawcett Columbine's recent series of new trade paperback editions of Updike's works is that — with the exception of the Rabbit novels as noted below — they are exact reproductions of the original Knopf hardback editions and so the pagination is identical. This will conveniently facilitate the locating of all Updike citations in these essays within those more accessible and inexpensive texts.

Furthermore, in order to facilitate easy reference all quotations from the Rabbit novels contain a combined set of page citations: for example, *Rabbit, Run* 237/203. The first page reference corresponds to the first edition Knopf hardback and the second to the 1995 Everyman's Library single-volume edition of the tetralogy, *Rabbit Angstrom.* If there have been textual changes in the later edition cited, the entry will contain the variation, e.g., "and as soon as she gets her little price (/contribution) leaves you with nothing" (*Rabbit, Run* 84-85/75). Fawcett Columbine has also reissued the four individual Rabbit novels in trade paperback, and in this case those new editions are produced from the same page proofs as the Everyman's Library tetralogy volume. To locate citations from that tetralogy volume in those new Fawcett Columbine editions, subtract the number of pages from the pagination in the Everyman's Library edition: *Rab-*

bit, Run, no subtractions necessary; *Rabbit Redux,* subtract 266; *Rabbit Is Rich,* subtract 623; *Rabbit at Rest,* subtract 1051. I owe thanks to Marshall Boswell for drawing my attention to this useful procedure.

John Updike's poem "Earthworm," which he describes "as perhaps my best-felt statement on religion," is included preceding his essay at his request. The book's epigraph is taken from an Updike article titled "Remarks on Religion and Contemporary American Literature," published in the journal *New Letters* (60, no. 4 [Fall 1994]: 80). The remarks were delivered at Indiana/Purdue University in Indianapolis, April 1994.

Besides my enormous gratitude to all the contributors for their fine scholarship and camaraderie, thanks are due to many persons for large amounts of encouragement and practical guidance as this book project metamorphosed its way into final form. Among them, my special thanks must go to Wayne Booth, W. Dale Brown, Jorunn Carlsen, Henry Carrigan, William Dean, Jack De Bellis, Robert Detweiler, Giles Gunn, Morton and Anita Kaplon, Robert McCoy, Ann-Janine Morey, David Silcox, Ralph Wood, Herb Yellin, Anthony Yu, and Jerome and Patricia Zeller. Updike's long-time associate and friend at Knopf, vice president and senior editor Judith Jones, and Kenneth Schneider, her tireless assistant, could not have been more cooperative, together with Michael Greaves, copyright and permissions manager there. Robert Gingrich II, my quietly efficient student assistant at Moravian College, uncomplainingly did the tedious work of checking the accuracy of citations. I am especially grateful for the help and support of many at Eerdmans, particularly Jon Pott, vice president and editor-in-chief, Charles Van Hof, Jennifer Hoffman, and Amanda Dombek. And to Ruth Linnea, my life's partner, goes an inexpressible gratitude accumulated over forty-five years of working together for common goals, one of which was this book.

James Yerkes
Bethlehem, PA

JOHN UPDIKE AND RELIGION

Earthworm

We pattern our Heaven
on bright butterflies,
but it must be that even
in earth Heaven lies.

The worm we uproot
in turning a spade
returns, careful brute,
to the peace he has made.

God blesses him; he
gives praise with his toil,
lends comfort to me,
and aerates the soil.

Immersed in the facts,
one must worship there;
claustrophobia attacks
us even in air.

— John Updike

Remarks upon Receiving the Campion Medal

JOHN UPDIKE

It is a thought-provoking, even disconcerting thing to be given an award as a "distinguished Christian person of letters," especially an award named for St. Edmund Campion. This brilliant Jesuit, a convert to Catholicism, was, history records, placed on the rack three times, in an effort to make him recant his faith. But, though tortured in body, he continued to debate brilliantly with Protestant theologians and won converts among them. He eloquently refuted the prosecution's trumped-up charges of sedition, but was nevertheless hanged, drawn, and quartered, at the age of forty-one, in 1581. How much of such persecution and agony, a recipient of the Campion Award cannot but wonder, would he endure for the sake of his religious convictions? It is all too easy a thing to be a Christian in America, where God's name is on our coinage, pious pronouncements are routinely expected from elected officials, and churchgoing, though far from unanimous, enjoys a popularity astounding to Europeans. As good Americans we are taught to tolerate our neighbors' convictions, however bizarre they secretly strike us, and we extend, it may be, something of this easy toleration to ourselves and our own views.

The Campion Medal was bestowed upon John Updike by the Catholic Book Club, in New York City, on September 11, 1997. The text of these remarks is reproduced here with his permission.

In my own case, I came of intellectual age at a time, the fifties, when a mild religious revival accompanied our reviving prosperity, and the powerful rational arguments against the Christian tenets were counterbalanced by an intellectual fashion that, a generation after Chesterton and Belloc, saw the Middle Ages still in favor as a kind of golden era of cultural unity and alleviated anxiety. Among revered literary figures, a considerable number were professing Christians — T. S. Eliot and W. H. Auden, Flannery O'Connor and Marianne Moore, Evelyn Waugh and Graham Greene, Rose Macaulay and Muriel Spark. The first recipient of the Campion award, Jacques Maritain in 1955, was the leading but far from the only figure in a movement to give Thomism a vital modern face; at another pole, philosophical existentialism looked to the Danish Lutheran Søren Kierkegaard as a founder, while the stark but expressive crisis theology of the Calvinist Karl Barth boldly sounded its trumpet against the defensive attenuations of liberal theology. Which is simply to say that when I showed a personal predilection not to let go of the Lutheran faith in which I had been raised, there was no lack of companionship and support in the literary and philosophical currents of the time. Had I been a young man in an atheist Communist state, or a literary man in the days when Menckenesque mockery was the dominant fashion, would I be as eligible as I am to receive this award? I am not sure. But in fact, yes, I have been a churchgoer in three Protestant denominations — Lutheran, Congregational, Episcopal — and the Christian faith has given me comfort in my life and, I would like to think, courage in my work. For it tells us that truth is holy, and truth-telling a noble and useful profession; that the reality around us is created and worth celebrating; that men and women are radically imperfect and radically valuable.

Although, as St. Paul as well as Luther and Kierkegaard knew, some intellectual inconvenience and strain attends the maintenance of our faith, at the same time we are freed from certain secular illusions and monochromatic tyrannies of hopeful thought. The bad news can be told full out, for it is not the only news. Indeed it is striking how dark, even offhandedly and farcically dark, the human condition appears as pictured in the fiction of Waugh and Spark and Graham Greene and Flannery O'Connor. We scan them for a glimpse of mollifying holiness and get instead a cruel drumming upon this world's emptiness. To be Christian in this day and age, as in the time of imperial Rome, is to be unorthodox, and readers should look elsewhere for the consolations of conventional sentiment and the popular, necessary religion of optimism.

While one can be a Christian and a writer, the phrase "Christian writer" feels somewhat reductive, and most writers so called have resisted it. The late Japanese novelist Shusaku Endo, a Roman Catholic and the Campion Medalist in 1990, observed of his Western peers, "Mr. Greene does not like to be called a Catholic writer. Neither did Francois Mauriac. Being a Christian is the opposite of being a writer, Mr. Mauriac said. According to him, coming in contact with sin is natural when you probe the depths of the human heart. Describing sin, a writer himself gets dirty. This contradicts his Christian duty." Endo went on to say that he could consider himself a Christian writer only insofar as he believed that, and I quote, "there is something in the human unconscious that searches for God."

And, indeed, in describing the human condition, can we, as Christians, assert more than that? Is not Christian fiction, insofar as it exists, a description of the bewilderment and panic, the sense of hollowness and futility, which afflicts those whose search for God is not successful? And are we not all, within the churches and temples or not, more searcher than finder in this regard? I ask, while gratefully accepting this award, to be absolved from any duty to provide orthodox morals and consolations in my fiction. Fiction holds the mirror up to the world and cannot show more than this world contains. I do admit that there are different angles at which to hold the mirror, and that the reading I did in my twenties and thirties, to prop up my faith, also gave me ideas and a slant that shaped my stories and, especially, my novels.

The first, *The Poorhouse Fair,* carries an epigraph from the Gospel of St. Luke; the next, *Rabbit, Run,* from Pascal; the third, *The Centaur,* from Karl Barth; and the fifth, *Couples,* from Paul Tillich. I thought of my novels as illustrations for texts from Kierkegaard and Barth; the hero of *Rabbit, Run* was meant to be a representative Kierkegaardian man, as his name, Angstrom, hints. Man in a state of fear and trembling, separated from God, haunted by dread, twisted by the conflicting demands of his animal biology and human intelligence, of the social contract and the inner imperatives, condemned as if by otherworldly origins to perpetual restlessness — such was, and to some extent remains, my conception. The modern Christian inherits an intellectual tradition of faulty cosmology and shrewd psychology. St. Augustine was not the first Christian writer nor the last to give us the human soul with its shadows, its Rembrandtesque blacks and whites, its chiaroscuro; this sense of ourselves, as creatures caught in the light, whose decisions and recognitions have a majestic significance, remains to haunt non-Christians as well, and to form, as far as I can see, the raison d'être of fiction.

PART 1

UPDIKE AND THE RELIGIOUS DIMENSION

As Good as It Gets

The Religious Consciousness in John Updike's Literary Vision

JAMES YERKES

> The motions of Grace, the hardness of the heart; external circumstances.
>
> Pascal, Pensée 507

It was a misguided understanding that led my wife and me to go and see Jack Nicholson, Helen Hunt, and Greg Kinnear in the 1998 film *As Good as It Gets.* Each of us had heard from different friends, our gender matches, that we simply must go and see it. It was said to be "uproariously funny" and "thoroughly delightful." One said, "I haven't laughed so hard in years." So when the young handsome gay artist was violently beaten to a pulp and left with face scars distorting him for life, and when the frantic single-parent waitress broke down in anguished, uncontrollable sobs, confessing that she longed once again just "to be held and fucked" by a man — well, we were totally unprepared. That sort of emotional assault on our expectations for some images from life's lighter side was not what we went to the movie for. We wanted *relief* from the world of violence, anguish, and dread.

But, of course, we did laugh uproariously, and a lot. And in deeply satisfying ways the film was thoroughly delightful. It even had a happy ending — young woman gets old man, young man gets darling dog, and dog gets bacon. What more could one want!? It was a movie we cried over — cried in laughter and cried in sorrow. It was a moving human story that powerfully intermingled the two faces of narrative art, comedy and tragedy, and there was insightful moral gain in the narrative. It raised and attempted to answer the deeply moral and religious question, "What is goodness?"

The next day as I sat down to write this essay, it dawned on me that the film was a genuinely Updikean tale. It was the truth. Life *is* a maddeningly turbulent and obscure mixture of laughter and weeping, pleasure and pain, hope and despair, carnival and labor, tenderness and violence, purity and lust, confidence and despair, faith and doubt. "One thing that's given me courage in writing," says Updike, "has been this belief that the truth, what is actual, must be faced and is somehow holy. That is, what exists is holy and God knows what exists; He can't be shocked, and He can't be surprised" (Plath, ed., 203). He says, "My books are all meant to be moral debates with the reader" in which the fundamental concern is to get the reader to ask the question, "What is goodness?" (*Picked-Up Pieces*, 502). Moreover, and more important for the context of this essay, he also plainly states, "The sense of the sacred or the religious, let's call it, certainly does play into one's art" (Plath, ed., 252).

But if this is so, how are we appropriately to understand what he means by this "sense of the sacred or the religious"? Put another way, what is the shape of the religious consciousness that Updike employs as he structures his literary world? What are the assumptions he invokes and the strategies he employs when he attempts to characterize it throughout his writings — a total now of fifty books? I will propose a definition and then fill out the analysis with justifications drawn mainly from Updike's memoirs, *Self-Consciousness;* James Plath's *Conversations with John Updike;* George Hunt's *John Updike and the Three Great Secret Things;* and Ralph Wood's *The Comedy of Redemption.*

Here is the definition: *the religious consciousness in Updike may best be characterized as our sense of an unavoidable, unbearable, and unbelievable Sacred Presence.* I will argue that in his understanding of religion a dialectically alternating value must be assigned to each of those adjectives: the Sacred Presence, God, in manner strikingly reminiscent of

Rudolph Otto's characterization of "the Numinous," always and at once *both troubles and inspires* human self-consciousness. To be more specific, the Sacred Presence is unavoidable, unbearable, and unbelievable in *both* a negative and a positive sense. The film title, as I understand it, is meant to suggest this same perspectival ambiguity in our consciousness, and it fits Updike here as well.[1] His view of the religious consciousness is "as good as it gets" — our awareness of the Sacred Presence in life is, by wrenchingly unpredictable turns, both astonishingly positive as an enabling gift and also frighteningly negative as a destructive threat. And there is no relief from the terrible uncertainty that this dialectically layered awareness thrusts upon us *qua* human. Even *qua* committed Christian believer, which Updike claims to be, this tension is never fully or finally resolved. Personal faith, for Updike and his mentor Kierkegaard here, is a stance of the will taken in the face of this unrelieved ambiguity, not as an escape from it. Faith of this transformative kind is a whole-soul response, not a descriptive observation. This essay has set itself only the descriptive task in addressing this unrelieved ambiguity.

If we are to assume, then, that "the sense of the sacred or the religious . . . certainly does play into one's art," how does Updike understand it to do so? First, from the standpoint of the writer, and in a Kantian manner, one feels unconditionally obligated to tell the truth. Truth-telling is the absolute credential for a fiction writer. A writer must deal unflinchingly with the good, the bad, and the ugly, with the unavoidable, the unbearable, and the unbelievable, as they actually appear in lived experience. "The first item of morality for a writer is to try to be accurate, to tell the truth as you know it . . . my overall theory, if I have one, is that the life of a piece of fictional prose comes from its relationship to reality, to truth, to what actually happens . . . A writer's job is to, by way of fiction, somehow describe the way we live" (Plath, ed., 120-21, 216). Second, in the process of such truth-telling, Updike believes that one in fact comes upon the awareness of Sacred Presence in human experience. For Updike, human self-consciousness, synchro-

1. The newspaper advertisement for the film trenchantly reflected this ambiguity: "A comedy from the heart that goes for the throat." The film's point, obviously, is that we experience life with the wildly vacillating sentiments of minimalist pessimism and maximalist optimism. At certain moments we stoically accept life's deliverances as the most we can expect and at other times as the best we could possibly imagine — precisely Updike's fictional world.

nized with its parallel world-consciousness, finds itself confronted willy-nilly with an awareness of the Sacred, with God. If you tell the truth about us, as Updike sees it, you have to record the religious dimension of human existence. That is the truth, and truth is holy, is sacred. Writers, he says, are "servants of reality" (182).

So, my definition of religious consciousness in Updike emerges only when one first recognizes how to understand the shape and movement of ordinary human consciousness. Humans are religious because in their self-consciousness they are driven by profoundly existential concerns — concerns about the meaning and purpose of their existence. Religion as an institution makes no sense at all unless it functions to address helpfully the fundamental questions that drive human consciousness: How did I get here? What am I to do here? What is my final destiny — if any — after here? Religion in the sense of personal and deeply self-conscious experience *is* the sense of an unavoidable, unbearable, and unbelievable sacrality that presents itself as the all-embracing context for that existential consciousness. "Like the inner of the two bonded strips of metal in a thermostat, the self curls against Him and presses. . . . God is a dark sphere enclosing the pinpoint of our selves" (*Self-Consciousness*, 229). Religion in the *institutional* sense consists of the human traditions, symbols, liturgies, and communities that help interpret, celebrate, and propitiate this *personal* sense of Sacred Presence. Humanity's personal religious experiences have given rise to the institutional forms, and not the other way around.

Fundamentally, human self-consciousness for Updike "is an existential desperation which all men being mortal feel" (Plath, ed., 160), and it involves "one's basic sense of dread and strangeness" (187) when confronting meaning-based questions: who, where, why am I? In a way, one could say that Updike sees himself and all of us hurrying toward death, and we are at different moments frozen and frenzied in our attempt to face that fact. Our anxiety about the possibility and necessity of death is, he says, "the natural product of having a mind that can foresee a future, which a dog, say, doesn't have. That is the human condition which leads us to theologians we can trust, leads us to church on a Sunday morning, leads us to pray in the space behind our eyelids" (250).[2] And in passing we need to note that Updike's constant

2. The fact that Updike has actually *read* theologians for guidance and has regularly *attended* church for worship is the anomalous fact that first led me — and ap-

portrayal of sexual encounter is an acceptance of the existential link between *eros* and *thanatos* — a link upon which, interestingly enough, both Freud and Kierkegaard insist. In sexual activity one seeks to fend off death rather than simply generate pleasure.[3]

Further, we find ourselves in a world where "making sense of it all" regularly seems maddeningly impossible. There is an opacity, an obscurity to the shape of our existence, an intransigence on the part of reality to yield to our desires — indeed, to our demand — for clarity, as well as for happiness. This is particularly true of the brutal churnings of nature in the destruction of all living forms. "I hate Nature," George Caldwell says in *The Centaur.* "It reminds me of death. All Nature means to me is garbage and confusion and the stink of skunk — *brroo!*" Yes, but — a favorite literary technique in Updike's fictional descriptions (Plath, ed., 33) — "Nature . . . is like a mother," says Pop Kramer, "she com-forts and chas-tises with the same hand" (*The Centaur,* 291).

This persistent "on the other hand" feature of Updike's descriptive dialectic is a hallmark of his view of our uniquely human existence. We are from time to time given pleasurable hints of meaning, a sense of transcendent beauty and support from the natural order, and also regularly crushed by blows of despair as we are consumed without mercy in its jaws. "He shares the Greek tragic conviction that the world's vitality is at war with its order," says Ralph Wood, "destroying itself even as it creates and renews" (*Comedy of Redemption,* 204). Thus, for Updike, in good Lutheran fashion, God is paradoxically both hidden and revealed in Nature's reality.

---

parently many other Protestants — to read him. A host of Jewish and Roman Catholic writers of stature so pursue their personal faith. Such Protestant writers of stature are, and have been, few.

3. One must be careful, however, not to assign sex only one meaning in Updike's work. Sexual experience for Updike is mythically or symbolically multivalent, as historian of religion Mircea Eliade would say. I believe George Hunt correctly suggests we must understand that sex in Updike's work "functions as a symbol, as 'a kind of code' for the myriad of complex symbols we associate with the word 'life,' a word more sizeable than 'sex.'" The obvious reason for this, he suggests, "is that it is the one great secret thing of which *all* his readers are aware, and so it becomes the most intelligible vehicle for his further exploration of those other two secrets [religion and art] to which readers are less sensitive" (Hunt, 210). Updike's focus on sexuality is therefore sized to other concerns, powerfully large though it is in human experience. For example, he observes that both religion and sex are "modes of self-assertion, of saying, 'I am'" (Plath, ed., 149).

Our existential torment involves the moral order as well as the natural order. Here the peculiar dilemma is that we are a creature torn open and chained Prometheus-like between two powerful forces — the drive of the body and the drive of the mind, or spirit. *The Centaur,* by Updike's own clear intention, symbolizes both the captive energies of physical embodiment, which generate suffering and pleasure, and the soaring energies of spiritual transcendence, which provoke anxiety and hope. In all his writings he has never failed to address the agonies and ecstasies these tangled energies generate in human life. Like Augustine, Pascal, and Kierkegaard, he sees the human soul as restless, longing for goodness, but driven by confused passions. The Pascal epigraph that he used for *Rabbit, Run* and that heads this essay could serve as the epigraph for his entire literary production. For Updike, the existential problem is not so centrally a matter of guilt as of anxiety (Plath, ed., 204). Moral panic fuels our anxiety, the anxiety of a life whiplashed in the moral storms generated by the personal desire for safety and freedom and by the relational concern for others that requires self-denial, risk, and suffering, as well as conformity and obedience. To understand our anxious moral dilemma is to realize that there is no perfect or final resolution to this personal storm and the social tragedies it ineluctably enacts.

Most of the time we simply do not know what to do with this moral anxiety. For Updike, to be authentically human — a favorite existentialist term — is to be ceaselessly driven and divided in our moral sense. "In other words," he says,

> a person who has what he wants, a satisfied person, a content person, ceases to be a person. . . . I feel that to be a person is to be in a situation of tension . . . a dialectical situation. A truly adjusted person is not a person at all — just an animal with clothes on. . . . Every human being who is more than a moron is the locus of certain violent tensions that come with having a brain. . . . you foresee things, for example, you foresee your own death. You have really been locked out of the animal paradise of unthinking natural reflex. (*Picked-Up Pieces,* 504, 509)

This human situation, argues Updike, like the film, is "as good as it gets." No free lunch. No easy solutions. No nirvanic quietude. Negotiating life is work — hard, grinding moral and physical work — ineluctably followed by our always anticipated personal death. To be religious is necessarily to exist inextricably inside of such excruciating tensions, spared nothing, parrying tragedy's punishing blows. And yet, to be religious is also to be seized and energized day by day, strangely, at some deeply intuited level, by something that answers to the word "hope."

Now if this hastily drawn sketch is the "truth" of the human condition, the truth of what Updike believes must be reported without favoritism or qualm, it will be there "in the midst" that the truth of the religious awareness of Sacred Presence, the presence of God, is to be found. It is a Presence that, as I have suggested, will be found to be unavoidable, unbearable, and unbelievable. It will be, necessarily, a contextual Presence both revealed immediately to self-consciousness and also mediated by our encounter with the world.

Let me then in a summative manner characterize Updike's understanding of the dimensions of this religious consciousness and explain my choice of those adjectival qualifiers. I want to emphasize that the following outline is intended to be suggestive, not exhaustive. It is offered in order to provoke in us as readers a new set of expectations as we approach Updike's writings with our own religious interests and concerns. There are five elements I want to identify in his view of human self-consciousness: a religious sense of (1) origin, (2) courage, (3) hope, (4) obligation, and (5) praise.

(1) *The religious dimension of human self-consciousness involves a sense of gratuitous, if deeply frightening, origin.* For Updike, this is the consciousness of the "floor" or foundation of our time-space existence. Speaking for himself, he notes, "my religious sensibility operates primarily as a sense of God the Creator" (Plath, ed., 103), but it is clear from his writings that he thinks this is a characteristic human sensibility. The issue is ontological, the surprising and gratuitous priority of being over non-being, as theologian Paul Tillich would put it. Augustine argued the same point in his *Confessions* (*Basic Writings,* 1:185-86), and 2,500 years ago the Greek philosopher Pythagoras put this peculiar awareness in the form of a question: Why is there something rather than nothing? The issue is not just or finally chronological — that is, the need for something temporally prior in order for anything to exist later. The issue is the power or ability for things to exist at all, for there to be any reliable matrix of passage in which things have the power to arise, flourish, and then, losing that power, perish. "The very existence

of the world provides [Updike] irrefutable evidence that we are not our own makers but the recipients of an unbidden gift," says Wood (*Comedy of Redemption*, 193).

The idea of existence being a gift and thus good is what makes the point ontological and not just temporal. It is also what makes that point unavoidable and, in a positive sense, unbelievable.[4] Updike once commented that his work searched for a "mystical sense of the real," and when asked what he meant he replied:

> I'm trying to capture . . . the wonder of the real which is very easy to ignore of course since we're surrounded by the real day after day and it's easy to stop seeing and stop feeling. . . . I'm trying to convey the fact that the creation of the world is in some way terribly good. We love being alive. (Plath, ed., 159)

In another context, commenting on his epic midlife poem "Midpoint," Updike speaks more philosophically:

> I think one of my independent philosophical obsessions was that there is a certain gratuitousness in existence at all. That is, however riddles [about human existence] are unraveled, why the void itself was breached remains permanently mysterious, and, in its own way, permanently hopeful-making. . . . I frequently find myself saying . . . be grateful for existence; that is, "nothing had to be." And that advice, I think, is religious advice. (Plath, ed., 100)

One needs to take heed of the term "mysterious" as well as "hopeful," however. Updike's interest in the new Hubble cosmology clearly has

4. Hunt, following Wayne Booth, who in his *Modern Dogma and the Rhetoric of Assent* notes how writers intuitively respond to the call of reality, suggests that Updike is indeed a "rhetorician of assent." He enacts in his art the claim that "'the great original choice between being and nothingness was, and eternally is, a fantastic, uncomprehensible act of assent rather than denial; the universe is, nothingness is not'" (Hunt, 213). If this essay, while claiming that religious awareness is ambivalent, seems to stress the ultimate power of the Yes over the No in religious awareness, it is because that is in fact Updike's own conclusion. The Yes *eventually* — not always obviously or in the short run of our frantic intervals of desperation — carries beyond the No the greater weight of assent: "He [God] is . . . a bottomless encouragement to our faltering and frightened being. His answers come in the long run, as the large facts of our lives, strung on that thread running through all things" (*Self-Consciousness*, 229).

a double edge in his writings. Beginning with "The Astronomer" in *Pigeon Feathers* and continuing through *Toward the End of Time,* he has made clear that we look out from planet Earth into an almost sickeningly dark and cold cosmos. If the void was breached and nothing had to be, and our existence seems at bottom a gratuity, it also feels in our darker moments lonely and suffocatingly frightening. Walter's visit with Bela the astronomer is hardly comforting in the way Updike draws the scene.

> I felt behind his eyes immensities of space and gas, seemed to see with him through my own evanescent body into gigantic systems of dead but furious matter, suns like match heads, planets like cinders, galaxies that were whirls of ash, and beyond them, more galaxies, and more, fleeing with sickening speed beyond the rim that our most powerful telescopes could reach. (*Pigeon Feathers,* 182)

Moreover, Bela himself, momentarily garrulous about the emptiness of New Mexico expanses, suddenly in his expression "confessed what he could not pronounce: He had been frightened" (185). The story closes with a question: "What is the past, after all, but a vast sheet of darkness in which a few moments, pricked apparently at random, shine?" (186). This is the perfectly matched sentiment of Ben Turnbull in *Toward the End of Time:* "What doesn't fall into the void?" (25). Indeed, the possibility of annihilation blossoms into panic as Ben works on his daughter's dollhouse in the basement.

> There was no God, each detail of the rusting, moldering cellar made clear, just Nature, which would consume my life as carelessly and relentlessly as it would a dung-beetle corpse in a compost pile. Dust to dust: each hammer stroke seemed dulled by cosmic desolation, each measurement for my rust-dulled crosscut saw seemed part of the grid of merciless laws that would soon extinguish me. (83)

So what have we here in the religious consciousness that testifies about our cosmic origin? Ambivalence. We have an elemental sense of hopeful gratuity that is regularly assaulted by a powerful sense of ineluctable futility. Our sense of things in Nature, as Pop Kramer noted, is Janus-faced mystery: our being is a gift, our non-being is inevitable. In the religious consciousness we are incessantly assailed by doubt, but moved at some elemental but never wholly assured level to hope — to the confidence that the world is, in some mysterious way, "terribly good."

(2) *The religious dimension of human self-consciousness involves a sense of unexpected, if constantly assaulted, courage.* If being is good, life is trouble. If to be religious is to have a gifted, though precarious, sense of "floor" to our existence, then it is also to have *a sense of being attended* in the midst of what is in fact, if we are honest, frequently a terrifying "maze" of tragedy and chaos. It would be tempting to say "a sense of being *guided*," but Updike has a not very sanguine view of our ability to figure out a sense of purpose operating in our lives. We are talking here in Lutheran terms about "the Left hand of God," which presents itself in our lives as pitiless destruction — individually, culturally, and historically.

> I've never really understood theologies which would absolve God of earthquakes and typhoons, of children starving. A god who is not God the Creator is not very real to me, so that, yes, it certainly *is* God who throws the lightning bolt and this God is above the nice god, above the god we can worship and empathize with. . . . I'm saying there's a fierce God above the kind God. (*Picked-Up Pieces*, 504)

This is the God of Calvin's horrible damnation decrees and Luther's *Deus absconditus.* Even more starkly, Updike fictionally records this dying accusation of President James Buchanan: "I am not troubled by the sins of men, who are feeble; I am troubled by the sins of God, who is mighty" (*Buchanan Dying*, 167). This is the sentiment behind the pitiless, gut-wrenching trauma described in *Rabbit, Run* as drunken Janice drowns her baby in the presence of a God, a Sacred Presence, manifestly there and deeply felt, who will not lift a finger to help (264/226-27). This is a God whose oppressive diffidence is morally unbearable and whose oft-touted loving-kindness is, in such moments, manifestly, in the most negative sense, unbelievable.

Where do such God-absconding experiences deliver the religious consciousness? "Absence is not a synonym for unreality," Wood reminds us. "This God is detected not so much by sight as by scent and footprint" (*Comedy of Redemption*, 193). The odd, incoherent reality we feel is the presence of an absent God, the God at once hidden and revealed. We have here another "yes, but." Along with the despair and anger elicited in such inscrutable moments, which a writer's truth-telling requires him or her to report, there is also something else to report. There is, among other things, the often neglected fact that we get up each day and go to work.

This impulse to keep on working, keep moving forward, albeit often numbed and plodding, is a "scent and footprint" of Sacred Presence at work in our midst. It is a religious impulse, as Updike sees it. For him, the determination expressed in work is the preeminent social virtue. In some paradoxical way, it is a sign of confidence that life, at least for one more day, somehow has meaning and purpose, for ourselves and for the others who depend on us. It is another ineradicable sign of faith in sheer existence, which, as we saw earlier, is the gift of God. We are, as it were, unexpectedly *drawn* forward, from beyond ourselves, beyond the sense of despair. If it is pointed out that many people crippled by depression do stay in bed and many troubled people commit suicide rather than face another day, I believe Updike would reply that these facts only demonstrate the obvious: we understand that they are ill in the face of life. As in many other matters, the exception proves the rule. To go to work — even under assault by the slings and arrows of outrageous fortune and when life seems like a tale told by an idiot, signifying nothing — is universally recognized as a sign of health and hope. "Religion," Updike says, "enables us to ignore nothingness and get on with the jobs of life" (*Self-Consciousness,* 228).

Courage to work is the courage to be. Going to work is the secular sign of a religious awareness and confidence, whether it is only latent and implicit or manifest and explicit. The sense of courage that propels us forward each day into the more obligatory tasks of life is for Updike something cumulatively reinforced, an impulse which carries the implication that there is an order to which I can contribute and for which I am obligated. It is a strangely motivated awareness that attends both our radical downs and our surprising ups. If *Rabbit, Run* shows us the natural legitimacy of the desire to be true to the unique, urgent personal energies within us, even when it entails causing others suffering, then *The Centaur* shows us the inevitable necessity for subordinating that urge to freedom in order to give one's life for others. The religious awareness, then, expresses itself in the surprising motions of courage that pull us out of bed from yesterday's depths of despair into today's "once again" routine. Courage is an ontological gift, but work is a temporal obligation — a vocation in the strict Lutheran sense of the term, a calling from God.

(3) *The religious dimension of human self-consciousness involves a sense of ultimate, but incessantly death-threatened hope.* If being is good, and life

is trouble, then help is available. Certainly the concepts of gifted origin and unexpected courage are a part of hope in human experience. Hope must have an ontological and moral ground if it is not to be confused with wishful thinking. Hope, one might say, is the deep-seated human confidence that the new is really possible, both the morally new and the ontologically new. But if hope has a ground and a workaday energy for Updike, it also has a temporal direction. It is, to use the appropriate theological word, eschatological. It has an end, a goal, a *telos.* In personal terms, the hope that our lives over time produce meaning that endures — indeed, that makes us think physical suffering and moral obedience are worthwhile — seems to require in us some latent sense that the meaning must and will endure beyond our death. And we are, we remember, the death-foreseeing animal. In Updike's novel *Toward the End of Time* Ben Turnbull comments, "if we can't take our memories with us, why go?" (74).

Here we come upon something aggressively central to Updike's concerns from the outset of his career, from what he calls his "angst-besmogged" Ipswich period, to the present (*Self-Consciousness,* 99). It was the urgent motive behind his much-quoted poem "Seven Stanzas at Easter" (*Collected Poems,* 20-21).[5] There is a convictional obstinacy here, some would even insist an embarrassing naivete, which many critics — religious and otherwise — find puzzling. With this conviction he certainly swims in a headstrong manner against the erosive intellectual tides of Enlightenment skepticism and postmodern pessi-

5. In this poem, written in 1960 during this Ipswich period, Updike gives a strictly physicalist interpretation of Jesus of Nazareth's — and by proleptic implication, our — resurrection:

> Make no mistake: if He rose at all
> it was as His body;
> if the cells' dissolution did not reverse, the molecules reknit,
> the amino acids rekindle,
> the Church will fall.

In *Self-Consciousness,* published in 1989, Updike's emphasis seems to fall instead on a claim for survival of personal identity or awareness, rather than a literal physical reconstitution. This in fact is the position now taken by many Christian theologians. This position, however, should not be taken as just a claim for the immortality of the soul — a Greek notion most notably advocated by Plato — but rather for the late Hebraic idea of a preservation of the individual identity accumulated through our bodily experiences in time and space.

mism. Human self-consciousness involves, he argues, "our persistence, against all the powerful post-Copernican, post-Darwinian evidence that we are insignificant accidents within a vast uncaused churning, in feeling that our life is a story, with a pattern and a moral and an inevitability. . . . That . . . the universe has a personal structure" (*Self-Consciousness,* 227). In other words, as the last chapter title of his memoirs suggests, there is something within human consciousness that insists "on being a self forever" (chap. 6).

Thus, if religious consciousness has a floor, as noted in the first point, it also has an open ceiling, a skylight of hope. Hope rises for individual human existence beyond the consumptively anxious "churnings" of space and time. "Anxiety" is the word we need to use here, for, as we saw, Updike is convinced that guilt is not the most fundamental category for explaining the deepest drives of the human psyche; it is rather the anxiety we feel about the survival of our individual identity that fuels our quest for meaning here and now. He thinks this concern is an implication of the question, judged universal, which occurred to him at a very young age: *"Why am I me?"* ("Midpoint," *Collected Poems,* 66; *Self-Consciousness,* 40-41). He argues, "The yearning for an afterlife is the opposite of selfish: it is love and praise for the world that we are privileged, in this complex interval of light, to witness and experience. . . . the basic desire, as Unamuno says in his *Tragic Sense of Life,* is not for some *other*world but for *this* world, for life more or less as we know it to go on forever: 'The immortality that we crave is a phenomenal immortality — it is the continuation of this present life'" (*Self-Consciousness,* 217). The point here is that Updike, right or wrong, thinks that the desire to escape the personal eradication death brings is necessarily inherent in human consciousness, and thus such desires and longings are religious elements.

The skeptical post-Enlightenment West, having turned away from the religious witness of hope in life after death in the Christian Apostles' Creed, for example, finds no credence for individual survival beyond death in its own creedalisms of atheism, naturalism, and humanism. But, says Updike, "An easy Humanism plagues the land;/I choose to take an otherworldly stand" ("Midpoint," *Collected Poems,* 96). Given both the delicious and the terrible texture of lived experience as reflected in the religious consciousness, such a view seems, alternately, as with his other characterizations, both unbelievable and believable.

> Our self is thrust into a manifold reality that is thoroughly gratuitous, and faith in an afterlife, however much our reason ridicules it, very modestly extends our faith that each moment of our consciousness will be followed by another — that a coherent matrix has been prepared for this precious self of ours. The guarantee that our self enjoys an intended relation to the outer world is most, if not all, of what we ask from religion. (*Self-Consciousness*, 217-18)

The transcendent value of the subject and the subjective is the heart of Updike's existentialist affirmation about religious consciousness, and he believes that Kierkegaard, though not alone in this affirmation, has intellectually preserved this truth for twentieth-century faith — and by extension, for all who philosophically resist modern materialist reductionism.

> By giving metaphysical dignity to "the subjective," by showing faith to be not an intellectual development but a movement of the will, by holding out for existential duality against the tide of all monisms, materialist or mystical or political, that would absorb the individual consciousness, Kierkegaard has given Christianity new life, a handhold, the "Archimedean point." (*Picked-Up Pieces*, 121)

The hope of the religious consciousness for Updike, despite all the frightening surface evidence to the contrary, is "That . . . the universe has a personal structure." Ours mirrors it, and it saves ours. That is the human hope faced in death.[6]

(4) *The religious dimension of human self-consciousness involves a sense of unrelieved and deeply conflicted moral obligation.* One might be entitled to ask after stressing the last point about hope whether religious motivation for Updike might not finally turn out to be simply a psychologically narcissistic strategy for coping with death, and as such fairly indifferent to the everyday gritty discipline of the moral life. Indeed, Wood is very

6. In an oft-cited line Updike confesses, "In the morning light one can write breezily, without the slightest acceleration of one's pulse, about what one cannot contemplate in the dark without turning in panic to God." He goes on, "Evidence of God's being lies with that of our own. . . . In the light, we disown Him, embarrassedly; in the dark, He is our only guarantor, our only shield against death" (*Self-Consciousness*, 226, 229). Reading that arresting line moved Nicholson Baker to write *U and I: A True Story*, a tribute (U meaning Updike) to Updike's positive influence on his own literary career.

hard on Updike for this very reason. The phrases he uses to criticize Updike here are "moral passivity," "deep tragic pessimism," and "ethical quietism" (*Comedy of Redemption,* 190). But, writes Updike,

> one believes not merely to dismiss from one's life a degrading and immobilizing fear of death but to possess that Archimedean point outside the world from which to move the world. The world cannot provide its own measure and standards; these must come, strangely, from outside, or a sorry hedonism and brute opportunism result. . . . Religion, once the self has taken its hook, preaches selflessness. The self is the focus of anxiety; attention to others, self-forgetfulness, and living like the lilies are urged, to relieve the anxiety. Insomnia offers a paradigm: the mind cannot fall asleep as long as it watches itself. (*Self-Consciousness,* 232)

It is here that I think Updike's Lutheran background has one of its firmest grips on his interpretation of the religious consciousness. Indeed, he identifies himself as the product of a "Protestant, Lutheran, rather antinomian Christianity" (234). His Lutheran view of the moral life is as nicely ambiguous as Calvinist Reinhold Niebuhr's view that sin is inevitable, but not necessary! Updike presumes that if it is true to our checkered moral experience that we do not seem able wholly to transcend the sins of hubris, concupiscence, and selfishness, then what one perforce must do is "sin boldly" (Plath, ed., 94-95). There is probably nothing so incomprehensible to purity-driven Calvinists as such outrageous advice. Here is a passage calculatedly meant to inspire even more Reformed Church apoplexy:

> Down-dirty sex and the bloody mess of war and the desperate effort of faith all belonged to a dark necessary underside of reality that I felt should not be merely ignored, or risen above, or disdained. These shameful things were intrinsic to life, and though I myself was somewhat squeamish about sex and violence and religion, . . . they must be faced, it seemed to me, and even embraced. (*Self-Consciousness,* 135)

Calvinist objections notwithstanding, the point that needs to be made here is that Updike does not take a fatalistic view of human moral failure. The moral life is much, much more dialectically complex in Updike than many of his critics suggest. There is recognition that moral effort succeeds, even if success is always temporary and never complete. For him that invites not despair, but serious moral effort:

> I came to the decision to write about the imperfect world — a world that is fallen. That's why many people find my books so depressing. But for me it isn't depressing to say that the world is imperfect. Here the work begins: One confesses this imperfectness more or less happily and starts to think about what one is to do with the world in this condition. (Plath, ed., 174)

For Updike the religious dimension of human self-consciousness operates under a serious sense of moral obligation. It is not, however, an obligation to some clear ethical code of specific actions. It is rather a Lutheran sense of obligation to love and serve the neighbor, even at one's own expense, but without the assumption that actions so motivated will always produce results unambiguously good on either side of the action. Moreover, sin for Updike may even be "oddly fecundating," as Wood suggests (*Comedy of Redemption*, 182) — that is, it is oddly tragic in producing the moral misery quintessentially requisite for moral wisdom. Still, this is *retrospective* understanding gained at great cost to oneself and to others. George Hunt names what is achieved "at least a muted reconciliation" (Hunt, 213). One does not sin in order to produce goodness, which is what genuine antinomianism means, but one does indeed learn a lot about goodness in sinning that would not be understood without it. Even in the dithering and dallying of the morally sloven Harry "Rabbit" Angstrom there develops a modest clarity about moral obligation. There is no celebration of "a sorry" or even genteel hedonism. Indeed, as Wood acknowledges, Harry learns that

> Laughter and enjoyment are nearly always derivative, . . . and but rarely intentional. They are serendipitous byproducts that issue from an acceptance of life's fundamental paradox: the inescapable linkage of joy and sadness, comedy and tragedy, carnival and labor, faith and doubt. When held together in unity and complementarity — and this requires a deep religious trust, a willingness to forego the idolatry of extremes — these dialectical opposites can be the means of grace . . . reconciled . . . by the enabling irony of life itself — and thus by the gracious God of life. (*Comedy of Redemption*, 229)

What Rabbit lacks, Updike tells us, is the *"going through"* character of Christianity,[7] and Updike suggests that "the struggle part of it — the

7. The passage is worth quoting: "Harry has no taste for the dark, tangled, vis-

winning-through" is a recognition of and response to the sense of obligation at the root of the religious self-consciousness (Plath, ed., 255). In different proportions and at different times, each of us is always both Rabbit and Centaur, and always *sub coram Deo.* That is the key: the moral struggle between the personal and the social good *is* a struggle because we all live, dimly or achingly, "under God's gaze." The drawn-in "eyes" of *The Centaur* make it clear from whence comes both this sense of obligation and this sense of judgment.

(5) *The religious dimension of human self-consciousness involves a sense of instinctually evoked, if tragically situated, praise.* Perhaps I could equally well have said a sense of gratitude. In some ways, this is the root sentiment that Updike thinks is discerned by all humans as they face the fullness of lived experience. "The instinct that life is good is where natural theology begins," he writes, the Hellish realities "of a profound and desolating absence" of God notwithstanding. Indeed, "my sense of things . . . is that wherever a church spire is raised, though dismal slums surround it and a single dazed widow kneels under it, this Hell is opposed by a rumor of good news, by an irrational confirmation of the plentitude we feel is our birthright" (*Picked-Up Pieces,* 91). This birthright is the rich plentitude of our existence seen as gift. The human consciousness drinks deeply the delight of life, even amidst the darkness of sin and death that presses on every side. "What bliss life is," says the mortally ill Ben Turnbull in Updike's *Toward the End of Time.* "Alive. A pitiable but delicious reprieve from timelessness" (299).

This natural astonishment at the goodness of existence is what causes Updike to believe that "the world wants describing, the world wants to be observed and 'hymned'." "So," he confesses, "there's a kind of hymning undercurrent that I feel in my work" (Plath, ed., 253). Indeed, "With writing, or generally with art, we show the world our admiration and express our thanks that we are here. I know that sounds somewhat strange, but it's my intention to describe the world as the Psalmists did" (175). Further, "I really never set out to be a Christian writer or theological writer. I'm just trying to announce with

---

ceral aspect of Christianity, the *going through* quality of it, the passage *into* death and suffering that redeems and inverts these things, like an umbrella blowing inside out. He lacks the mindful will to walk the straight line of a paradox. His eyes turn toward the light however it glances into his retina" (*Rabbit, Run,* 237/203).

a sense of wonder the surprise that I'm here at all" (203). "He envisions human existence," says Wood, "as a tragic conflict of opposites that, by faith in God's grace, can nonetheless be affirmed as good . . . as containing, within its own tragic dialectic, the surprise of goodness" (*Comedy of Redemption*, 178).

Witness, for example, the poignant "All joy belongs to the Lord" scene in *The Centaur.* George recollects walking as an anxious boy with his father, the minister, through dark and dangerous streets in Passaic, New Jersey.

> From within the double doors of a saloon there welled a poisonous laughter that seemed to distill all the cruelty and blasphemy in the world, and he wondered how such a noise could have a place under the sky of his father's God. . . . he remembered his father turning and listening . . . and then smiling down to his son, "All joy belongs to the Lord."
>
> It was half a joke but the boy took it to heart. *All joy belongs to the Lord.* Wherever in the filth and confusion and misery, a soul felt joy, there the Lord came and claimed it as his own; into barrooms and brothels and classrooms and alleys slippery with spittle, no matter how dark and scabbed and remote, in China or Africa or Brazil, . . . wherever a moment of joy was felt, there the Lord stole and added to his enduring domain. . . . The X-rays were clear. . . . [He] discovered that in giving his life to others he entered a total freedom. . . . and in the upright of his body Sky and Gaia mated again. Only goodness lives. But it does live. (*The Centaur,* 296-97)

So, whether hymning the wonder of the created order or of human self-consciousness, both the creature and the writer respond with praise even when surrounded by the squalor of sin and death. Updike the writer is that boy mentioned above. The world *can* be hymned because God is creatively, if often hiddenly, present in and under all of its forms — personal and social, natural and cosmic. Being is good, life is trouble, help is available. Goodness lives. This is the deepest intuition that sustains the religious consciousness and evokes its praise.

A few coda comments are appropriate here. John Updike is not a theologian, even though he is very well-read indeed in some aspects of Christian theology. His work will not therefore register the precision of answers for which trained theologians often want to press. Those who look for such precision will be disappointed. He is a writer, and he deserves the latitude which that art form permits and requires. Though he freely acknowledges that he writes from inside a life deeply influenced by Christianity, as a writer who sets out, we recall, to "describe the way we live," he has also on occasion firmly stated that he does not want to be considered a Christian writer. When reminded that his theological hero Karl Barth once observed that "Christian art" is well intentioned but ultimately impotent, Updike replied:

> But I've never really offered [my work] as Christian art. My art is Christian only in that my faith urges me to tell the truth, however painful and inconvenient, and holds out the hope that the truth — reality — is good. Good or no, only the truth is useful. (Plath, ed., 104)

I am a trained theologian. I live and work as a member of the Christian church. So what has that to do with my exegesis of the religious consciousness in Updike's literary vision? Something quite important, I believe. I have endeavored to perform a kind of Husserlian "epoche" or bracketing of validity or "truth" questions and tried to describe how Updike sees the contours of human self-consciousness as religious. In setting out my understanding of Updike's views I have tried to resist talking overmuch in traditional theological terms about problems such as natural vs. revealed religion, divine transcendence vs. immanence, high vs. low christology, or exclusivist vs. inclusivist salvation. One can certainly do this in relation to his views, and Christian theologians should do this in other contexts, but I have felt it my first obligation here to clarify as best I could in what sense Updike thinks all humans are experientially religious in the awareness of God as Sacred Presence.

As a theologian, however, I have always maintained that Christian doctrines are not answers to questions nobody asks, but proposals for answers to questions everybody asks. They are questions of ultimate concern and concerned questions about what is ultimate. Updike the writer attempts to describe the questions everybody asks, and at root he sees these questions emergent from the religious dimension of human self-consciousness. One may agree or disagree with this analysis of human self-consciousness — the overwhelming majority of contemporary academics and the literary elite certainly *do* disagree with him — but all Updike as writer wants his readers to do is to check out their own experience. That is the final test to which he appeals for the validity of his insights as writer. He does not think one needs to be "Christian" to see things this way. He just thinks one has to open one's eyes and be honest, be truthful.[8]

8. Perhaps the most controversial theological issue in any interpretation of Updike in these matters is this: what, exactly, is the limit of natural human ability to experience and interpret the truth of God's reality in nature and culture? Many commentators want to insist that Updike is a theological Barthian here. To condense the issue, Calvinist theologian Karl Barth argues that, with regard to the ability of natural reason to know God truly, we are, to use Calvin's own striking metaphor, "blinder than moles" (*Institutes* 2.2.18). It is assumed that this is Updike's view as well, since he always alludes to Barth's writings so favorably. Instead, I have taken very seriously Updike's important observation in 1993 that "I only really took out of Barth what I wanted and what I needed. There's a lot left-over that I didn't use" (Plath, ed., 254). Furthermore, one should note his own clear statement as early as 1976 that what Barth said "with resounding definiteness and learning [about God] . . . joined with my Lutheran heritage and enabled me to go on. . . . I'm not a good Barthian" (102-3). With these comments in mind, I would argue that if Updike seems to scramble in his fiction and personal comments what theologians call "natural" and "special" revelation, it is because ultimately his understanding of human religious consciousness follows Luther more directly than Barth on those issues.

But what Updike clearly does take from Barth is Barth's stubborn insistence against the naive optimists of Enlightenment rationalism that there can be no climbing to the truth of God on terms we independently lay down in advance. Any true knowledge of God is a function of God's gracious enablement, which is why Luther was less exercised about the rational knowledge of God than about an experientially personal way to find "a gracious God." Updike does not think humans are "naturally religious" if that means that we independently from our side generate or manipulate the sense of God, the Sacred Presence, according to our own interests. God's self-revelation in our religious awareness is both a gift and a judgment, which we find present without and beyond our efforts. In authentic religious awareness the movement is always from God to us, not the reverse. We do not struggle to find God in our consciousness; we struggle to deal with the God whom we find already confronting us there — even if we attempt to explain or evade what is confronting us by giving it some other name. This point of view means that our experience of God is more a matter of being found than of finding, of being known than of knowing, of being corrected than of being correct.

There is probably no clearer witness to this Updikean conviction than divinity professor Roger Lambert in *Roger's Version:* "'The church preaches, I believe, and the Old Testament describes, a God Who acts, *Who comes to us,* in Revelation and Redemption, and not one Who set the universe going and then hid. The God we care about in this divinity school is the living God, Who moves toward us out of His will and love, and Who laughs at all the towers of Babel we build to Him'" (22). Barth is invoked approvingly by name in that dialogue. Again, Lambert insists, "'A

This is an important matter to a theologian like me. I understand the plethora of religious traditions and communities throughout history to have emerged because such religious consciousness is at work wherever humans have been, are now, or ever will be found. Indeed, he seems anthropologically quite correct in this descriptive sense when he notes, "How remarkably fertile the religious imagination is, how fervid the appetite for significance; it sets gods to growing on every bush and rock" (*Self-Consciousness,* 226). As a theologian I see Updike's work articulating Calvin's *Divinitatis sensum,* the universal sense of the divine, and Luther's understanding of God's ambiguity in human experience as always both hidden and revealed. I also accept Paul Tillich's view that humans are incorrigibly moved to ask religious questions, and that one asks such questions already under the impact of anticipated answers (Tillich, 61).

It is important to realize that it is this presumed linkage of question and answer which allows Updike to move so quickly, and to some so confusingly and heretically, from description of the religious dimension of consciousness, as I have tried to outline it, to specifically biblical and creedal language. In fact, that is what gives his writing such power in American and Western culture: he shows the experiential connection between real life and the otherwise, for so many, apparently irrelevant mouthings of Christian language about something called good news. This is the linkage he shows in his earliest memoir, "The Dogwood Tree," when he wonders how he got "branded with a Cross" as a boy in Shillington, Pennsylvania (*Assorted Prose,* 181). From then on he recognizes in himself "an obdurate insistence that at the core of the core" of human experience "there is a right-angled clash" of opposites "to which, of all verbal combinations we can invent, the

---

God Who is a mere fact will just sit there on the table with all the other facts: we can take Him or leave Him. The way it is, we are always in motion *toward* the God Who flees, the *Deus absconditus;* He by His apparent absence is always with us'" (219). All the italics are Updike's. Notice especially the motion symbolism. Lambert is Updike here, and, as the language clearly attests, this is Updike's more characteristically Lutheran position — to which Barth's modern witness, as he stated, is thus joined. In Luther, the special revelation of God in Jesus Christ fulfills — expands and reorients — the effects of natural revelation; it does not replace it in God's economy of self-disclosure within human experience. But it is natural revelation that shapes Updike's view of the human religious consciousness — deeply and troublingly ambivalent, though ultimately sustaining — and it is that which I have sought to describe in this essay.

Apostles' Creed offers the most adequate correspondence and response" (181). Note carefully: "correspondence and response," *correspondence to questions* that arise in the religious dimension of human experience and *the response of proposed answers* in Christian creedal language.

How then might one characterize, in capsule form, the baseline religious consciousness in John Updike's literary vision? Perhaps it would sound something like this. Here is human life: thin ice, hot passions, hard facts; "in the night sky, blackness is not all. . . . The Truth arrives as if by telegraph: / One dot; two dots; a silence; then a laugh" (*Hugging the Shore*, 547; "Midpoint," *Collected Poems*, 96).

This is as good as it gets.

From the standpoint of the Christian witness of faith, however, it is not at all a bad place to start. When facing down all of life's terrifying ambiguities, we do, after all, as Updike suggests, end with a laugh and not a sneer. Even if always and everywhere never at our own command, there are, as Pascal witnesses, always and everywhere, "motions of Grace."

The Obligation to Live

Duty and Desire in John Updike's *Self-Consciousness*

AVIS HEWITT

James Yerkes has appropriately remarked that John Updike's religious sensibility is captured effectively in the title of the 1998 film *As Good As It Gets.*[1] The ambiguity of that phrase with its implication of both the most one can expect and the best one can imagine does indeed betray an overarching tension running throughout Updike's work. In his 1989 autobiographical text *Self-Consciousness,* Updike speaks of his life as an attempt to establish "rapport if not rapture" with God (257). That is, he has some provisional peace or tentative trust in his relationship with his God as Creator even though his real desire is for some sense of lofty and ecstatic transport for himself as creature. Updike's religious sensibility centers upon an energizing point of tension that, like the tension between peace and ecstasy, finds different labels in different contexts. As early as 1968 he articulated this perspective: "To be a person is to be in a situation of tension, is to be in a dialectical situation" (Plath, ed., 34).

This dynamic so pervades his work that Updike challenges readers

1. See Chapter 1 in this volume, "As Good as It Gets: The Religious Consciousness in John Updike's Literary Vision."

to find even in his memoirs the nature of that dialectical tension. Ralph Wood has written that for Updike "God himself has rendered our existence double, planting us amidst the contraries of inward and outward life" (*Comedy of Redemption*, 181). Particularly in *Self-Consciousness*, readers search for the tension that shapes Updike's memoirs as a means of discovering what has shaped his life. We care intensely about this issue because the man himself is not only an archetypal American success story but also the most lyrical teller of the archetypal American individual story. In his forty-year career Updike has become the spokesperson for our collective private lives. The Rabbit tetralogy that spans four decades and *In the Beauty of the Lilies* that covers four generations — and thereby most of the twentieth century — penetrate our contemporary American ways and days extensively, insightfully, and in painstakingly apt detail. Often we are ashamed to claim affinity with his blatantly flawed protagonists, yet finally we are forced to admit an insider's knowledge of these groping and ego-driven characters. Updike's narratives betray an unsettlingly candid understanding of the individualized yet prototypical contemporary American self.

His people strive then settle, reach then retrench in a restless motion that we hope is forward because we see its resemblance to the movement of our own lives. We ourselves unwillingly yet inevitably inhabit that narrow edge between an unleashed infinity of desire and the drudging drawbacks of duty — what we want to do relentlessly revised by what we must do. Once in an interview Updike revealed that his books "are all meant to be moral debates with the reader" and to raise such questions as "'What is a good man?' or 'What is goodness?'" (*Picked-Up Pieces*, 502). Somehow we assess how successfully we are living a good life by how skillfully we negotiate between the affinities of our inner lives and the afflictions of our outer lives.

On the one hand, almost every one of his fictional enterprises applies some currently popular solution — divorce, wife-swapping, therapy — to our perennially problematic creaturely lives, solutions that result in less than goodness. On the other hand, he recognizes that humans are by nature unfulfilled, confronted constantly with their own limitations and incompleteness. Our fight against these limits produces desire, the impulse that drives us forward. For Updike, desire can be specifically erotic: "I do buy Freud's notion about the radical centrality of sex. It's somehow so, isn't it? All kinds of activity, all the getting of money, are a forum for preening" (Plath, ed., 16). It can also be more generally egoistic: "My mind when I was a boy of ten or eleven sent up its silent screams at the thought of future aeons — at the thought of the cosmic party going on without me" (*Self-Consciousness,* 217). In fact, yearning spans very focused desires within the moment to the desire for an infinite number of moments. Ultimately our desires converge in the yearning to live forever.

Initially Updike's ploy for insuring perpetuity seems to involve a simple exchange: I offer God belief, and he offers me immortality. But perhaps immortality is more accurately the by-product of a compelling worldview. For Updike Christianity is the intersection of the physical with the spiritual as represented both in Christ's incarnation and in his cross. He endorses this convergence, this paradox, early in his career by affirming the "obdurate insistence that at the core of the core there is a right-angled clash to which, of all verbal combinations we can invent, the Apostles' Creed offers the most adequate correspondence and response" (*Assorted Prose,* 181). The element of Christian belief to which Updike most clearly subscribes is Christ as God Incarnate. That notion allows him to forestall the threat of nothingness, the sense of futility that comes to those who see life as limited to the strictly material realm. "Religion enables us to ignore nothingness and get on with the jobs of life," Updike writes in *Self-Consciousness* (228). Yet instead of seeing the issue as settled, his overwhelming urge is to revisit it, to wrestle with its particulars. For him the world holds two kinds of people: the ones for whom nothingness presents no problem and the ones for whom it is "an insuperable problem, an outrageous cancellation rendering every other concern, from mismatching socks to nuclear holocaust, negligible" (228). And Updike aligns himself clearly with those in the latter category.

One example of this is a compelling family photograph that graces the inside covers of *Self-Consciousness,* commemorating the 1909 fiftieth anniversary of his paternal great-grandparents. Most of us would glance only for a nostalgic moment at the thirty faces staring from the page, but for Updike the photo becomes a manifestation of banished existence. "Isn't this," he asks, "the fascination and terror of old photographs, their irrefutable evidence that photons once bathed vanished and disassembled worlds just as brightly as they now bathe ours?" (201). His musings about our individual places in the march of generations is a pervasive element of his memoirs. In them he initially presents little Johnny as a lonely only child, one who would rather retain a sense of his own singularity while observing those around him than give himself over enthusiastically to a sense of community. Furthermore, his observations invariably result in speculation about ultimate questions, our relation to one another and to God. He confides that he afforded his parents and grandparents an easygoing tolerance because those "distracted and needy" members of the household that nurtured him were "Depression-shocked" and seemed less in harmony with the world than he. Consequently, he "acquired an almost unnatural willingness to make allowances for other people, a kind of ready comprehension and forgiveness that amounts to disdain, a good temper won by an inner remove," based on the assumption that if he were "nice and good," they would "leave [him] alone to read [his] comic books" (256). To be left alone to observe and to hymn God's creation seems somehow Updike's inherent inclination.

Yet aloneness makes for hollow hymning. His novels and short stories boast a wealth of affiliations — albeit entangled ones — among his often autobiographical fictional protagonists. A man can be in lone pursuit of God and adhere perhaps to the first great commandment, but the second, which is "like unto it," requires heart ties. In the 1977 study that introduced the relationship between Karl Barth's theology and Updike's fiction, William Neal argues that both writers endorse our responsibility to relate "upward to heaven and beyond it to God, and downward to the other earthly creatures and to the mineral world [as well as] outward to [our] fellow-man" (Neal, 23). *Self-Consciousness* substantiates Updike's struggle between these horizontal and vertical relationships, perhaps for him another manifestation of "the right-angled clash." When we are fortunate, both desire and duty pull us out of the self toward our fellow creatures and toward God, creating the self-consciousness that allows for God-consciousness.

The self of which we are conscious is both an autonomous obligation and a social and collective creation. The self we are dutifully obliged to steer through our years of accountability and intended autonomy seems at times a yoke:

> Even toward myself, as my own life's careful manager and promoter, I feel a touch of disdain. Precociously conscious of the precious, inexplicable burden of selfhood, I have steered my unique little craft carefully, at the same time doubting that carefulness is the most sublime virtue. (*Self-Consciousness*, 257)

Paradoxically we need the intimacy and attentiveness of relationship to confirm that same identity: "Only in being loved do we find external corroboration of the supremely high valuation each ego secretly assigns itself" (*Assorted Prose,* 233). Updike, surely the most implicitly theological of our contemporary authors, sees both our singularity and our sociability. We bear the burden of autonomous identity, yet require external corroboration for the identity that we forge. The obligation to self and the obligation to others meet in what Updike has defined as "the obligation to live."

In the fifth memoir of *Self-Consciousness,* "A Letter to My Grandsons," Updike gives Anoff and Kwame (to whom the book is dedicated) a piece of wisdom that he inherited from *his* maternal grandfather: "We carry our own hides to market." He explicates this perspective as "putting the responsibility where it can be borne, on a frame made to fit" because it gives us a "partial release from tribal obligations — our debt of honor to our ancestors and our debt of shelter to our descendants." For Updike these duties matter but are not all that must matter: "These debts are real, but realer still is a certain obligation to our own selves, the obligation to live" (*Self-Consciousness,* 211). He then expands upon his particular meaning of the infinitive: "to live" is to nurture that "something [which is] intrinsically and individually vital" and which must be "defended against the claims even of virtue." He admonishes this new generation of Updike males not to "quench [their] spirit" or "hide [their] light beneath a bushel basket" or "bury [their] talent in the ground of this world" (211). Yet the prophet Micah reminds us: "What does the Lord God require of us? That we seek justice, love mercy, and walk humbly with our God" (6:8). God does not require that we seek personal, individual fulfillment.

Updike's fictional characters, however, frequently put private volition ahead of public virtue. A representative story, "Separating," illustrates the principle that choosing to seek one's own desires often throws one into a clash with conventional virtue. In it, a philandering protagonist tucks his elder son and namesake into bed after having told him on the drive home from the commuter train that he is leaving the boy's mother and thereby his four children. When the stoical son fails to make an emotional display but simply asks a level-headed "Why?" the father admits that he does not know. Although ostensibly the plan had been to marry another woman, one living in a house they had just passed on the drive home, that no longer seems significant compared to what he is doing to his family. His central realization is that his own father would never have put the private, ego-driven happiness of Eros love first: "My father would have died before doing [this] to me" (*Problems,* 129). The balance between "tribal obligation" and "the obligation to live" tips toward the self in Updike's narratives.

As we hear the protagonist hurt his son in order to please his own marital tastes of the moment, we are reminded of the societal justification such choices find these days. Roger Lundin has pointed out in *The Culture of Interpretation: Christian Faith and the Postmodern World* (1993) that since construction has replaced discovery as the main metaphor for the mind's activity in modern times, we have shifted our perceptions inward; rather than finding truth, we construct interpretations of reality that let us "live contentedly in a world where nothing is at stake" beyond a manipulatable sense of "feeling good" or supposed well-being (Lundin, 41). The distinction between the good and "feeling good" is vast, as wide a gap as righteousness is from "Right on!" — the phrase that has encouraged many to do what they want when they want in recent decades. Charles Taylor tells us in *Sources of the Self: The Making of the Modern Identity* (1989) that there seems "no conceptual place left for a notion of the good as the object of our love and allegiance . . . as the privileged focus of [our] attention or will" (C. Taylor, 3). The tension between inner volition — our heart's desire — and outer virtue — God's desire for our lives — has slackened amid current therapeutic confusions between loving ourselves and loving selfishly.

Updike's perspective on these issues throughout *Self-Consciousness* must be traced in increments. First, we must note the way in which the center of gravity in each of the six memoirs is an explicit statement of God-consciousness. Second, we must unpack the nature of God made evident in Updike's prose. Finally, we must investigate ways in which duty and desire, virtue and volition might meet. And if so, how so?

What we encounter in interacting with *Self-Consciousness* is that Updike chooses to map his life by enumerating his infirmities rather than his achievements. In fact, his memoirs reflect acute self-consciousness in both its senses: the positive level of attuned surveillance that monitors and manages the making of one's way through the world, and the less positive level of feeling awkwardly ashamed of one's presentation of self. The ailments and disadvantages that have created this awkwardness — from psoriasis, stuttering, and dental deterioration to his small-town, non-affluent upbringing — have also shaped him. Psoriasis encouraged him to the solitude of the writing desk because he felt he did not *look* good enough to pursue a vocation that brought him daily face to face with people. Stuttering helped him keep focused on writing once fame had allowed him the option of extensive lecture tours because he felt he did not *sound* good enough. Some reviewers have in fact been so disdainful of the physical imperfections he divulges in *Self-Consciousness* that he seems justified in having been embarrassed about such sufferings all along. What we come to see, however, is Updike's having reenacted in this text, by recounting these mundane yet deeply real creaturely humiliations and stumblings, the brokenness of a humble and contrite spirit that allows us to come before God. Implicitly he reveals self-consciousness, not only as awareness but also as awkwardness, to be our primary — perhaps our only — means to God-consciousness.

In the opening memoir, "A Soft, Spring Night in Shillington," Updike focuses on re-creating the streets and scenes of his hometown, contrasting its current features with those from his boyhood. As his tour opens and as it ends, Updike bullets his prose with the singular italicized Heideggerian term *Dasein.* This Old High German word for "being there" also invites reference to the philosophical project of Martin Heidegger, the "everyday Being-in-the-world" and "the structure of worldhood" around which he has shaped much of our century's perspective.[2] The narrator's immersion in the scene alludes as well to Heideggerian "thrownness," the notion that each of us is a situated, lo-

2. Martin Heidegger (1889-1976) in his early *Being and Time* (*Sein und Zeit,* 1927) indicted contemporary persons for failing to address and assume responsibility for their nature as *Dasein,* human existence in respect to its radical temporal and historical character — hence the use of the term here. Michael Inwood explains the connection between *Dasein* and "thrownness" as "the fact that *Dasein* is 'always already' in a specific situation that determines the possibilities available to us" (Inwood, 52). Heidegger was a watershed German philosopher; his early works contributed significantly to existentialist thinking in the first decades of this century — for example, Jean Paul Sartre — and his later works were powerfully influential in the philosophies of Hans-Georg Gadamer, Jacques Derrida, and Michel Foucault. Updike reviewed Heidegger's *Discourse on Thinking* (1966) for *The New Yorker* on 20 August 1966; the review was later included in *Picked-Up Pieces* (126-27). Updike at that time characterized Heidegger's views as "a humanism tied to a mysticism shorn of theology" (127). Still, it is evident he finds Heidegger's concept of *Dasein* quite helpful in his memoirs.

cated consciousness by the time we are a consciousness at all. This immersion in the world runs concomitantly with our sense of self. While this understanding gives us a finite sort of freedom within limited and confined lives, it also gives us an expanded sense of self. We are not simply a quickened corporeal entity with a Social Security number; we are the streets and houses and people and activities that texture our lives. Consequently, Updike revealed to Melvyn Bragg in a 1990 interview that he "gets very excited" each time he returns to Shillington, finding himself "begin[ning] to talk very rapidly and jump around a lot, just being in the blocks, the streets" (Plath, ed., 222). We know from *Self-Consciousness* that he loves Shillington "not as one loves Capri or New York, because they are special, but as one loves one's own body and consciousness, because they are synonymous with being," and that if "there [is] a meaning to existence, he [is] closest to it here" (*Self-Consciousness*, 30).

As he guides our tour, Updike re-creates the houses that once lined the streets of his town and its satellite "string-towns," their garages and alleys and packed-in tidiness. He resurrects Stephens' Luncheonette where he spent a sizable portion of his adolescence learning to smoke and blow smoke rings, posturing, and daydreaming after school. He nods to that moment of only-child loneliness that is almost a leitmotif of the text. Half the high school poured into Stephens' Luncheonette immediately after the day's last class, but within an hour everyone who lived in walking distance or had a car — that is, everyone except the author himself — had gone home, leaving him with the husband and wife owners and with the pinball machine. His father, Wesley, a math teacher at the high school, sometimes kept the young Updike waiting hours for a ride to the farm eleven miles away. Apparently any teacherly duty or athletic committee responsibility seemed better than reentering the life dominated by his wife and in-laws on the Hoyer homestead.

Updike recalls for us the post office, the funeral home, the town hall, the drug store, and the spot on Lancaster Avenue where, as a five-year-old child, he had been struck by a car and dragged for a distance while still clutching his Sunday School nickel (8). He takes us to Henry's Variety Store and Rollman's Camera Shop and to the "rec hall" where Betty Zimmerman had taught him to dance during the war, even though his only-child status had made him "shy and clumsy in the give and take and push and pull of human interchange" (12). We meet a classmate, a principal, several teachers, and learn the floor plan that forms the educational plan — the smart side and the slow side — of the elementary school. We meet the doctor who delivered him and the barber who cut his hair. Nearing his childhood home, we pass the trolley tracks and ice plant that are no more. We learn the outlines, the fates of several neighbors as we pass the addresses from which they had neighbored young Johnny. When we reach his own, 117 Philadelphia Avenue, he waits "to feel something" and feels "less than [he] had hoped," but senses at least that the "blunt, modest" street and house actually hold something "precious" and "mystical" that he has "parlayed into a career, a message to sustain a writer book after book" (24).

As Updike muses about the relative status and affluence his child self had observed among his own family and the neighbors, a steadily stronger theme of vindication and finally vengeance emerges from the text. In pondering the blows fate dealt his father and both his grandfathers, the humiliations they suffered, he relishes the extent to which he has "shown" this unsuspecting town an unequivocal Updike success: "more people had heard of me now than had ever heard of Philadelphia Avenue" (30). In vividly recounting the repeatedly broken nose, aggravated hernia, and varicose veins his father suffered, as well as an outsider's ostracism from local club membership and a tired teacher's disrespect from students, Updike calls Shillington the place where he had "waited in ambush to take [his] revenge" (33). Then he elaborates on ways in which waiting and ambush have shaped him.

Two sensations of childhood held for him repeated bliss: first, his "awareness of things going by, impinging on [his] consciousness and then sliding away toward their own destination and destiny" — that "sweetness of riddance" that would seem to contradict his obsession with immortality (34); and second, "the sensation of shelter" where he can be "out of the rain, but *just out*," a mode mindful of the cold writerly objectivity to which both he and Nathaniel Hawthorne have confessed:

> The experiencer is motionless, holding his breath as it were, and the things experienced are morally detached from him: there is nothing he can do, or ought to do, about the flow, the tumult. He is irresponsible, safe, and witnessing. (35)

In the second memoir, "At War with My Skin," the child who crouched under the overturned wicker lawn furniture, watching the rain misting around him, "happy almost to tears," is superseded by the young man entering the world with skin that periodically betrays his efforts to fit seamlessly into the larger society. The first memoir had closed with this God-conscious notion: "Rain is grace; rain is the sky condescending to the earth; without rain, there would be no life" (41). But this very rain also stimulates his own singular awareness out of the vast awareness among us all: "Billions of consciousnesses silt history full, and every one of them the center of the universe. What can we do in the face of this unthinkable truth but scream or take refuge in God?" (40). He examines "the oddity of consciousness being placed in one body rather than another, in one place and not somewhere else," and the notion of *Dasein* recurs. In a particularly Heideggerian moment he sums up his experience that night in Shillington: "I had propelled my body through the tenderest parts of a town that was also somewhat my body" (40), allowing the Emersonian Me/Not Me dichotomy to yield to the larger view of creatures and Creator that Updike's vision unrelentingly dramatizes. In a moment of self-possession and autonomy he confesses that life, from the age of thirteen on, has "felt like not quite my own idea" — he had strongly disliked the move to the farm — but "Shillington, its idle alleys and darkened four-square houses, had been my idea" (41).

"At War with My Skin" provides the same close correspondence between outer circumstance and inner self. His psoriasis was inherited from his mother, with whom in early years he shares parts of the treatment: sunbathing and the pus-like, tar-like ooze of the medicine, Siroil. In the same way that the first memoir highlighted rain, descending to us as grace, letting us be washed clean and given the chance to flourish, this memoir showcases sun: "To be forgiven, by God . . . a tactile actuality . . . the sun's weight on my skin always meant this to me: I was being redeemed, hauled back into mankind, back from deformity and shame" (68). Here Updike the family man and steadily more successful writer makes his home in Ipswich, Massachusetts, and grows his family to the symmetrical sum of two sons and two daughters. They experience sufficient prosperity that he can rent a room for writing in downtown Ipswich, and at lunch the stationwagoned "wife and quartet of children . . . plump and brown in their bathing suits" would pick him up for a noontime swim and picnic at the beach: "to walk down the boardwalk in procession, myself the leader and evident support of so much healthy flesh — what pagan, bourgeois bliss!" (59).

Paradoxically, his need for the curative power of the sun prompted many other manifestations of bourgeois bliss — not only the yearly January trips to the Caribbean to get enough extra sun on his skin to hold back the lesions until hot rays returned to New England in the late spring, but also his choices of family and work and milieu:

> Why did I marry so young? Because, having once found a comely female who forgave me my skin, I dared not risk losing her and trying to find another. Why did I have children so young? Because I wanted to surround myself with people who did not have psoriasis. Why, in 1957, did I leave New York and my nice employment there? Because my skin was bad in the urban shadows. (48)

Having found Ipswich, in part because "this ancient Puritan town happened to have one of the great beaches of the Northeast" (48), Updike experiences the greatest sense of affiliation he has known, joining clubs and serving on committees and enjoying a recorder group and a poker group: "In Ipswich my impersonation of a normal person became as good as I could make it" (54). He felt that "the sisters and brothers [he] had never had were now on the phone or at the back door" (52), and he enjoyed "a rush of wonder" that he had "come to be part of this" (53). The problematic "pelt" that might have separated him painfully from his fellow creatures had actually propelled him into sociability instead:

> An illusion of eternal comfort reposes in clubbiness — an assurance that members of tribes and villages have extended to one another for millennia, the assurance that no earthly adventure, from puberty to death, is unprecedented or incapable of being shared and that one's life is thoroughly witnessed and therefore not wasted. (55)

Yet, for all the exuberance of such a reassuring passage as this one, the span of years that informs the second memoir seems yet another version of the growing-up years in Shillington. In fact, he admits that these Ipswich years had "a raw educational component," that he came into them "know[ing] very little of how the world worked" and enjoyed instruction in such myriad aspects of middle-class adulthood as the proper backhand stroke, the use of a wallpaper steamer, and the secret of mixing a good martini or dancing the Twist. He confides that he and his wife must have looked to their children quite old to be "still taking lessons, in how to be grown-up" (55). And just as a child sheds his nest to enter the adult world, Updike shed this second-time nest of warm familial and clubby entanglement. As the layers of skin come off to reveal the new creature, so in middle life the Ipswich "impersonation" peeled away, as he forsook his wife and children and allowed his newest layers of self to emerge.

Updike implies that previous selves would no longer work, just as many elements of life may lose their effectiveness simply because they have long *been* effective. We grow immune. The January trips to the Caribbean at first included the family and then did not; the varieties of treatment for psoriasis at first worked and then worked less well. A new discovery, methotrexate, has worked in recent years, but will likely, given the way of the world, wear thin in its combative powers. Seeing life as a long combat against the inevitable encroachment of death, he also sees his true and psoriatic self as at last winning out over all efforts at concealment:

> when I am at last too ill for all these demanding and perilous palliatives, the psoriasis like a fire smoldering in damp peat will break out and spread triumphantly; in my dying I will become hideous, I will become what I am. (78)

In the third memoir, "Getting the Words Out," Updike reverts a third time to childhood to pick up the thread of affliction where it began — with a sidewalk quarrel between himself and Eddie Pritchard, who called him "Ostrich" (79). The contours of his stuttering stem from that moment, as he carefully explains: stuttering occurs when he finds himself in a false position that he feels compelled to rectify. He becomes overwhelmed with how much about him needs explaining, all of which is "subsumable under the heading of 'I am not an ostrich'" (80). Stuttering stems from as well as creates difference. It is one more way in which he is separated out. He thinks that most people have "a settled place they speak from; in me it remains unsettled, unfinished, provisional" (80); he believes that the "paralysis of stuttering stems from the dead center of one's being, a deep doubt there," and is perhaps "a kind of recoil at the thrust of [one's] own voice, an expression of alarm and shame at sounding like yourself, at *being* yourself, at taking up space and air" (87). When stutterers displace their ordinary voice because of a cold or an accent or singing, the problem disappears. It is some need to own and affirm the self that creates the trauma.

At the center of this memoir is the image of the throat: "how strange, that there is not more erotic emphasis upon it. For here, through this compound pulsing pillar, our life makes its leap into spirit, and in the other direction gulps down what it needs of the material world" (91). The overarching dynamic of this chapter is Updike's leaps and gulpings. From his shy Shillington uncertainties to his splendid New York and New England successes, he has leapt from obscurity to opulence in the best Franklinian and Horatio Alger style, yet he chokes on what he has gulped down. He begins to suffer attacks of asthma, a variation on the tightened and blocked throat that has blighted him since childhood. Desperate to desert the secure nest he has created, he finds that he both literally and figuratively can no longer breathe in its atmosphere. He recalls an especially baleful bout of asthma that occurred once when he took his wife and children to visit his parents and almost actually physically suffocated from the demands made on him by the simultaneous roles of husband, son, and father. Escape seemed injurious but inevitable. Finally, after twelve years of attempting to wrest himself free, his chance came because of his allergy to cat dander. In fact, he once caught his younger son throwing the cat down the cellar stairs in angry exasperation as the boy realized that the cat was facilitating his father's desertion: rather than get rid of the cats, "it seemed easier to get rid of me" (101). Updike neither excuses nor blames himself for this rupture that reopened his throat passages. One must breathe because one has the obligation to live.

The fourth memoir, "On Not Being a Dove," manifests the benefits of having cleared his throat. Even though his ambivalent stance was unpopular in the artist and writer circles to which he belonged, he articulated it during that conflicted era of American life and chose to replay it for us two decades later. It is the antithesis of his clubby and affiliated period in Ipswich, a turning back to the genteel poverty and overt patriotism of his boyhood. He finds the issue not solely military and political: "I feel in the dove arguments as presented to me too much aesthetic distaste for the President"; furthermore, he sees the self-interest that underlies the chaotic protesting and acknowledges that he too "would be glad to be freed of all the duties of living in a powerful modern state — while continuing to accept, of course, the benefits" (114-15).

The liberals voted as Democrats "out of human sympathy and humanitarian largesse" while remaining securely within the upper middle class. The Democrats were the party that helped the poor. By contrast, Updike's family voted Democratic out of crude self-interest: they had simply *been* poor. His argument here is that we should "come clean" about our motives, that we must embrace reality: "down-dirty sex and the bloody mess of war and the desperate effort of faith all belonged to a dark necessary underside of reality" as "shameful things" that are "intrinsic to life" (135). His theological stance is similar:

> A dark Augustinian idea lurked within my tangled position: a plea that Vietnam — this wretched unfashionable war led by clumsy Presidents from the West and fought by the nineteen-year-old sons of the poor — could not be disowned by a favored enlightened few . . . pretending that our great nation hadn't had bloody hands from the start, that every generation didn't have its war, that bloody hands didn't go with having hands at all. (135-36)

Acknowledging that this stance directly reflects the notion of original sin, he continues to square it with the human condition. He says that our deeming "war [to be] madness is like saying that sex is madness"; if one is a "stateless eunuch," then the madness can be sidestepped, but most of us "must make [our] arrangements in the world as given" (141).

As the fourth memoir winds away from its center, Updike contrasts his "deadpan churchgoing" with the bohemian and disenchanted stance most writers were displaying toward religion. For him, atheism provokes "repulsion" because of "its drastic uninterestingness as an intellectual position" (141), and he sees the "psychological tensions" generated by our "enchantment" with Christianity as the basis for what has transpired in Western culture from Boethius to Marcel Proust (142). The argument for an original sin position regarding Vietnam mingles with his own debts as sinner. Those who served in uniform — Mailer, Roth, Vonnegut — have earned commenting. What has Updike earned? He remembers Kazin's review accusing him of "dazzling" and "brilliant" prose that yet failed in "conveying [the adult world with] its depths and risks" (149). Has he indeed stayed too successfully out of harm's way?

In a deft rhetorical move that merges his creaturely afflictions with his spiritual stance, Updike spends the last ten pages of "On Not Being a Dove" in the dentist's chair. His dental ordeals seem at first a mundanely unfitting conclusion to arguments about America's intervention in Vietnam. Finally, however, it becomes obvious that the citizens of rich and powerful countries are privileged to undergo the pain of dental repair because they are blessed with the wealth and technology that can save their teeth. They suffer in part because they have been privileged to enjoy the refined sugar treats that generate the dental difficulties. Updike equates confronting the debt we owe our dentist with the debt we owe our country, pondering how he would have faced Iwo Jima or Normandy if that lot had fallen to him: "I flatter myself that I would tuck my head down with the others, jump waist-deep into the shocking, surging water, and wade numbly forward. If hit in the gut with a bullet, I would grunt and fall on the wet sand and wait for the next blow of a distant God" (162). His hope about his response in extremity stems from something a British officer taught Hemingway during World War I: *"By my troth, I care not: a man can die but once; we owe God a death . . . and let it go which way it will, he that dies this year is quit for the next"* (163; italics in original). Now alongside "down-dirty sex and the bloody mess of war and the desperate effort of faith" we align the owed death. Before the obligation to die, however, comes still the obligation to live.

In the fifth memoir, "A Letter to My Grandsons," Updike wrestles with the myriad branches of the family tree, the Pennsylvania and New York and New Jersey and Old World roots and offshoots. Intermingled with his interpretations of work and worship and race relations in America are enough facts and anecdotes to provide his grandsons some modicum of security in their own efforts toward self-consciousness: "I was an Updike, and this distinctive name conveyed that I was somebody, from a line of somebodies" (197). Surely this is one of the most valued familial assurances the fledgling members of a clan can be given. Near the end of the essay he foreshadows the argument of his final and most philosophical memoir. At this point he provides three pages of background identification regarding those thirty family members pictured on the inside covers at the 1909 wedding anniversary. These "vanished souls and lives" echo those "billions of consciousnesses" who have passed through God's earthly creation since its genesis. Moreover, "every one of them [has been] a center of the universe" and every one of them a "somebody" (40). Yet each passes from the scene after so brief a turn that we yearn to understand the significance of having participated at all. In the sixth and last memoir, Updike comments on that significance.

"On Being a Self Forever" wrestles with the possibilities of immortality. Is the self that one would be forever the self derived from self-consciousness? Generally, yes. To introduce his argument, Updike marshals a new list of minor sufferings that mark him as a unique creature: the specks in his vitreous humor, his artist's habit of tracing images with a mental finger, the scraps of old songs that float into his head, his rehashing inner voice, the glitch in the *d* that comes when he signs his name, and the graphite remains of a pencil wound from junior high. He wonders whether such a flawed, idiosyncratic self deserves "to persist forever, to outlast the atomic universe." The body peaks and then declines. If disembodied spirits go somewhere "in the vast spaces disclosed by modern astronomy" (214), then where? The looks and laws of Heaven that derive from biblical passages hinge on the physical and material resurrection articulated in the Apostles' Creed, but what will the resurrected, even if restored, body *do?* And where will it wait? Updike confesses that attempts to be specific about the afterlife appall us. In having lost much of our capacity for reverence and awe, we have also become resistant to "vague reassurance" (216).

Even though it seems that any endlessly sustained condition would be intolerable, what we do wish to sustain is "the self as window on the world"; the thought of shutting it seems as unbearable as the notion of "the cosmic party going on without [us]" (217). Citing Miguel Unamuno's *The Tragic Sense of Life* for the particular sort of immortality we crave, for "the continuation of this present life" (217), Updike confesses that the life we now experience, life with its fascinatingly endless change, is what we love about being alive: "the resolution of old adventures and the possibility of beginning new ones"; therefore, all we ask from religion is "that each moment of our consciousness will be followed by another" (217). He sees selves as continually dying and giving way to new and slightly altered versions: "That we age and leave behind this litter of dead, unrecoverable selves is both unbearable and the commonest thing in the world" (226). In the morning light we can stand it, but in the darkness we cannot contemplate it "without turning in panic to God." We do not like that feeling of "immense sliding" that takes away the world with all its "bright distractions and warm touches." Our fervid appetite for significance convinces us that "our life is a story, with a pattern and a moral and an inevitability," and that "our subjectivity . . . dominates, through secret channels, outer reality," providing the universe with "a personal structure" (226-27).

Throughout *Self-Consciousness* Updike appears to have premised his narrative on a certain significance and pattern. In fact, when "the impalpable self cries out to [God]," the answer from him finally comes "as the large facts of our lives, strung on that thread running through all things" — a "consecration of what is" (229). Now he admits that his belief in God originated in a syllogism: "If God does not exist, the world is a horror show. The world is not a horror show. Therefore, God exists." His admission does not dismiss human suffering but simply acknowledges that existence "does not feel horrible; it feels like an ecstasy. . . . The world is good, our intuition is, confirming its Creator's appraisal as reported in the first chapter of Genesis" (230). Finally, he explains his sense of the elusive nature of institutionalized Christianity and its "signs of belief," which almost no one took seriously: "when you moved toward [it] it disappeared, as fog solidly opaque in the distance thins to transparency when you walk into it" (230). In spite of that, however, he decided that he *would* believe. His use of Chesterton, Eliot, Unamuno, Kierkegaard, and Barth have aided him in constructing a life based on that decision, and in this observation he affirms it: "Wherever there is a self, it may be, whether on Earth or in the Andromeda Galaxy, the idea of God will arise" (232) — and from God, the hope of immortality. In his relentless naming of immortality as a central issue of belief, Updike aligns himself with Unamuno's "stubborn child" adamancy in *The Tragic Sense of Life:* "I do not want to die — no; I neither want to die nor do I want to want to die; I want to live forever and ever and ever. I want this 'I' to live — this poor 'I' that I am and that I feel myself to be here and now" (Unamuno, 51).

In the closing pages of the text, Updike visits his mother, circling back through his past as he has done countless times since leaving home for Harvard in 1950. Old family friends that they encounter in town comment on how much he looks like her, a moment that he artfully juxtaposes with contemplating his own photo hanging in the hallway that had been taken when he was a child of five.[3] Even though

3. The postmodern gesture of photographing that photo is one that Updike chose himself. He has used the resultant art on the dust jackets and mass-market paperback editions of *Self-Consciousness*.

"little Johnny" with "his tentatively smiling mouth" and "his dark and ardent and hopeful eyes" has "got [Updike] into this" (*Self-Consciousness*, 238), he represents simply the past while his mother serves dually: "My mother was my future, as well as my past" (242). Implicitly Updike, by turn, is past as well as future for her: her unpublished fiction stands somewhat vindicated by the prolific and celebrated career of her son. Her passion and talent and calling have moved forward in time farther than she alone was able to carry them.

We are reminded of the tribal obligation that Updike has weighed in his writing to the newest members of the Updike tribe, Anoff and Kwame. In warning them that such obligations must not supplant "a certain obligation to our own selves, the obligation to live," he creates space for making choices that might seem noticeably self-serving, ones that could "be defended against the claims even of virtue" (211). Yet he has not made many such choices — or at least not revealed them. Yes, he left his wife and four children in order to regain his breathing capacities, but generally in the life he interprets for us here others have not figured as prominent characters. No true love or arch rival or bosom friend gets cast. Yet his motions in response to parents, wives, children, and friends have shaped his circumstances. As the epigraph to *Rabbit, Run* he chose a quote from Blaise Pascal's *Pensée 507:* "The motions of Grace, the hardness of the heart; external circumstances." His memoirs have hymned the complex interaction of the three, but the shift in punctuation — a comma joins the first two while a semicolon separates them from the last — indicates that our circumstances are shaped by the tension between our hard hearts and God's gift of grace. These contraries are kept taut by love, which helps to explain Christ's use in the second great commandment of self-love as a measure of how well we are loving others. Whether we love from desire or from duty is ultimately subsumed in our having loved at all.

C. S. Lewis points out in his Afterword to the third edition of *The Pilgrim's Regress* that we must come "at last into the clear knowledge that the human soul was made to enjoy some object that is never fully given — nay, cannot even be imagined as given — in our present mode of subjective and spacio-temporal experience" (204). Desire moves from the erotic impulse, which is ultimately a Kierkegaardian attempt to fend off death, to the yearning for an enlarged plane of awareness, a greater consciousness — great enough to allow for consciousness of God. God has created our separateness from him in order that we might move toward him. Lewis writes in *The Problem of Pain* that "He caused things to be other than Himself that, being distinct, they might learn to love Him, and achieve union instead of mere sameness," and that "it is not God's purpose that we should go back into that old identity [of sameness] . . . but that we should go on to maximum distinctness there to be reunited with Him in a higher fashion" (151). This "higher fashion" implies Updike's own notion of the "obligation to live" because, paradoxically, the self cannot be fully honoring of God that does not hold in some way separate from God. This fits the Updikean scheme that his prose relentlessly explores. Consequently, he concludes *Self-Consciousness* with the explicit desire to "achieve rapport if not rapture" with God. In the space between whatever mutual affinity is denoted by *rapport* and the ecstatic transport, even to a heavenly at-one-ment with Christ, which he may intend by *rapture*, John Updike has hymned for us late-twentieth-century readers his representative twentieth-century American life. The world he gives us here calls us to live at the crux of that right-angled clash, at the nexus of duty and desire, at that level of affinity and sometimes transport which his perspective illuminates.

The Pocket Nothing Else Will Fill

Updike's Domestic God

JAMES A. SCHIFF

In a preface to a special printing of *In the Beauty of the Lilies,* John Updike explained that in his seventeenth novel he was attempting

> to tell a continuous story, of which God was the hero. I invited Him in, to be a character in my tale, and if He declined, with characteristic modern modesty, to make His presence felt unambiguously, at least there is a space in this chronicle plainly reserved for Him, a pocket in human nature that nothing else will fill. ("Special Message," ii)

Updike's comment, however playful, is provocative, even startling. Though God is invoked on many occasions in that novel, one never conceives of him — at least I didn't — as being an actual character, much less the hero. In *Lilies* as in other novels by Updike, characters debate and search for signs of God's existence, yet those theological exercises have always seemed simply an added layer, something that while in no way insignificant was nevertheless supplementary to the central human action. Though I am well aware of the many critics who have viewed Updike as a religious writer, he has always seemed to me to be foremost a domestic writer, concerned with how individuals exist inside and outside of households. I continue to view him in these terms. His statement regarding *Lilies,* however, leads me to pose what I believe is a useful and fairly crucial question: What exactly is the role of God in Updike's fiction, and where does one find this God?

Further fueling my desire to explore the relationship between Updike and God is the fact that Updike was basically ignored in Alfred Kazin's recent and much praised critical study, *God and the American Writer.* Though Kazin halts his historical survey at Faulkner, he nevertheless makes a brief, dismissive reference to Updike in an Afterword: "John Updike, modestly acquiescent to religious tradition, opens his novel *In the Beauty of the Lilies* with a minister's loss of faith, but never tells us what was lost — and why" (Kazin, 259). Kazin's remark, which I will later consider, suggests to me that a good deal more needs to be said.

As for Updike's personal orientation to God, Updike, unlike many of his literary contemporaries, is a believer: "I do tend to see the world as layered, and as there being something up there" (Plath, ed., 50). What is up there, though, cannot be articulated in simple terms. Updike's God is dualistic and paradoxical. As Updike explains, "there's a fierce God" who throws lightning bolts and causes earthquakes, and "the kind God" whom "we can worship and empathize with" (33). According to Ralph Wood, Updike "finds . . . a God who is double if not duplicitous in character: a Power making for terror no less than wonder, a Savior who redeems but also a Bungler who must be forgiven" (*Comedy of Redemption,* 190).

Continuing in this paradoxical vein, Updike's God is hidden yet visible, absent yet present. As many of his readers know, Updike has long maintained a Barthian position in which God is "Wholly Other" and thus absent from this world. In a 1963 review of a new translation of Karl Barth's *Anselm,* Updike quoted and appeared to agree with the Neoorthodox Swiss theologian, who stated, "There is no way from us to God. . . . The god who stood at the end of some human way . . . would not be God" (*Assorted Prose,* 273). Though removed and hidden, Updike's God nevertheless reveals himself and leaves traces for humans to find. In an early interview, Updike explained that his parents and grandparents had a tendency to "examine everything for God's fingerprints" (Plath, ed., 12). Years later he added that in the cornucopia of items displayed at Henry's Variety Store in his hometown of Shillington, Pennsylvania, he found "a single omnipresent manufacturer-God [who] seemed to be showing us a fraction of His face, His plenty" (*Self-Consciousness,* 11). God, then, for Updike, is in the details and abundance of existence. As the narrator of "The Blessed Man of Boston, My Grandmother's Thimble, and Fanning Island" explains, "A piece of turf torn from a meadow becomes a *gloria* when drawn by Dürer. Details. Details are the giant's fingers" (*Pigeon Feathers,* 245). Updike's God is both there and not there, such that his existence lies within a dialectical tension that can never be resolved. God is beyond the finite world yet reveals himself within it.

In his fiction Updike often explores the question of God's existence by positing a dialectic. Consider his first novel, *The Poorhouse Fair,* in which the humanist prefect Conner and the aging Hook debate the existence of God. A lyrical novel that favors the character and perspective of the Christian, Hook, *The Poorhouse Fair* emphasizes the glory of God's presence over the despair of his absence. When Conner asks, "What makes you think, God exists?" the wiser and far more likable Hook responds, "There is what of Cre-ation I can see, and there are the inner spokesmen" (112). Typical of Updike's protagonists, Hook sees a magnificent, mysterious pattern in the natural world, which suggests God's existence: "That part of the uni-verse which is visible to me, is an unfailing source of consolation" (114).

Though writers have long found signs of God's presence in the bounty of nature, particularly the untamed, majestic beauty of the American landscape, Updike goes further. He finds God not only in nature, as one sees through the arguments of Hook, but in other places as well, such as human sexuality, inanimate objects like furniture, craftsmanship and art, games such as golf and poker, human vitality, and simple domestic scenes. Whereas Emerson and Thoreau experienced transcendence outdoors in the natural world, Updike finds a mode of revelation, attributable to God, in domestic objects and details. Consider, for instance, Thomas Marshfield's declaration in *A Month of Sundays:*

> But it was, somehow, and my descriptive zeal flags, in the *furniture* I awoke among, and learned to walk among, and fell asleep amid — it was the moldings of the doorways and the sashes of the windows and the turnings of the balusters — it was the carpets each furry strand of which partook in a pattern and the ceilings whose random cracks and faint discolorations I would never grow to reach, that convinced me, that *told* me, God was, and was here, even as the furnace came on, and breathed gaseous warmth upon my bare, buttonshoed legs. Someone invisible had cared to make these things. (22-23)

Marshfield sees God's hand working beneath or through human hands, and he finds manifestations of the divine in the everyday tangible. His most intense physical religious experience occurs not on a mountain peak but rather comically in a bathroom during a bout with constipation, when "a great force as if manually seized my bowels, and my body, like a magnificent animal escaped from its keeper. . . . It was a thrust from beyond" (222). Updike is unique in endowing the human and domestic with the same spark of divinity that is often found in the great outdoors.

Elsewhere Marshfield explains how he finds God operating beneath the surface of golf and poker games. "A power greater than myself" (181) allows Marshfield to hole a shot with a 7-iron, and he later describes "watching the breath of the Lord play across the surface of the cards" (196). God is "an omnipotence that moves and creates everywhere, that 'potently does everything in everything'" (199). Marshfield thus views the physical world as transparent, and he asserts that through careful observation "we dissolve the veneer our animal murk puts upon things, and empathize with God's workmanship" (191).

Given that twentieth-century depictions of provincial middle-class American life are often satirical — consider, say, the work of Sinclair Lewis — one is not likely to discover traces of divinity in such settings. For Updike, however, God permeates every aspect of human life so that his presence is felt in and around households. Writes Updike, "there is a color, a quiet but tireless goodness that things at rest, like a brick wall or a small stone, seem to affirm. A wordless reassurance these things are pressing to give." Though this reassurance is not necessarily incontestable evidence of God's existence, Updike suggests the possibility of there being something greater beneath the physical surface: "Blankness is not emptiness; we may skate upon an intense radiance we do not see because we see nothing else" (*Assorted Prose,* 186).

One begins then to gain a better understanding of Updike's highly descriptive prose style, which, depending on one's perspective, can be magnificent or self-indulgent. Updike's style, as it builds through an accumulation of details and images, works to replicate the abundance of God's world. Updike, who articulates his style as "a groping and elemental attempt to approximate the complexity of envisioned phenomena" (*Self-Consciousness,* 103), strives to imitate the richness of creation. Relying on complex imagery and metaphorical, baroque language, his style expresses the pattern of interconnection that the author suggests is behind all creation:

> The day's rain lifted; the high yellow house hove clear of spray; the many gray connections between below and above were snapped. The unpainted wood of the tables was soaked black. Drop by drop the colored bulbs slipped their thin jackets of water. A few of the women ventured into the open, treading distastefully the drenched lawn in which the circular cobwebs of the grass spiders showed like mirrors left lying in the grass. The song of the birds was especially strident. Hook from the porch heard what he rarely heard, a bobolink. Mrs. Lucas came down from her room, her legs better. The musicians laid their instruments aside. The inmates of the home, already united in expectation of the holiday, had passed as a group through two turns of fortune: the rain, and the rain's abatement, which last joined them together in a mood of raucous, cruel exhilaration quite unlike the sweet and moderate expectation of the morning. (*Poorhouse Fair*, 127-28)

Through language Updike captures the breadth and potency of creation, which stands as evidence, for Hook as well as the author, of a divine presence in the world. In a novel that debates God's existence, everything from the characters to the land to the craftsmanship of the poorhouse edifice can be seen as masks of God. "Imitation is praise. Description expresses love," writes Updike, who, by re-creating the world, composes a personal hymn to God (*Self-Consciousness*, 231).

Yet God's presence is hardly absolute or constant; it must always be reaffirmed and rediscovered. As Marshfield explains, "Even were the sky a neonated 3-D billboard flashing GOD EXISTS twenty-four hours a day we would contrive ways to doubt it" (*Month of Sundays*, 213). From Harry Angstrom to *Toward the End of Time*'s Ben Turnbull, Updike's protagonists doubt and vacillate, seeing the world at one moment as a horrible void and at the next as an emblem of God's majesty.

While I have suggested that God is often transparently present in Updike's domestic realm, upheaval within a household can quickly lead characters to doubts and questions about God's existence. Consider the short story "Pigeon Feathers," in which teenager David Kern's belief in God is shaken after reading H. G. Wells's denial of

Christ's divinity. Yet before David even reads Wells, we learn in the story's opening that his world has become disoriented by the family's recent move to the country:

> When they moved to Firetown, things were upset, displaced, rearranged. A red cane-back sofa that had been the chief piece in the living room at Olinger was here banished, too big for the narrow country parlor, to the barn, and shrouded under a tarpaulin. Never again would David lie on its length all afternoon eating raisins and reading mystery novels and science fiction and P. G. Wodehouse. (*Pigeon Feathers*, 116)

The narrator explains that a blue wing chair, formerly in the guest bedroom, a room David had been afraid of, was now placed before the parlor fireplace: "it was disquieting to have one of the elements of [the guest room's] haunted atmosphere basking by the fire, in the center of the family." David realizes that, "like the furniture, he ha[s] to find a new place," so he then tries "to work off some of his disorientation by arranging the books" (117). Though domestic disorder does not literally generate David's doubts and fears, it contributes to them.

After reading Wells, David is suddenly "visited by an exact vision of death: a long hole in the ground, no wider than your body, down which you are drawn while the white faces above recede" (123). Following this "revelation of extinction" (128), David searches for hope and reassurance — which ultimately comes as he buries the pigeons that he has killed: "Across the surface of the infinitely adjusted yet somehow effortless mechanics of the feathers played idle designs of color, no two alike, designs executed, it seemed, in a controlled rapture, with a joy that hung level in the air above and behind him" (149). David has worked through his doubts and darkness to arrive at "this certainty: that the God who had lavished such craft upon these worthless birds would not destroy His whole creation by refusing to let David live forever" (150). Like the aging Hook, David locates God in creation.

Yet, as critics have pointed out, one must be attentive to irony. According to Robert Luscher, David's "affirmation of God's existence, a rudimentary version of the theological argument from design, is more important as a strategy to cope with his fear of death rather than as a genuine religious commitment" (Luscher, 32). Is God simply the antidote to fear and terror? Perhaps, yet Updike seems genuine in his belief that something, some intentional force, has shaped this world. As he writes, "One believes not only to comfort one's self but for empirical and compositional reasons — the ornate proposed supernatural completes the picture and, like the ingredient that tops up and rounds out the recipe, gives reality its true flavor" (*Self-Consciousness*, 233-34). Utter gloom and bleakness seem unreal to Updike, who writes, "As in the night sky, blackness is not all" (*Hugging the Shore*, 547).

Given that domestic upheaval in Updike's work often leads characters to question God's existence, it is not surprising to see those same domestically dissatisfied figures searching for something loosely or tangentially associated with the divine. Consider Harry Angstrom in *Rabbit, Run*, who views his domestic arrangement as a "mess" (31/29): "The clutter behind him in the room — the Old-fashioned glass with its corrupt dregs, the chock-full ashtray balanced on the easy-chair arm, the rumpled rug . . . clings to his back like a tightening net" (14/14). Harry yearns for something greater: a better domestic situation, a life that will allow him to make fuller use of his talents. Similar to *In the Beauty of the Lilies*, a novel that associates personal energy with the presence of God, Harry is searching, among other things, for the return of God in his life.

When Harry espies his son Nelson through the window of his parents' house, he views that house in direct contrast to his own: "[Nelson's] little neck gleams like one more clean object in the kitchen among the cups and plates and chromium knobs and aluminum cake-making receptacles on shelves scalloped with glossy oilcloth. His mother's glasses glitter" (*Rabbit, Run*, 20-21/20). When objects "gleam," "glitter," or are bathed in light in Updike's writing, it is often because they are touched by God. In *Lilies* Essie literally "glows" from the light God favors her with, and in a Wilmot family discussion "God" and "the Light" are used synonymously: "Some would say God did nothing to Clarence. If there was any doing, it was the other way around. My brother turned and ran from the Light, is the sad truth of it" (*In the Beauty of the Lilies*, 152). In his memoirs Updike explains:

> The sun's weight on my skin always meant this to me: I was being redeemed, hauled back into mankind, back from deformity and shame. The sun was like God not only in His power but also in the way He allowed Himself to be shut out, to be evaded. (*Self-Consciousness*, 68)

In Updike's work, light, which serves as an emblem of God, both reveals and glorifies.

Because Harry's present life lacks light and glory, he searches for the quintessential "it," which he locates at moments on the golf course and in sexual relations. For instance, as he makes pure contact with a golf ball and projects it far into the distant sky, Harry cries, "That's *it!"* (*Rabbit, Run,* 134/116). Though the "it" isn't necessarily God, one sees it as a certain kind of energy and force, a godliness that is breathed into him, enabling him to perform at his best.

Similarly in *Couples,* characters are searching for either a return of or a replacement for God. America, according to Piet Hanema, is *"unloved": "God doesn't love us any more. . . . We're fat and full of pimples and always whining for more candy. We've fallen from grace"* (*Couples,* 200). Because God is no longer present in their homes, these characters search elsewhere for hope and transcendence. As Freddy Thorne, the group leader, explains, "People are the only thing people have left since God packed up. By people I mean sex" (145). Yet sex, in spite of the temporary transcendence it bestows, proves an equally unstable replacement, and God ultimately makes his presence known in *Couples* through the destruction, by "God's own lightning," of Tarbox's Congregational Church (441).

If God can strike a church with lightning, then perhaps he has not wholly absconded. In *Roger's Version,* the desire to find God becomes an obsession for computer science graduate student Dale Kohler, who attempts to see and render him as a visual presence, a revelation on the computer monitor. According to Dale, our effort to chart the origin of the universe reveals so many coincidences and perfect mathematical figures that the odds that it happened as it did, by chance, are astronomically low. Consequently, Dale concludes, "there's no intrinsic reason for those constants to be what they are except to say *God made them that way"* (*Roger's Version,* 14). Working from his knowledge of physics, religion, and computer science, and utilizing his computer to increase his visual range, Dale is determined to demonstrate that "God's face is staring right out at us" (20).

For Dale the computer offers a new mode of vision that allows him, like God, to see simultaneously from a multiplicity of angles and perspectives. As Updike states, "We have surrounded our consciousness with vastness — vast libraries, vast galaxies, vastly complex molecular and atomic entities — and in the miniaturized guts of a computer the complication of God's (so to speak) world meets an equivalent complication we have created" (*Odd Jobs,* 857). Perched in "his Tower of Babel" (*Roger's Version,* 246), Dale works at his computer screen, crashing together data, rotating images, and varying his perspective in hopes that the computer will seize upon a sign from God. Resorting to all the computer tricks and knowledge he has, Dale battles furiously against his invisible opponent, God, hoping for a sign and yet fearful that "It hates [his] seeking It, and will extract vengeance if he finds It" (248). In a brief flicker, Dale sees on the screen "a mournful face" that quickly vanishes (244). Shortly thereafter he detects

> A hand, patched of colors as if dabbled with glowing camouflage paint but its form emergent, even to palm creases. . . . Its relaxation is curious. Is it relaxed because it has been slain, a hand nailed limp to the cross? (248-49)

Dale attempts to print the Christ-like image, but the result is faded, and further attempts at reproducing the commands that generated it fail. Inevitably, Dale's majestic effort to see the unseeable proves unsuccessful.

Roger Lambert, Dale's opponent, is delighted. Maintaining the Barthian position, Roger is steadfast in his belief that God cannot be known or seen by human eyes, unless God so chooses. Echoing Barth, Roger states, "The God we care about in this divinity school is the living God, Who moves toward us out of His will and love, and Who laughs at all the towers of Babel we build to Him" (22). Roger associates God with yearning and views our "longing for God . . . when all is said and done, [as] our only evidence of His existence" (67). We are "always in motion *toward* the God Who flees, the *Deus absconditus*" (219), and the "silence He maintains [is] so that we may enjoy and explore our human freedom" (281). Perhaps the difference between the views of Roger and Dale can be best understood through Updike's statement, "A loud and evident God would be a bully, an insecure tyrant, an all-crushing datum instead of, as He is, a bottomless encouragement to our faltering and frightened being" (*Self-Consciousness,* 229).

Dale's attempt in *Roger's Version* to see a personified creator provides transition to *In the Beauty of the Lilies,* the novel in which God is said to be the hero. God is first invoked in *Lilies'* epigraph, which comes from Julia Ward Howe's "Battle-Hymn of the Republic":

In the beauty of the lilies Christ was born across the sea,
With a glory in his bosom that transfigures you and me:
As he died to make men holy, let us die to make men free,
While God is marching on.

The stanza reveals central themes of the novel: the inherent sadness of what Updike refers to as America's "Protestant estrangement," in which Christ was born "not on this side of the ocean" ("Special Message," i); the martial aspect of American Christianity; the national drive toward freedom; and the fact that God is an active presence who is "marching on." In *Lilies* one either marches on with God and America or is left behind.

In the novel's opening section, Presbyterian minister Clarence Arthur Wilmot suddenly realizes *"There is no God"* (*In the Beauty of the Lilies,* 10). Through this recognition, which transforms Clarence's life and the lives of his descendants, one begins to understand God's role in the novel. Clarence now feels "numb" and "hollow," and his world changes dramatically: "Life's sounds all rang with a curious lightness and flatness, as if a resonating base beneath them had been removed" (7). Without God, Clarence is empty and lacks those characteristics — will, energy, confidence, ambition, hope, even voice — which once filled him. God is associated with vitality and drive, and without him one simply stops trying.

As to Kazin's remark that Updike "never tells us what was lost — and why," I disagree. We see exactly what was lost: Clarence's energy, his desire to struggle forward with his life. In addition, we see how this loss affects succeeding generations of Wilmots. Kazin is correct, however, in his assertion that Updike never explicitly tells us why — which, of course, is the beautifully crafted mystery of *Lilies.* Though Clarence claims that his loss of faith was not volitional and that "the reasons came . . . from outside . . . from above," Rev. Thomas Dreaver from the Presbytery challenges him: "Much of what we blame on the above comes from within" (81). If one agrees with the sermon Clarence is unable to finish, then men and women are offered a "choice" regarding belief: "If we cannot feel God's hand gripping ours, it is because . . . we have not reached up" (54). Clarence's renunciation stands as a personal failure, a refusal to "reach up." For whatever selfish, intellectual, perverse, or mysterious reason, Clarence has simply given up. Though he has, in a sense, followed the national movement toward greater freedom by "liberating" himself from the enslavement of belief, he has simultaneously opted against the American ethic of continuing the struggle.

Like his father Clarence, Teddy Wilmot views God as hidden, yet for the son God exists — not so much as the glorious creator, but as an unkind presence who should be blamed and resisted. Convinced that God betrayed his father, Teddy holds a grudge: "You're not going to get me to go sing the praises of God, after what He did to Father" (152). Later Teddy explains, "It seemed to me God could have given Dad a sign. To help him out. Just a little sign would have done it, and cost God nothing much" (410). Cautious and fearful, Teddy resists all opportunities that come his way, opportunities presumably from God. Teddy wants no relationship with or dependence upon God, opting instead for a quiet feud. As his wife Emily explains, "It's as if after whatever it was that happened he just wants to get through this vale of tears with — what did they used to call it during the war? — minimal damage. It's as if he won't give God any satisfaction" (269). Like most of the women in the novel, Emily maintains a belief in God: "He's not silent with me," she asserts (201). Teddy, however, refuses to engage in the human struggle that God has engineered.

Of all the Wilmots, Teddy's daughter Essie has perhaps the most intimate and unique relationship with God. For Essie, God exists absolutely and is experienced physically:

> God was in the clouds and had sent Jesus to earth to make Christmas and Easter, and His love pressed down from Heaven and fit her whole body like bathwater in the tub. The fact that Jesus came down meant that God wasn't just up there but was all around them, invisible, not like a ghost, who would be scary, but like blood in your veins that you can sometimes hear when your ear is against the pillow and that the doctor can feel when he puts his cold fat fingers smelling of antiseptic on your wrist. (233)

God is present in light, which nourishes and shines upon Essie, bringing out her beautiful vitality. He is also present in rain: "It always made her excited when it rained, as if God was touching her somehow" (264). A palpable presence who exists inside and outside of her, God provides Essie with confidence, energy, and ambition. It is he who has given her her talents and drive to succeed, and it is he who protects her and answers her prayers. He is a companion — someone she blames, loves, thanks — and he confirms to her that she is indeed special.

Whereas God is a palpable presence for Essie, he is conspicuously absent from her son's life: "[Clark] was jealous of his mother; she had had a God, here under the cozy close sky of Basingstoke, and in her Hollywood egotism hadn't bothered to pass Him on to him" (408). Clark wonders, "Who was this God everybody talked of but no one ever met?" (408). In his ramblings he arrives at a Colorado ranch where he encounters Jesse Smith, a figure who claims to be the new messiah. Says one of Jesse's followers, "I'm betting Jesse's the real thing. Some might say it's mighty strange for the Lord to come again in the form of a limited, gun-crazy guy like Jesse, but that's the Lord's style, to work in mysterious ways" (471). Clark desires God because he believes God can provide opportunities that will, perhaps, enable him to become a hero. Again, God is associated with vitality, yearning, and the desire to do one's best. Furthermore, one could interpret Clark's decisions during the final months of his life — to join the Temple, to shoot Jesse and save the children — as part of a desire to meet God. By throwing himself so wholeheartedly into the operations of the doomed Temple, Clark moves at an accelerated pace toward his death, which may also bring him closer to God.

What makes *Lilies* such an intriguing novel is the transition Updike posits in twentieth-century American culture. Refusing to believe that God is dead, Updike suggests that God has simply become transformed, so that an individual is more likely to experience his presence in a movie theatre than in church. Whereas God for Updike typically exists in the visual and textual surface of the domestic material world, in *Lilies* movies overwhelm and provide a substitute for that world. God's domestic light pales beside the heavenly light of the cinema:

> [Essie's] set-back gray house, with her father in the yard and her grandmother in the kitchen, and Mr. Bear upstairs waiting on her bed, where the day's light was leaking away above the spines of the radiator with their secret pattern of twisting ivy, struck Essie suddenly as

> sad, and insubstantial, a ghost house, seen by the light of the silvery movie world whose beautiful smooth people rattled all those words at each other and moved through their enormous ceilingless rooms with such swiftness and electric purpose. (252)

With its larger-than-life gods and goddesses, emanating as images of light moving across and conquering the darkness, the cinema replaces the church as the dominant locus of yearning, passion, mystery, transcendence, and fulfillment. Projecting enormous images of stars who epitomize beauty and grace, the movie world stands as a heaven to which the masses aspire.

Though a sadness pervades *Lilies* because of the way in which the religious impulse has become distorted and belittled through cinematic surrogacy, the need for God nevertheless continues. In America, "this land of promise where yearning never stops short at a particular satisfaction but keeps moving on, into the territory beyond" (333), God stands as the embodiment of longing. He is what the Wilmots need and seek as well as that which gives them the confidence to continue their struggle. Much as in the early stories of Genesis, the model Updike had in mind when he wrote *Lilies* ("Special Message," i), God is a character — a figure whom four generations of Wilmots blame, thank, search for, and argue with. Furthermore, each of these four generations of Wilmots seeks a career that involves delivering messages, both human and divine, to the world. As a minister, Clarence delivers God's word to his congregation; his son Teddy delivers mail to his community; Teddy's daughter, Essie, emerges as a silver-screen goddess delivering emanations of light to moviegoers; and Essie's son, Clark, becomes the PR man for a new American messiah and delivers his own message of heroics via television. Struggling with, searching for, and encouraged by God, the Wilmot family, following Clarence's initial failure, continues the effort to deliver, often heroically, some personal version of God's message. In effect, they serve as masks of God.

In *Lilies* God is an animating force whose presence breathes light and hope into individuals, and whose absence deflates and renders them hollow. Interestingly, Updike's female characters — Stella, Emily, and Essie — are the firmest believers and have the most assured sense of divinity. This belief provides them with personal strength. Clarence, Teddy, and Clark, on the other hand, are without God, which renders them, respectively, weak, fearful of risk, and unsuccessful. Whereas most of Updike's women seem to know precisely what they want, his men worry and flounder.

In *Lilies* as well as in other Updike works, God can be found in the furniture and moldings and window sashes of households, and also in the light and rain and weather that come from above. Furthermore, God is present in the body and mind of certain characters, endowing them with energy and confidence, stirring them toward desire and grandeur.

For more than four decades Updike has been praised for his ability to depict the visible, tangible world with great fidelity, and though his prose style and eye for detail largely account for this success, so does his integration of a divine presence within that picture. Updike's domestic world becomes all the more real, vital, and glorious through the subtle, mysterious presence of a transcendent creator. Though one cannot always locate God precisely and unequivocally in Updike's work — God is beneath the surface, pushing through, as well as above the world, providing light and hope — such an ambiguity clearly attests to the author's artistic achievement since God, in life as in fiction, is never easily or clearly found.

When Earth Speaks of Heaven

The Future of Race and Faith in Updike's *Brazil*

DILVO I. RISTOFF

> We can catch at a truth from a distance as well as up close; I refuse to disown my Brazil as unrealistic. A country's sense of itself is an activating part of its reality, and this sense derives in part from outsiders. Because others have romanticized and sexualized Brazil, Brazil is saturated in romanticism and sexuality. Sex, between masters and slaves, conquerors and indigines, has shaped its identity as an image of the world that is coming, one world of many mixed colors.
>
> John Updike (*Brazil*, "A Special Message," Franklin Mint Edition)

Reviews of John Updike's novel *Brazil* are mostly negative, with reviewers complaining that the book in no way lives up to the quality expected from this well-known and widely acclaimed writer. Merle Rubin, for instance, argues that "a great deal of beautiful writing, arranged like a blossom-heavy vine over the trellis of an elegantly structured plot, has been used to dress up a story that is little more than a collection of clichés about women, men, blacks, whites, Indians, settlers, love, sex, class, and money" (Rubin, 15). Similarly, Erich Eichman writes: "[This is] a curious and unsatisfying novel that blends realism with some South American variety of exoticism. The result is neither magical nor transporting, although one suspects that it is meant to be. . . . Maybe the idea of the novel and the challenge it posed was more compelling than its execution" (Eichman, 28). Barbara Kingsolver, while concurring that the text exemplifies rape fantasies, racist remarks, and political incorrectness, is more generous with her praise. She compliments the work as "good-natured and bent on self-parody" (Kingsolver, 1), much like the Rabbit tetralogy, which also parodies our weaknesses, fantasies, and illusions.

All critics of the novel agree on one point: because of its formal unevenness, its hasty generalizations, and its confusing juxtaposition of the realistic and the fantastic, *Brazil* is hardly Updike's best work. Although I find it easy to agree with this assertion, I would argue along with James Schiff that Updike has written "a vision of Brazil" (*John Updike Revisited,* 157) and contend that much remains to be said about this intriguing text, especially with regard to Updike's treatment of its theme of eternal love and faith in a time and place of apparent godlessness, brutality, and permissiveness devoid of societal norms. Is Updike's Brazil merely an arena in which the rules of the game are dictated by the forces of chance, or is it indeed, as Alice and Kenneth Hamilton once put it, a moving picture of "those aspects of earth which can speak to us of heaven" (Hamilton, 248)? Or, to sound even more like the Hamiltons, "Does the [Brazilian] universe, blindly ruled by chance, run downward into death; or does it follow the commands of a Living God whose Will for it is life?" (249). If our answer to these questions favors God, what kind of God exactly is this? What values does this God stand for? What kind of life does this God affirm?

It is essential to realize that the novel re-creates the romance of Tristan and Iseult — more specifically, Joseph Bédier's version of that story. Beyond the obvious similarities between Bédier's text and *Brazil* — which include similar character names, identical scenic descriptions, parallel plot developments (such as exchanges of solemn vows and symbolic gifts and the presence of presages), a shared determination to live and die for love that is complicated by the obstacles of familial resistance, wicked enemies, infidelities and separations, and dramatic rescues and miracles that are not enough to circumvent a tragic ending — Updike explicitly recognizes in his Afterword to the text that "Joseph Bédier's Tristan and Iseult . . . gave me my tone and basic situation." At its most fundamental level, therefore, *Brazil* is the traditional story of Tristan and Iseult revisited, rewritten, and transplanted to twentieth-century Brazil.

The leading question raised by this novel for Updike afficionados and scholars is why this internationally acclaimed and cosmopolitan author would choose for his scene a country that, in the minds of his preferential readers, is still dominantly associated with the primitive Amazon region rather than recognized as a modern, urbanized nation of 150 million people? His choice of setting seems especially strange if we recall, as Sérgio Augusto pointed out in an article in the newspaper *Folha de São Paulo* in December 1991, three months prior to Updike's visit to Brazil, that historically "when they return to their [native] countries, writers forget Brazil" (Augusto, 5,1). To support his argument, Augusto cites Jean Paul Sartre and Graham Greene as examples of forgetful authors who did not write a line about Brazil after leaving there. One gets the impression that Updike read and was influenced by that article in *Folha de São Paulo* and was determined not to pass into history as one more illustrious and ungrateful visitor to Brazil. He answers Augusto's tacit challenge, not with a commentary, but with a whole novel. It is an uncommon novel, unfair in its descriptions at times (it is true), written perhaps in too great a hurry, but nonetheless one that serves as an answer from a mind that sees in Brazil something worthy of attention, something that might affirm a faith which is constantly pursued yet still lacking in America.

A secondary query that arises when reading the novel is why, for the first time, Updike does not include even a single American character. The answer to this question reveals an underlying truth that posits Brazil as a microcosm for the world at large. Nowadays, love between individuals is not impeded by conflicts between aristocrats or nations at war but by sociological issues — especially race, class, and gender relations — that modern societies have transformed into centers of power and sources of social and political conflict. It is impossible to read Updike's *Brazil* without being constantly reminded that these issues are motives triggering every action performed and every sentence uttered by the characters in the novel.

Although all of the aforementioned sociological issues are central to the focus of the novel, none assumes greater importance than that of race relations, which is key to character and plot development.

Updike's adaptations of the protagonists of Bédier's romance are Tristão, a nineteen-year-old black youth living in the slums of Rio, and Isabel, a wealthy, white, eighteen-year-old girl who resides in Copacabana. They meet on the beach and, as if bewitched by the same magic potion that made Tristan and Iseult inseparable, fall madly in love at first sight. Aware of the pressures that surround them and could potentially separate them, they elope. Marriage, however, does not circumvent difficulties, and the exiled lovers are forced to retaliate against both physical and intangible threats such as hired gunmen, racial discrimination, betrayal, economic exploitation, ignorance, and all the hardships of life in the jungle and in large urban centers. As in Bédier's romance, one by one these modern and primitive monsters are defeated. Thanks to the magic performed by an Indian shaman whom they meet in the jungle, the color of their skins is reversed. After this dual transformation, they finally manage to enjoy for a time the pleasures of Brazilian bourgeois life without interference or discrimination.

The race issue pervades the novel, which in fact begins with an attempt to portray Brazil as a racial democracy. The setting of the first scene is Copacabana Beach, described as a multiracial paradise: "Black is a shade of brown. So is white, if you look. On Copacabana, the most democratic, crowded, and dangerous of Rio de Janeiro's beaches, all colors merge into one joyous, sun-stunned flesh-color, coating the sand with a second, living skin" (*Brazil,* 3). In Updike's Brazil racial identity ultimately disappears, for black is not fully black, nor is white entirely white. Both colors lack an intrinsic, original, and positive definition. They become the result of something more, the nuances of a third color — a neutral color that contains them both. Even in their contrasts, Isabel and Tristão both incorporate this racial ambiguity. In the same way that Isabel is figuratively depicted as foreign as a white woman, Tristão is ironically described as having "pure African blood, as pure as blood can be in Brazil" (7). The underlying implication could not be clearer in both cases: in Brazil, pure race and pure blood are fictions.

The narrator's obsession with racial issues is present on every page of the novel. Each character is invariably described in terms of race and color, not only revealing a narrative awareness that is incompatible with true racial democracy, but also suggesting that perhaps there is a hidden, motivating force that makes writing this novel a necessary exercise for Updike, as if the story were his metaphor for the shaman's theory of substitution and transposition: "When something here is placed *there,* something there must be placed *here*" (186). The shaman believes that only God or Monan can create, but Updike demonstrates his own brand of generative power, not merely by creating a revised Tristan and Iseult narrative, but by examining a dilemma (mirrored in his own personal life and also distinctly American) and rendering it almost invisible, Brazilianizing it through sociocultural and religious magic.

This heightened narrative awareness requires us to take a closer look at the novel's underlying concerns with race, most visibly demonstrated in the character descriptions. Isabel is initially white but later becomes black; Tristão is first black and later white. Isabel's mother is descended from the Andrade Guimarães family, said to have Moorish blood, which would explain "that drop of darkness which makes a true Brazilian beauty" (77). Isabel's father comes from the Portuguese Leme family and has a thin bluish skin (as bluish as Tristão's, suggesting that perhaps Tristão and Isabel are brother and sister). Each of Tristão's brothers seems to belong to a different race altogether and functions as a representative of the Brazilian miscegenation that the narrator observes in all parts of the country. If we analyze the novel's characters one by one, we see that all of them without exception — from the bellboy at the hotel in São Paulo to the butler in Brasília to the policemen, hired gunmen, and gold miners at Serra do Buraco — are described as having traits that identify them as originating from more than one race. In Updike's Brazil, pure races are replaced by multiracial compositions, and the nation becomes (theoretically at least) the ideal place for love between individuals of different races to fulfill its potential. Updike's novel argues the obvious: that in a society where racial identities are not clearly definable and where miscegenation is commonplace, interracial unions are more easily accepted. At the end of the novel, Tristão and Isabel's acceptance without restrictions into Brazilian urban society and their integration into the Paulista and Carioca social circles proves that, once certain impediments are overcome, interracial marriage could allow the Brazilian version of Tristan and Iseult to have a happy ending.

The unfortunate reality, however, is that neither the beginning, middle, nor end of the novel is happy. In picaresque mode, Updike constructs scenarios that reveal to us, moment by moment, the rich complexity of Brazilian race relations. The nearly endless display of prejudice and discrimination throughout the novel includes racially motivated verbal and physical harassment, manifestations of national pride in the Freyrean vein, constant dislocations of the racial issue to the realm of social class, and even practical examples of what the publisher of *Folha de São Paulo,* in one of its books on the subject, termed "cordial racism."[1] For example, after years of cohabitation with his maid of Indian blood and "taciturnity," Uncle Donaciano decides to marry her. He insists that his opposition to Tristão and Isabel's love affair has nothing to do with race and everything to do with economics. When Isabel confronts him on the issue, saying, "I thought this was a country where each man made himself regardless of color," Uncle Donaciano replies emphatically, with the conviction of someone who has read his Gilberto Freyre[2] and thus knows what goes on in the world: "I do not speak of color. I am color-blind, like our constitution, in tune with the national temperament we inherited from the grand-spirited sugar planters. This is not South Africa, thank God, or the United States. But a man cannot make himself out of thin air, he must have materials" (23). Since Donaciano actually does marry his maid,

1. *Racismo Cordial: a Mais Completa Análise sobre o Preconceito de Cor no Brasil,* edited by Cleusa Turra and Bustavo Venturini (São Paulo: Editora Atica, 1995). The English translation of the Portuguese title is *Cordial Racism: The Most Complete Analysis of Color Prejudice in Brazil. Folha de São Paulo* is the Brazilian newspaper equivalent to *The New York Times.*

2. Gilberto Freyre (1900-1987) was a prominent Brazilian sociologist and writer. At eighteen he went to study in the United States, first at Baylor University and later at Columbia University, where he defended his dissertation "Social Life in Brazil in the Middle of the 19th Century." His most famous work is *Casa-Grande & Senzala* [*The Masters and the Slaves*], first published in Portuguese in 1933 — the first of a series of books concerned with the understanding of Brazilian social and racial relations. Often defined as "a conservative revolutionary," Freyre achieved notoriety among intellectuals for his understanding that the underlying fundament of Brazilian society is that of a racial democracy. His views, although not uncontested by other sociologists, are generally acknowledged to have contributed significantly to the country's optimism and self-reliance. Besides *The Masters and the Slaves: A Study in the Development of Brazilian Civilization* (New York: Knopf, 1956), other Freyre English titles are *New World in the Tropics: The Culture of Modern Brazil* (New York: Knopf, 1959), and *The Mansions and the Shanties* (New York: Knopf, 1963).

All Freyre quotations in this essay are my own translations from the Portuguese *Casa-Grande & Senzala* (Rio de Janerio: n.p., 1989).

his words acquire certain credibility and perhaps serve to convey Updike's own point of view.

Donaciano's vision, however, conflicts with other discussions that take place in the novel and show that Updike, much in accordance with his well-known style, avoids the excessive predominance of any single voice. If compared to most of his short stories and novels, *Brazil* seems to be a novel written backwards. Updike's usual pattern involves a hero who represents middleness in conflict with the marginal forces of history, or with what Linda Hutcheon calls "the ex-centrics." In *Brazil,* however, the opposite happens: the ex-centric protagonists have nothing in common except their physical attraction and love for one another. Their life stories are totally disparate, as are their social class, color, race, educational level, and societal relations, and these differences encompass both extremes of what would usually represent the marginal in other Updike works. A clear ideological definition of these marginal forces is absent, and in *Brazil* it is evident that the protagonists are in conflict with establishment values. In other words, Tristão and Isabel have between them the most profound differences imaginable. Through the force of emplotment, however, they redefine themselves as a unit that opposes itself to the oppressive and repressive forces of Brazilian society, more because of their passionate belief that they were born for each other and are therefore destined to spend their lives together than because of any merely intellectual or political conviction. For each point of view presented in the novel and with which the reader feels tempted to identify, however, there is another perspective that contradicts or complements it. For instance, we can discern at least two counterpoints to Donaciano's lecture on marriage as economic necessity. As another example, when Isabel meets with her classmates from the Universidade de Brasília in a smoke-filled bar, political discussion (mixed with subtle processes of seduction) becomes inevitable, and the racial issue, brought to the surface because of the recent assassination of Martin Luther King and the rebellions that ensued in various American cities, quickly takes center stage.

Sylvio begins the debate by baiting Isabel: "In the United States . . . the blacks have reduced Washington to rubble in the wake of Martin King's assassination. In Chicago and Baltimore, too. The end is near for the lily-white imperialists of the North." Surprisingly, Isabel answers as if denying the events themselves: "The blacks will never revolt, there or here. They are too happy and good. They are too beautiful. Always it was so. The Indians died of slavery; the blacks rose above it, of their own great natures. Because they are superior, they let themselves be treated as inferior . . . they are able to live in our hideous twentieth century — live, and not merely survive" (99-100). "I think you romanticize them, darling," answers Isabel's roommate. "We all do, to spare ourselves guilt over their abysmal condition. And they conspire with us, is the insidious thing, by being so damned picturesque." Ana Vitória, their pedantic classmate, concludes: "So does contemporary sociology romanticize, following after Gilberto Freyre, that master of self-congratulation. If Brazilians did not romanticize, they would have to awaken to their realities, and the realities of Karl Marx" (101).

It is apparent from this conversation and from other dialogues in the novel that Updike (as he admits in the Afterword) has read Freyre's *The Masters and the Slaves,* titled in Portuguese *Casa-Grande & Senzala.* It is also evident that, although he is interested in problematizing Freyre's optimism with regard to racial attitudes, Updike's narrator shows more sympathy for Isabel's naive suppositions than for the Marxist, anarchist, and fascist arguments expressed by the other students in the group.

Similarly, the cordial racism of the hotel clerk in São Paulo is no accident. This same clerk sends a message to Tristão and Isabel later in the novel begging their pardon for not allowing them to stay at the hotel. His explanation: "The reason you were turned away was not racial prejudice on [my] part, but respect for the feelings of the other guests, many of whom come from abroad, from less tolerant societies" (60). Although laughable at times, this kind of cordial or ashamed racism, when associated with the predominant presence of easy-going and (self-termed) "color-blind" Uncle Donaciano, confirms that Updike perceives Brazilian race relations as more acceptable than those in America. The clerk's behavior, when considered as a sociological construct, also reveals that Updike was strongly influenced by the tenets of Freyre. What liberates the text from these Freyrean paradigms is the explicit and implicit racism faced by the two lovers from the beginning to the end of their trajectory, in the cities, the country, and the primitive jungle.

Even the murder of the newly white Tristão by black street boys on Copacabana Beach must be perceived as a crime motivated by racial hatred (in this case of racism against whites). As the boys stab Tristão to death, the omniscient narrator interprets the thoughts behind their actions: "[They] slashed and stabbed at the crouching, toppling white man, as a lesson to all such white men who think they still can own the world" (255). Strangely, the most tragic moment in the novel is also the most ironic, since the now white and rich Tristão, accepted by society but still unhappy because he cannot fully penetrate the world of the Lemes, tries in vain to explain to the street boys that he is not a foreigner, as they imagine, but one of them, someone able to understand them. His last, useless words are emblematic of his final, failing effort to reestablish his origins: "I am one of you" (254). Tristão's tragic end confirms Updike's earlier admission that even the most democratic beach in the world is not exactly a paradise.

Despite the lengthy list of petty and great racial cruelties in the novel, however, it is possible to infer that an attitude of general approval of the Brazilian racial experiment predominates in the narrator's mind. This tacit acceptance is quite evident in the repeated comparisons of Brazil with the United States and South Africa, where, as the narrator puts it, "a white man and a black wife would be [more] conspicuous and poignant" (207-8). It is certainly no accident that Updike's narrator impregnates the words of various characters with ideas espoused by Freyre — ideas that try to distinguish the Brazilian process of colonization from other such processes, especially those of the Northern Hemisphere, by attributing its singularity to the racial indeterminacy of the Portuguese colonizers. In this respect, it is worth recalling Freyre's words:

> The singular predisposition of the Portuguese for hybrid and slave-based colonization in the tropics can be explained to a large extent by their ethnic, or rather cultural, past as a people undefined between Europe and Africa. Neither intransigently of one or the other, but of both. The African influence simmering under the European and adding a burning touch to sexual life, to food, to religion; the Moorish and black blood running in the veins of a large whitish population not predominating in certain regions of dark people until today. (*Casa-Grande,* 3)

The narrator shares this understanding. When we perceive, for example, that the novel tries to characterize Uncle Donaciano, Salomão, Isabel, and Isabel's mother as having inherited from their Portuguese ancestors some Negroid physical traits and some Moorish or black blood, and that miscegenation is a commonplace thing, it becomes evident that Freyre is not an object of mockery but, quite the contrary, somebody whose ideas exert strong influence over John Updike.

Not even white Tristão manages to escape from Freyrean descriptions. When Tristão explains to Isabel's father the profound love he feels for his daughter, linking her name with an abundance of adjectives praising her virtues, old Salomão, a learned man, identifies in his tone something profoundly sad and attributes the despair to typical Portuguese melancholy. Salomão's digressions, however, do not stop there. In a total identification with the voice of the narrator, he thinks: "No less an authority than Gilberto Freyre assures us that, had not the early colonizers imported Africans to cheer up their settlements, the whole Brazilian enterprise might have withered of sheer gloom" (*Brazil,* 229). These are words from the novel. Freyre's own words, however, are not very different:

> It was also the Negro who brought life and great happiness to Brazilian domestic life. The Portuguese, melancholy by nature, in Brazil became dejected, dismal; and what to say of the Caboclo: quiet, suspicious, almost sick with sadness. Contact with him only increased the Portuguese melancholy. It was the laughter of the Negro that erased all this vile sadness into which the life in the Casa-Grande had sunk. It was the Negro who brought life to the June festivities, who animated the folk dances, . . . carnivals, and Christmas. (*Casa-Grande,* 514)

Since Tristão is a black man who became white, his sadness obviously could not have Portuguese roots. How to explain it then? Updike's narrator once again finds support for his theory in Freyre: "And yet the Africans themselves suffered such homesick sorrow in the New World that a word was coined for it, *banzo,* a kind of black *saudade*" (*Brazil,* 229). It may not be mere coincidence that in Freyre's text, *banzo* is defined immediately after the discussion of the African's capacity to bring joy to the master's quarters and to festivities in general. Freyre writes: "But the life of Negroes, slaves of white yoyos and yayas, was not only made of happiness. There were those who committed suicide by eating earth, hanging themselves, poisoning themselves with weeds and potions of shamans. Banzo put an end to the life of many. Banzo — the longing for Africa. There were many who were so banzoed that they became paralyzed and idiotic. They did not die: just suffered endlessly" (*Casa-Grande,* 516).

To a large extent, the origins of Updike's text are explained by the Freyrean comprehension of race relations in Brazil. It is not my purpose here to judge the merits of this perspective, but I do believe it is important to register that Updike's admiration for Freyre's views does not merely stem from his unhappiness with American racial relations. Updike's espousal of Freyrean theory also pertains to the fact that racial tensions in America had recently and directly affected his own family life. And this fact, perhaps more than his affinity for Freyre, explains the hidden origin of the text.

It is important to remember that John Updike has mulatto grandsons from the marriage of his daughter to a black man from West Africa. In *Self-Consciousness,* his autobiography published in 1989 (five years before *Brazil*), Updike reveals the origins of *Brazil* in a long letter to his grandsons. In addition to articulating a new take on Tristan and Iseult, this letter begins with the same fundamental thesis as the novel about the nonexistence of pure races and the world's natural preparation for a future racial democracy. His very first sentence in the letter, later repeated *ipsis verbis,* becomes the matrix underneath the opening paragraph of *Brazil.* Whereas the novel starts with the idea that in Rio de Janeiro black and white are shades of brown, the missive to his grandsons begins by affirming that "We are all of mixed blood" (*Self-Consciousness,* 164). After considering the type of blackness of his son-in-law, he writes: "Genealogists tell us that we are all cousins, with common ancestors surprisingly few generations in the past. . . . Your two parents are about as black and white as people can be, and that helps make them a beautiful couple" (164-65).

What future does Updike foresee for his grandsons in the United States? He does not mince words to explain it:

> When Anoff was born . . . my instinctive thought was that he would do better if his parents settled in Ghana; that is, I trusted an African country to treat a half-white person better than my own country would treat a half-black. Now, I wonder. . . . An ideal colorblind society flickers at the forward edge of the sluggishly evolving one. Slim black models pose in *Vogue,* and well-dressed, professional blacks work in the downtowns of the major cities: neither of these things was true of the America I grew up in. Further, the Latinization of North America — the influx of Hispanics — has softened the color line and the singularity of the original black population imported from Africa

by pale planters from northern Europe. America is slowly becoming yours, I want to think, as much as it is anyone's. (195-96)

Updike's optimism for the racial future of American society is grounded in his memory of the civil rights movement and its practical consequences with regard to affirmative action. He evaluates these actions as signifying an improvement in race relations, opening up unprecedented spaces and possibilities of social mobility for American blacks. Simultaneously, however, he fully realizes that being an American is synonymous with being constantly reminded that the individual is nothing but "one site in a web of racial tension and mutual ethnic watchfulness" (205). For Updike this watchfulness is so real that he uses his letter to call the attention of his grandsons (who could not yet read) to the fact that the day will come when his white skin will separate them from him, for it will become a cause of suspicion and uneasiness. It is highly likely, he suggests, that in the future they will not enjoy a greater proximity than they now achieve during the unconscious and innocent moments they spend together. When Updike recalls that as a child he always found it extremely easy to consider the United States as his country and "an easy country to love," he acknowledges that the situation will probably be different for his grandsons, should they decide to make the United States their country, because "though exactly half white, you will be considered black" (197).

The origins of *Brazil* are, therefore, at least threefold: Bédier's *Tristan and Iseult* text, Freyre's *The Masters and the Slaves,* and Updike's own life. Since Bédier's romance and Updike's personal history inevitably become interwoven with his fiction and since Updike had an acute awareness of the difficulties of making this story palatable for his North American readers, he decided to filter it through spatial and cultural dislocation. Thus Brazil, in the final analysis, becomes a bridge, working less to connect Brazil to the United States and more to link Updike's wishes for a better racial future for America to his certainty that the imagined future (for the time being) can only become real in a fantastic, exotic, religiously and psychologically distant country.

Updike's work is, therefore, markedly similar to that of the shaman he created within it: *Brazil* is "magic" in its transpositions, and it negates finding ultimate meaning in the realm of logic and transplants the search for truth to the realm of faith. Much like the shaman, whose primitivism interferes with urbanized and civilized Brazil by causing colorblindness and reducing racial prejudice, Updike's "magic" connects Brazil to the United States by hoping that the imagined primitive in his native country will eventually interfere with the imagined civilized. Since this translocation operates mostly in the realm of faith, a few words must be said about the role of religious awareness in the novel.

It is important to recognize that different forms of religious understanding, not just that of Christianity, are present from the beginning of the novel and involve all its major characters. For example, the first reference to Tristão tells us that "He believed in spirits and in fate" (*Brazil,* 4), and it is from spirits that he receives assurance that approaching Isabel is the right thing to do. Isabel, though hardly religious at all, carries within her spiritual values that result from her mixed experiences of education with the nuns at a Catholic school and of the spirituality of the Brazilian masses. Uncle Donaciano, the pragmatic bon vivant, clearly expresses belief in immortality and heaven as he passionately remembers his brother's deceased wife Cordelia. The novel presents an understanding that we are all creatures under heaven, that is, creatures of God: "Like pious peasants of the Old World, they believed that this heaven, which sent them its news on invisible waves, directed its smiling, soulful face toward them personally, just as the impalpable dome of blue sky above is centered precisely upon each upward gazer" (9-10). In other words, in the relation between humanity and the universe, the old dichotomies that guide our reasoning (center and periphery, metropolis and satellite, civilized and primitive) disappear in Brazil. Our position in the universe is as gazers, centered under the sky, each one as capable as the next person to capture the heavenly messages present in the "invisible waves."

This premise explains the role of Granny, Tristão's grandmother. Originally from the state of Bahia, where Christianity and African faiths have combined to form one inextricable religious syncretism, Granny represents extrasensory perception and an ability to foretell disastrous events. Though living in Rio, far from the spirits of the forest, she can "smell bad luck coming. It smells like flowers, it smells like the forest. The old forest, it is coming back, it will eat all the poor! Oxalá, have mercy!" (42). Granny's god, Oxalá, the greatest of the Orixás, originates from natural forces and is summoned to Candomblé religious gatherings through songs and the powers of mediums.

Granny possesses such calling abilities and powers and behaves as if spirits are warning her about what awaits Tristão and Isabel.

Granny's premonitions about the fate of her grandson and his lover unfortunately materialize. The laws of the jungle bring the lovers bad luck, and their journey into the remote reaches of the Mato Grosso places them simultaneously in direct contact with the cruelties inflicted by the "representatives" of Christian colonizers and with the shaman of a tribe so remote that Christianity has not yet reached it. Ironically, when Isabel asks the shaman to perform the magic of whitening her lover and he demands some form of payment, she believes that her only valuable possession is "a little cross covered with jewels." She goes on to explain that "A cross is the symbol of our God. It means both agonizing death and endless life. In this sign my people are conquering the world" (187). Isabel, however, unwittingly carries with her something of greater value than the bejeweled cross, worth many cruzeiros in the white man's world but worth nothing to the shaman, who associates it with bad luck. More precious than the religious faith embodied in her cross is the ring Tristão gave her and the love between them that it symbolizes. The ring is fitting payment for the services the shaman will perform because it will help make his magic happen. As he explains to Isabel, "It holds both of your spirits" (187). Ironically, the shaman's perception of value associates the miracle of giving and loving with a ring stolen from an American tourist.

The role of religion in *Brazil,* therefore, seems designed to bring the lovers together. Roman Catholicism (the religion of Isabel and her family and the official religion of the country), Candomblé (the religion of Tristão and his family and the unofficial religion of the populace), and the shaman's primitive magic all coincide with the forces of Brazilian history as presented by Gilberto Freyre. Even the character changes occurring in the novel (which have been the object of harsh criticism by many reviewers), when brought into the context of Freyrean sociology, lose some of their stereotypical charge. Updike's manipulations do bring the political incorrectness of his characters to the surface, but the underlying inferences are supported not only by an ugly reality but also by descriptions and arguments from one of Brazil's finest sociologists. By allowing his characters to be reborn into a new racial contract, with all its values, demands, and prejudices, Updike reaffirms not only his expressed conviction that art must not sacrifice its essential energy in order to be politically correct (Couto, 1,7) but also his repeated commitment to a form of representation that is above all realistic and not necessarily pleasing to our senses.

That Updike relies so heavily on contested Freyrean views may place him at odds with other interpreters of Brazilian society, but it also clearly shows his concern with finding a safe and believable ground upon which to unfold the actions of his characters. We may dislike her graphic comment, but black Isabel's insight that "Being a white woman fucked by a black man is more delicious . . . than a black woman being fucked by a white man" (*Brazil*, 204) has a direct connection to Freyre's *The Masters and the Slaves.* Isabel's explanation here of her new racial perception clearly parallels Freyre: "The [white woman], to a descendant of the masters of colonial Brazil, had the exaltation of blasphemy, the excitement of political defiance; the latter transaction [that of the black woman and the white man] savored of mundane business" (204). Isabel has not only changed the pigmentation of her skin — she has also acquired an understanding of race relations that has a historical tradition and a special political significance. Schiff may be right when he claims that in Updike's Brazil "pigment is destiny" (*John Updike Revisited*, 170), for there is no doubt that pigmentation implies social relations and expectations that directly affect the individuals involved. Only in an ideal world can skin color be perceived as something separate, in itself, and unimportant.

Updike's Brazil, however, is not the ideal world of Bédier, where magic can perform all miracles. His Brazil is only contaminated by magic and religion, not guided by it. It is a place where magic, religion, and love have their limitations and can no longer act upon reality with their twelfth-century strength. Yet both Updike's and Freyre's Brazils still seem to have inherited enough energy from their singular histories to allow race, religion, and political differences to play important roles in daily life. Updike re-creates Tristan and Iseult's story in order to deal with personal and national anxiety over American race relations. Consequently, even if we question the realism of its representations, *Brazil*'s setting has to be construed as a technical device created by Updike to add another perspective to and inform discussions about the complex racial situation in America, not only in Brazil. It is ultimately an affirmation — not of religion, or race, or ideology, but of love and faith in the future of America.

The *Brazil*ian universe, therefore, speaks to us of a God who, although in the background and never taken seriously by the characters, reminds us of life beyond the deadness of materiality. Although it is still possible for the spiritual to impress itself upon dark matter in the remote forests of the Mato Grosso, in urban Brazil materiality gains precedence over the spiritual. The final scene of the novel is illustrative: When Isabel lies next to her dead husband on Copacabana Beach, trying to iterate Iseult's gesture of willing herself to death, the miracle does not happen. As the narrator puts it, "There would be no miracle today. . . . The spirit is strong, but blind matter is stronger. Having absorbed this desolating truth, the dark-eyed widow staggered to her feet, tightened her robe about her nakedness, and let her uncle lead her home" (*Brazil*, 260). Thus Updike fosters an understanding that the miracle worlds of Bédier and the shaman do not encroach upon the crowded beaches of Rio. In Bédier's text, Iseult prayed to God, lay down by the dead Tristan, and "so gave up her soul, and died beside him" (Bédier, 202). Iseult's death is thus an essentially religious experience.

In Updike's text, on the other hand, there is no room for religious prayer, and Isabel, who earlier screamed that "There is no God, our lives are a terrible accident!" (*Brazil*, 159), is condemned to live — not, however, before realizing what Rabbit discerns in the Rabbit novels: unless the Divine breath of life is with us, we are nothing but "rotten meat" or "the piece of litter" (260) Tristão has become. Deep in her soul, however, Isabel keeps more than the lesson taught to her by the nuns — that her God means both agonizing death and endless life. She also retains the lessons gleaned from Tristão — that there is a God, and that our lives hold purpose. The purpose of their union, as he argued with Isabel, was "to prove love — to make for the world an example of love" (159). That Isabel is unable to die, as Schiff accurately suggests, makes *Brazil* one of the saddest versions of Tristan and Iseult's story (*John Updike Revisited*, 172). If God does make endless life possible, as in the Christian paradox, then Isabel and Tristão will be together again only when death unites them.

Updike 2020

Fantasy, Mythology, and Faith in *Toward the End of Time*

DAVID MALONE

"How could such a gifted writer produce such a lousy book?" This reaction from *The New York Times'* book reviewer Michiko Kakutani sums up a prevalent, vehemently-disappointed response to Updike's novel *Toward the End of Time.* Reviewers have objected most strenuously to two elements of the novel: the character of Ben Turnbull, the novel's protagonist, and Updike's failure to integrate the novel's science fiction elements with its more realistic attributes. Kakutani calls Turnbull "a narcissistic and dirty-minded old man — self-absorbed, bitter and malicious" (Kakutani, E1). Sven Birkerts huffs that "Those who regard women as worthy to walk beside men will twig early on to the fact that Ben is a pig," and laments that after his diagnosis of prostate cancer Ben does not walk "a path of redemptive suffering" (Birkerts, 5).

Kakutani is also unimpressed with the way Updike handles the novel's futuristic setting. She complains that the presentation of the year 2020, following the devastation of nuclear war and the collapse of the American government, has not been "fleshed out": "Updike's future," she notes, "looks very much like the present" (Kakutani, E8). David Foster Wallace quantifies the disparity between the novel's post-apocalyptic setting and its actual subject matter by setting up a list detailing the amount of space Updike gives to various topics in the novel: "the Sino-American war" (0.75 pages), "Ben Turnbull's penis and his various feelings about it" (7.5 pages), Turnbull's misogynistic observations (36.5 pages), or "flora around Turnbull's home, plus fauna, weather and how his ocean view looks in different seasons" (86 pages) (Wallace, 1).

Even reviewers who find the novel praiseworthy seem to find its science-fiction aspects intrusive; most would seem to agree with Joyce Carol Oates (and Kakutani) that "the futurist setting seems merely coincidental to Ben's experience" (Oates, 117). For the most part, these reviewers choose not to address the scene when the doe that eats Ben's bushes transforms into a young woman; science-fictional elements such as the metallobioforms, a nonorganic species that has evolved from human machinery and garbage; Ben's sexual relationship with Doreen, a fourteen-year-old girl who lives in his woods; or the breaks in the narrative where Ben takes on the voice of an Egyptian grave robber or Saint Mark or a guard in a Nazi concentration camp. Oates dismisses these and other nonrealistic occurrences as Ben's "fantasies of more passionate lives" (117) and, with the other positive reviewers, focuses instead on qualities that could be found in any of Updike's other, realistic novels: the "beautiful accuracy" of his descriptions of the natural world and the inner life (Pritchard, A20), the novel's "ultra realism" (Atwood, 10), the narrator's "Whitmanesque ability to absorb the natural world and reveal its organic unity" (Schiff, "Updike's Meditation," D4), and the exploration of "ancient and yet ever new metaphysical and religious questions" (Yerkes, "Beyond Time," 1079).

I tend to align myself more with the Updike detractors than the Updike admirers: the typical Updike protagonist seems to me enormously self-involved, charmless, and resentful of women, a WASPy version of the annoying character Woody Allen always plays, with the added detraction that Updike's protagonists are rarely intentionally funny. Nevertheless, I find myself unable to agree with either camp's assessment of *Toward the End of Time.* It's not simply that I find Ben Turnbull less sympathetic than the admirers apparently do and less repulsive than the detractors; it's that I think both sets of reviewers have neglected important elements of the work, particularly what Updike once referred to as his "sense of life as many-layered and ambiguous" (Plath, ed., 45). To read this novel as an inept attempt at realism or a thinly disguised expression of the author's opinions and feelings is to be content with merely a single layer of meaning and thereby to miss the richness and complexity of myth, philosophy, theology, and social comment that blend and clash throughout the work.

One of the reasons why these reviewers have read *Toward the End of Time* as a realistic novel is that most of them have little experience with strategies for reading non-realistic writing. According to science fiction writer Orson Scott Card, realistic fiction and science fiction require two different reading approaches: when we read realistic fiction, we already share with the author certain basic assumptions about what reality is, and therefore when we encounter what Card calls "a strange juxtaposition of familiar words," we expect "the term to be metaphorical, to express an attitude toward or give a new understanding of something that is part of the known world" (Card, 93). Science fiction requires a different strategy, because we are unfamiliar with the world of the story and need to be told by the writer what exists in this world, what can and cannot be done. Therefore, when we encounter strange juxtapositions of familiar words, we expect "the term to be literal, to have a real extension within the world of the story" (93). Card uses the example of the markedly different responses of members of one of his classes to a science fiction story that contained the term "reptile bus": the practiced science fiction readers imagined a bioengineered, dinosaurian vehicle, while those who had never read science fiction understood the term metaphorically, picturing an ordinary bus divided into jointed sections slithering over the pavement.

What is challenging about applying this strategy while reading *Toward the End of Time,* and what seems to have annoyed many of its reviewers, is that Updike plays on our expectations that he will write nothing other than a realistic novel. The novel dwells, in its first pages, on the conflict between Turnbull, a sixty-six-year-old retiree, and his wife, Gloria, over what to do about a deer that has invaded their garden and is eating their plants. The tension between Gloria's drive to chase the deer away, or have it killed, and Ben's ambivalence toward this plan (and toward Gloria) seems to locate the novel in the familiar terrain of the domestic, realistic novel, the commonplace, closely observed setting we think of when we think of Updike. Our expectations could easily overpower the small suggestions of the unfamiliar that Updike drops along the way. The first oddity, that the Siberian tiger has been rendered extinct by the recent war (*End of Time,* 5), barely registers, and Ben's revelation that Massachusetts now uses a new form of currency called the "welder" (8) occurs in the middle of an argument with Gloria and is not explained any further. The revelation that Ben is writing in January of the year 2020 is similarly diffident (22).

Even when something terribly unrealistic happens — while Gloria is away, the deer from the garden "becomes . . . a young lean-bodied whore, whom [Ben] invite[s] into the house," has sex with, and then sends off in a taxi — we seize with relief on Ben's statement, "I tell myself she is a fantasy, a branching not existent in the palpable universe" (35). Similarly, when Ben mentions, as part of his narration of his ongoing sexual relationship with Deirdre, the doe-turned-prostitute, that Gloria may or may not be dead and states, "I have a memory of wheeling and shooting her with Charlie Pienta's shotgun through the living-room window, but when I went back inside there was no body" (41), we grope for the realistic answer and finally receive one a hundred pages later when, a few days after May Day, Gloria returns, tells Ben, "You *never* listen when I tell you where I'm going," and claims that she's been at a conference in Singapore (141-42).

Updike further complicates the issue by providing Turnbull with some of Updike's own personal history: an ex-wife married straight out of college (*Self-Consciousness,* 99-102; *End of Time,* 69); a pair of grandsons with an African father (*Self-Consciousness,* 164; *End of Time,* 71-72); and a "strikingly majestic New England home" that "looks out onto the distant Atlantic from the top of a hill" (Plath, ed., 186; *End of Time,* 4-6). These details work to fulfill the reader's expectation that realistic novels will contain bits and pieces of the writer's life. They may even suggest to some readers that Updike includes the fantastic elements to draw attention away from the fact that he is writing about himself. At one point in the narrative, for example, Turnbull describes some of the childhood toys that he keeps in a bushel basket in his barn — "a tin Pluto who when wound up would whirr himself to the edges of a table and then, his weight shifting to a sideways wheel near his nose, magically turn back from danger" and "bas-relief Mickey Mouse blocks" (*End of Time,* 80) — items that an Updike afficionado will recognize as toys from Updike's own childhood. In one interview, Updike describes "a little funny tin Pluto dog that used to turn on the table in a way I can remember. It's in a bushel basket, and when you wind it up it still runs" (Rothstein, C21), and in *Self-Consciousness* he refers to a bushel basket containing a set of blocks "featuring, along with the numbers and letters, Walt Disney characters from Mickey Mouse to Horace Horsecollar . . . painted only on the raised parts" (104). It seems odd that a fictional character born in 1953 should have toys from the author's childhood in the 1940s, and Turnbull underscores the discrepancy by pointedly failing to recognize them, writing, "The toys seem older than I. . . . Could these toys have belonged not to me but to my father . . . ?" (*End of Time,* 80). To the reader most comfortable with realistic conventions, this discrepancy would seem to authorize a realistic reading: despite the futuristic guise, Turnbull is Updike, writing about growing older in the 1990s.

By combining the fantastic with the realistic without providing any clear demarcation between the two, Updike seems to be trying to thwart readers' expectations of him as a realistic novelist and to create a space in which he can address issues beyond the usually narrow focus of the realistic novel. Science fiction author James Morrow notes that unlike most authors of mainstream literary fiction, who "confine themselves to their various ethnic heritages and interpersonal relationships" as though "the big issues (does God exist? from whence springs decency? what sort of species is *Homo sapiens?*) were either settled or not worth discussing" (Morrow, xi), science fiction writers are always didactic — one writes about the future in order to critique the present. The unrealistic elements of *Toward the End of Time* free Updike — and, potentially, the reader — to explore a multiplicity of political and cultural meanings in the work.

The reviewers' complaints about *Toward the End of Time* are, in fact, a cranky echo of Updike's comments in a review of Marge Piercy's 1970 novel *Dance the Eagle to Sleep.* Although "Piercy places her history in a futuristic time," Updike writes, "the styles and equipment and brand names are all of our time" (*Picked-Up Pieces,* 394-95); he also notes that the novel's reference to the twenty-five-year history of the Cold War places the action in 1970. "No matter," Updike comments. "The futuristic conceit frees her to work on a large scale" (395), presenting characters and events that could not be contained in a conventionally realistic novel: "Piercy's heroes would be kings; that attempt failing, she caricatures them as gods" (395). The application of these observations to Updike's own novel seems appropriate in at least two ways: the novel's fantastic elements both expose the reader to grander themes than the conventional realistic novel usually pursues and, under their realistic veneer, associate the characters with the gods and heroes of ancient myth.

Consider, for example, Turnbull's relationship with Deirdre, the doe/prostitute. A reader who refuses to be bound by realism's conventions has the freedom to read this transformation as something other than Ben's fevered fantasy. The transformation of doe into woman is not, after all, an unfamiliar story: it calls to mind the parallel tale of Actaeon in Ovid's *Metamorphoses,* in which the young hunter happens across the goddess Diana bathing and, as punishment, is changed into a stag:

> she set
> a long-lived stag's horns on the head she'd drenched;
> she made his ear-tips sharp, stretched out his neck,
> and changed his hands to feet, arms to long legs,
> and cloaked his body with a spotted hide.
>
> (*Metamorphoses,* 84)

After his transformation by Diana, Actaeon is killed by his own hunting dogs, while the deer in the garden is killed by a hunter Gloria hires. Like Diana, Gloria oversees the hunt, pushing Ben out into the garden with a gun, and telephoning around, "searching for men with rifles or bows and arrows and an atavistic hunger for venison" (*End of Time,* 6); Ben even refers at least once to her "pale fire" (20), an allusion that yokes her, like Diana, with the moon.

Another parallel might be made with the story of Io, whom Jove pursues, rapes, and then transforms into a heifer in order to save himself from Juno's jealousy; Juno, for her part, pierces Io's breast "with an invisible, relentless goad," and drives "the frightened girl across the world — /a fugitive" (*Metamorphoses,* 32). In this case, Gloria's animosity toward the deer is, like Juno's persecution of Io, related to the dalliance with her husband; Ben's ultimate acquiescence to Gloria's wishes — he describes himself as following her orders "as blindly as Assyrians in the time of Hammurabi followed Ishtar's" (*End of Time,* 14) — parallels Jove's relationship with Juno, forever pursuing women and then abandoning them to similar fates once Juno's jealousy is aroused.

Updike's reference to Ishtar suggests an additional mythical connection with Inanna, the Sumerian queen of heaven, counterpart to the

Babylonian Ishtar. On her ascent from the underworld, Inanna sends demons to search for her husband, Dumuzi, whom she has elected to take her place in the underworld; as he attempts to flee the demons, Dumuzi calls out to Utu, the god of justice:

> Change my hands into the hands of a gazelle.
> Change my feet into the feet of a gazelle.
> Let me escape from my demons. (Wolkstein and Kramer, 81)

Utu turns Dumuzi into a gazelle, allowing Dumuzi to escape Inanna's demons for a brief time before he is ultimately captured. Deirdre's gender would seem to argue against her being identified as Dumuzi, but Updike suggests that both woman and deer are somewhat sexually ambiguous: Ben describes Deirdre's body as "lithe as a boy's" (*End of Time*, 60) and her back as "heartbreakingly boyish" (75), and Ben and Gloria disagree about the deer's sex from the novel's first pages — "The deer had seemed to me clearly a large doe, but to my wife, in her animus, the creature was a 'he'" (9) — and, despite Ben's corrections, Gloria continues to refer to the deer as "he" even after it has been killed (322).

I do not wish to argue that any one of these versions of the "human being turned into animal" is absolutely parallel to the events in the novel nor to claim that Updike means to portray Gloria as being more like Inanna than Juno or Diana; Updike's intent seems, instead, to be to build his novel around characters and events from a variety of mythic traditions. Once we start thinking about myth, it soon becomes clear that *Toward the End of Time* is riddled with references to other literary works: Gloria's death/disappearance in the winter and reappearance in the spring, "a few days" after May Day (141), parallels Ishtar/Inanna's descent into the underworld, as well as the myth of Proserpina, dividing her time between the earth and the underworld. Ben dreams of walking out of Boston, following Gloria on "an obscure path" that takes them "among the building tops" and across "the perilous gulf" until they are "together on the opposite side" (91), suggesting parallels with Orpheus and Eurydice and, perhaps, Dante and Beatrice. Ben's first wife, Perdita, plays Diana, too: when, as a newlywed, he takes Polaroids of her skinny-dipping in a lake, she takes them from him, refusing to part with them even after they divorce and he claims the photographs as his property.

Updike has insisted that "books should have secrets, like people do" (Plath, ed., 36); most reviewers of *Toward the End of Time* seem to have assumed that the novel's secret is that Ben Turnbull is the latest in a long line of protagonists who, in Wallace's words, "are all clearly stand-ins for the author himself" (Wallace, 1). It seems to me, however, that the real secret is that this interpretation is not precisely true: *Toward the End of Time* is in many ways a more playful book than its reviewers have realized, enticing readers to confuse its protagonist with its author and to rationalize away the richness of its mythic allusions and events in favor of something more mundane. As in *The Centaur,* natural events in *Toward the End of Time* are, in Updike's words, "meant to be a kind of mask for the myth" (Plath, ed., 51) — but without the earlier novel's explicit naming, and indexing, of the mythic characters, and with the added distinction, thanks to the science-fictional setting, of moments where mythical events break through the mask of natural events. In the words of its first epigraph, this novel is "pierced by that/ Occasional void through which the supernatural flows."

Reading for the mythological provides an interpretive context for what in a naturalistic reading would be seen as confusing or arbitrary details. Ben's description of Gloria as "my naked queen of tilth" (*End of Time,* 140) can be read literally, allowing us to understand Gloria as a Demeter figure. Ben's observation, "My wife is a killer. She dreams at night of my death" (6), which in a realistic reading indicates primarily an old man's paranoia and misogyny, suggests in a mythical context Robert Graves's White Goddess, a distillation of all goddesses of fertility, love, and death into a single figure whom Graves explains as "the White Goddess, or Muse, the Mother of All Living, the ancient power of fright and lust — the female spider or the queen-bee whose embrace is death" (Graves, 24). Gloria's "beautiful, trim sternness" (*End of Time,* 14), "pale fire" (20), "red lips" (141), "ice-blue eyes" (8), and "crown of ash-blond hair" (14) bear a certain resemblance to Graves's description of the White Goddess — "a lovely, slender woman with a hooked nose, deathly pale face, lips red as rowan berries, startlingly blue eyes and long fair hair" (24). Atwood has noted that Gloria, Deirdre, and Doreen form a "Gravesian trio of crone, Venus and maiden" (Atwood, 10), three aspects of the White Goddess; Updike hints at this essential connection between the characters when Ben notes that the returned Gloria sounds like Deirdre and thinks, "I wondered if one of them had absorbed the other" (*End of Time,* 144). Graves's description of the central poetic theme — "the God of the Waxing Year" fights a "losing battle with the God of the Waning Year for the love of the capricious and powerful Threefold Goddess, their mother, bride and layer-out" (Graves, 24) — finds certain parallels in Updike's story. The scenes in which Ben speaks in other voices highlight times when one power or belief system is challenged by its successor: the invasion of the pyramids by agnostic grave-robbers (*End of Time,* 61-66); the clash between early, Judaic Christianity and St. Paul's "anti-social" theology (123-34); the pillaging of an Irish monastery by Viking invaders (215-22); a violent confrontation between a concentration camp guard and a Jewish prisoner, within the context of an imminent Allied invasion (241-43). Ben's customary weakness in the knees when he holds one of his grandchildren (106-7, 193) seems a sort of instinct to surrender to the generation that will succeed him, parallel to the Irish monk's instinct to "crouch beneath" (222) the invader who is poised to kill him. And the continuing descriptions of plants in the Turnbulls' garden that Wallace finds so self-indulgent convey the same story: a particular plant blooms for a time, then decays, and is succeeded by the blooms of other species.

Even a passage near the novel's end describing yellow leaves on the tops of willow trees and "some strange trees (oaks, I think, of a special sort) [that] have bleached almost white in turning and yet do not drop their leaves, rather like trees abruptly killed by lightning" (330), gains a certain interpretive resonance in the light of Graves's assertions that in Greece the willow "was sacred to Hecate, Circe, Hera and Persephone, all Death aspects of the Triple Moon-goddess" (Graves, 173) and the oak is "the tree of Zeus, Jupiter, Hercules . . . Thor, and all the other Thunder-gods" (176): if Gloria correlates with the deadly aspects of the White Goddess, Ben correlates with "the sacred oak-king" who was annually "killed at midsummer" (*End of Time,* 179), a connection that at least suggests a symbolic interpretation of Ben's midsummer prostate operation and subsequent impotence. Finally, Graves connects the oak tree with the letter "D" (Graves, 176), a yoking that may provide some insight into the otherwise baffling question as to what induced Updike to choose such alliterative chapter titles: "The Deer," "The Dollhouse," "The Deal," "The Deaths," and "The Dahlia."

The latter half of the novel has a number of parallels with the Gilgamesh epic. Like Gilgamesh, Turnbull seems to be on a sort of quest to discover the meaning of death, eternity, and immortality (Gardner and Maier, 6), and Gilgamesh's lament to Utnapishtim — "What can I do, Utnapishtim? Where can I go?/A thief has stolen my flesh./Death lives in the house where my bed is,/and wherever I set my feet, there Death is" (245) — could easily be Turnbull's own. The adolescent squatters in Turnbull's woods, who seem, upon first meeting him, wild and hostile, can be seen as, in aggregate, roughly parallel to Enkidu, an uncivilized man brought into being in the wilderness by the gods to be Gilgamesh's rival (*Epic,* 5-6). Upon their first meeting Enkidu attacks Gilgamesh, but after fighting him Enkidu admits Gilgamesh's superiority and becomes his close friend (18); when the gods sentence Enkidu to death for various offenses he has committed against them with Gilgamesh (59), Gilgamesh mourns in anguish over the body of his friend (69-72) and sets off on his long quest for eternal life (75-94). In similar fashion, the adolescent boys initially extort protection money from Ben and threaten his property (*End of Time,* 163-70), but before long he is their de facto partner, offering them advice on the best ways to extort money from his neighbors for a percentage of their profits (203); sharing the sexual favors of Doreen, the boys' fourteen-year-old companion (236); and thinking, "I loved these willing boys, so superior, in their readiness and accessibility, to my own grandsons" (225). When the boys' extortion efforts attract Gloria's attention, leading to the group's being destroyed by metallobioforms, Ben grieves and feels responsible, thinking, "Had I been there to counsel them, they might all still be alive" (275). And Ben's actions in the novel's final pages, searching through the basement for the bulb of the dahlia that Gloria grew the previous summer, acquires greater resonance in parallel with Gilgamesh's search in the sea beneath the earth for a plant known as "The Old Man Becomes a Young Man," which will restore the eater's youth: Gilgamesh, unlike Ben, finds the plant he is looking for, but has it stolen by a snake before he can partake of it (*Epic,* 106-7).

These mythical parallels, combined with the novel's futuristic setting, allow Updike to explore several familiar themes in ways that mere realism would not allow. In Updike's post-apocalyptic America, for example, society has come undone: the economy and government have collapsed, the police are powerless, and Ben, who makes monthly protection payments to local hoodlums, notes that "In the breakdown of order, the criminal element has proved to be the only one with the resources and ruthlessness to rule" (*End of Time,* 46). This is a world, like that of myth, without stability: the inhabitants are, it seems, only one word or gesture away from offending a god and being transformed into an animal or plant, from being served their children for dinner, from being ripped into pieces by loved ones in a bacchanalian frenzy. All that is left after the collapse of society, Ben sums up, is "Paganism. Imported Oriental gods, fraudulent magi and seers. The decline of Rome" (122).

This setting allows Updike to dramatize the theme of conflict between the individual and his or her social structure that he has been exploring at least since *Rabbit, Run.* In that novel, Rabbit leaves his wife and child in response to his "inner urgent whispers," but, as Updike has pointed out, "the social fabric collapses murderously" (Plath, ed., 33). The variation Updike presents in *Toward the End of Time* is that society falls apart and, as many reviewers have complained, Ben Turnbull is so attentive to his "inner urgent whispers" that he barely notices. This is not, in fact, as fantastic as the reviewers claim. After all, Ben is rich, a condition that affords many individuals the opportunity to block out tragedy and focus on their own concerns. If anything, this aspect of the novel is a realistic tribute to the insulating power of wealth: by converting the United States into a Third-World country whose residents are eager to cross the border into economically sound Mexico, Updike is free to explore the gap between rich and poor that exists within developing countries, as well as the ease with which most of us can ignore the devastation, armed conflicts, and poverty taking place in other countries or other neighborhoods.

Because he is wealthy, Ben can afford to tell Deirdre, "I don't much care what happens in the world" (*End of Time,* 121). He even finds himself appreciating some aspects of the post-apocalyptic chaos, noting that "One advantage of the collapse of civilization is that the quality of young women who are becoming whores has gone way up" (40). Updike counters Ben's callousness with the example of Deirdre, for whom the collapse of civilization has less benign effects: to avoid poverty and violence, she moves in with Ben, at the price of having to submit to his sexual whims and moments of cruelty. Ben may have found civilization confining, but for people like Deirdre, Updike suggests, civilization is a great benefit. Ben himself admits that the twenty-year-olds who are becoming prostitutes "would once have become beauticians or editorial assistants, nurses or paralegals" (40-41), would have had greater autonomy had civilization not collapsed. As Deirdre tells Ben, shortly before she leaves him:

> "When there was government, there were things like the FBI and the Federal Reserve Board to keep things stable. There was structure. . . . Structure is worth paying quite a lot for. Without it, you just get survival of the brutes." (121)

At one level, then, *Toward the End of Time* is a subtle criticism of Ben's solipsistic view of life, using both the negative example of his brutish callousness toward others' misfortune and an image pattern that suggests the effect that Ben's way of life has on people around him. Deirdre is regularly associated with oil: her pubic hair is "so oily it would have been iridescent in a stronger light" (44); she has a "headful of wiry oily wool" (54); "oily whiffs spring from her flesh and hair" (117); and, attending Easter services with her, Ben notices her "oiled curls" (117). Other oppressed characters in the novel share Deirdre's oiliness: Manolete, one of the young squatters, has "eyes like globules of oil" (201), and the Jewish concentration camp prisoner has eyes "like globules of black oil" (242). The oil in Deirdre's hair may suggest some kind of anointment; it also seems to be connected to the variety of metallobioforms that Updike has named "oil-eaters" (110). These oil-eating "trinkets" (111) destroy Manolete and his companions, a connection that reduces the characters to a kind of fuel; this imagery ultimately comes into focus with Ben's observation that his "faithful servant" of a house "pursue[s] an independent life, like a motherly, stationary megatrinket" (298). The implicit message, that the powerful maintain their lifestyles by cannibalizing the marginalized, is probably intended to be more rueful than outraged: as Updike said of readers who were bothered by Rabbit's hardness of heart in *Rabbit, Run*, "I meant to say, 'We're all hard of heart like this; don't get mad at him'" (Rothstein, C21). Everyone who enjoys the luxury of debating the moral decisions of fictional characters is an oil-eater of one kind or another.

Despite the novel's attention to social issues, Updike's central concerns in *Toward the End of Time* are overwhelmingly religious. The novel's setting in the year 2020 is enormously ironic because Ben Turnbull could not be more myopic: he is a mythic figure, living in a post-apocalyptic world, married to a goddess who dies and returns from the dead, and sleeping with a woman who used to be a deer, and yet he understands himself to be nothing more than an upper-middle-class retiree, and he labors to bend the fantastic events he experiences to fit that paradigm. His assertion when, late in the novel, he hears an unfamiliar noise — "There had to be a rational explanation" (*End of Time,* 333) — is a sort of credo for his actions throughout the novel as a whole: he will believe nothing that fails to conform to his narrow definition of the rational.

In *The White Goddess,* Robert Graves notes that "the common people of Christendom" have, on the whole,

> discarded their religious idealism . . . and come to the private conclusion that money, though the root of all evil, is the sole practical means of expressing value or of determining social precedence; that science is the only accurate means of describing phenomena; and that a morality of common honesty is not relevant either to love, war, business or politics. (Graves, 476)

Ben fits Graves's profile quite well: he seems to have nothing but contempt for anything that is not scientific, accusing even himself at one point of "pre-scientific stupidity" (*End of Time,* 33) and complaining that "priests . . . continue to practice their grotesque trade on this doomed planet even into this age of scientific enlightenment" (329); he even boasts "I never read fiction," calling its "little hurly-burly . . . more proof that we are of all animals the most miserable" (46). His most persistent explanation for the fantastic events that permeate his narrative draws on a theory of quantum measurements that postulates the branching out of parallel universes when specific actions, such as the measuring of a quantum particle, are performed (16). His use of the concept, however, seems illogical: if the universe branches out at the moment, for example, when Ben thinks of shooting Gloria, creating parallel universes in which Gloria is and is not shot, it would seem impossible for the version of Ben in a universe in which Gloria is dead to backtrack through that moment of branching into a universe in which Gloria is still alive. Any universe in which Gloria was shot will always contain the moment of her death, whatever its future branchings might be. Updike underscores the point with his second epigraph, which states that we could not know we were branching into duplicate selves "because our consciousness rides smoothly along only one path in the endlessly forking chains"; Ben's attempt at a rational, scientific explanation for the phenomena of his life collapses because he can remember events that did not occur on his "path." He prefers to believe an illogical "scientific" explanation rather than acknowledge that other explanations might exist.

In addition to science, Ben's other sacred article of faith is money. The Emily Dickinson poem Ben overhears on his car radio (85) — which refers, incidentally, to a "Color . . . That Science cannot overtake/But Human Nature feels" — ends with the lines that Ben transcribes as "something about *encroached* (it sounded like) *upon a sacrament*" (85); a quick dip into Dickinson's *Complete Poems* — Updike helpfully provides the poem's number on his copyright page — reveals the actual lines to be "As Trade had suddenly encroached/Upon a Sacrament" (Dickinson, 395). The lines seem an apt description of Ben's attitude toward the sacrament of marriage, which he seems to see largely in terms of trade. He refers to Perdita as "the first woman I slept with on a contractual basis" (*End of Time*, 91), and his marriage to Gloria has a financial aspect as well. He notes that upon meeting Gloria his mother told him, "Those teeth are worth investing in" (259), and by marrying Gloria he is able to leave behind the financial insecurity of his childhood and first marriage for a house filled with the inherited wealth of Gloria's "splendid ancestors" (61). If he is a type of Gilgamesh, he is a Gilgamesh who chose not to reject Ishtar's proposal of marriage, with its promise of power and wealth: "a chariot of lapus lazuli and gold," and "kings, lords, and princes bowing before him" (*Epic*, 51). Sex in general is, for Ben, less sacrament than trade: early in the novel, he writes that he is no longer interested in the passionate affairs of his youth and would prefer to seek out prostitutes and "put the problem of my erratic erections to them like a tricky tax matter laid before a well-paid accountant on a clean, bed-sized desk" (*End of Time*, 21); introducing one of his sexual encounters with Deirdre during which the pair negotiate prices for particular acts, he notes, "Our lovemaking had some of the excitement of an auction" (42). His sexual access to Doreen seems to be a payment for the help he has given her adolescent companions, and he scrupulously abides by the terms of their contract — "no penetration" (236-37).

Ironically, Ben's scientific materialism leads him to take a brutish view of life. He tells Deirdre that male cruelty is biologically inevitable, since "The killers survive, the killed drop out of the genetic pool.

Same reason . . . women are masochistic. The submissive ones . . . make the babies and the scrappers don't" (53-54). Ben's naturalistic view focuses on the body and its urges rather than the promise of democracy; he effusively hymns his penis as

> Stout and faithful fellow! My life's companion. I loved it, or him; erectile heat suffused my system with the warm blood of well-being; for these pumped-up instants I felt no need to justify my earthly existence; all came clear. (187)

If Ben is meant to be a Jovian figure, then his name, "Turnbull," is particularly appropriate. He is Jove turned bull in pursuit of Europa, ignoring any other aspects of himself in pursuit of the pleasures of brute, animal existence. As Ovid writes:

> And so, great Jove
> renounced his solemn specter: he — the lord
> and father of the gods — whose right hand holds
> his massive weapons; three-pronged lightning bolts,
> the king whose simple nod can shake the world —
> takes on the semblance of a bull.
>
> (*Metamorphoses*, 72)

As a young father, Ben had wrestled with the problem of materialism and mortality, convinced that there was no God, "just Nature, which would consume my life as carelessly and relentlessly as it would a dung-beetle corpse in a compost pile" (*End of Time*, 83); his struggle mirrors Updike's biography, even to the details of feeling crushed by his mortality building a dollhouse for his daughter in a cellar. Unlike Updike, however, who responded to his ontological crisis by reading Karl Barth and falling in love with other men's wives (*Self-Consciousness*, 98), Turnbull, with his innate materialism, seems to have ignored theology altogether, merely beginning his first affair, noting:

> My marriage, I knew, was doomed by this transgression, or by those that followed, but I was again alive, in that moment of constant present emergency in which animals healthily live. (*End of Time*, 84)

The view of life that Turnbull advocates suggests what Updike has criticized as

> an easy humanism that insists that man is an animal which feeds and sleeps and defecates and makes love and isn't that nice and natural and let's all have more of that.
>
> But this is omitting intrinsic stresses in the human condition — you foresee things, for example, you foresee your own death. You have already been locked out of the animal paradise of unthinking natural reflex. (Plath, ed., 61)

In place of this easy humanism, Updike says he takes "a rather darker view. We must of necessity lose our humanity all the time" (62).

By the end of *Toward the End of Time,* Ben has come closer to losing his humanity in Updike's sense in literal and mythical ways: the operation for prostate cancer, which causes him to lose a "bit of [his] animal self" (*End of Time,* 331), seems a sort of death and rebirth, and the death of the deer can be read as a sort of substitutionary act, the killing of a scapegoat in Ben's place.[1] Most dramatic, however, is what seems to be nothing less than an encounter with God. The science fiction setting allows Updike to introduce an extraterrestrial object that Turnbull refers to as "the torus," an enormous pale ring floating "beyond the clouds but lower than the moon," demonstrating that "somewhere in the universe mind has triumphed over matter, instead of antagonistically coexisting with it as on our planet." However, Turnbull speculates, the torus is "composed of a substance impalpable on Earth," and "the minds, or giant mind, behind this perfectly circular intrusion into our skies do not, and does not, communicate"; he questions if "there can be no more language between above and below than between a man and an underground nest of ants" (153-54).

In these descriptions, the torus bears the characteristics of God in Neo-orthodox theology. In a review of one of the works of Karl Barth, Updike quotes Barth as responding to a "naturalistic, humanistic, demythologized, and merely ethical" version of Christianity with the affirmation, "There is no way from us to God. . . . The god who stood at the end of some human way . . . would not be God" (*Assorted Prose,* 273). Updike goes on to explain that "The real God, the God men do not invent, is . . . Wholly Other. We cannot reach Him; only He can reach us" (273-74).

1. If we read the deer, mythically, as a metamorphosis of Deirdre, we can see even more specifically Christian overtones, since Updike spins a brief connection in the Easter Sunday scenes between Deirdre and the risen Christ (*End of Time,* 117).

Late in the novel, the torus seems to reach out to humanity, its ring expanding to encircle and pass over the earth, and as it does so Turnbull describes himself as being flooded with "a creamy, weightless sense of irreversible reassurance" (*End of Time*, 231). While the torus is around the earth, he experiences what seems to be the ecstasy of a saint in the presence of God:

> I would not die, I realized; all would be well. All the fleeting impressions I had ever received were preserved somewhere and could be replayed. All shadows would be wiped away, when light was everywhere and not confined to loci-stars, hot points, pinpricks in nothingness. But just the concept of light, born of combustion and atomic collision, was too harsh for the peace that was promised with the torus. . . . Time was a provision that would be rescinded; its tragedy was born of misperception, an upper limit of conceptual ability such as keeps the bee bumbling among the clover and the faithful dog trotting, loving but puzzled, at his master's heels. (232)

After the torus has passed, people throughout the world are unable to reach a consensus as to what they have experienced. "Everyone had seen it; everyone had felt it," Ben writes, but their explanations of their experience conflict. Psychologists postulate "theories of mass hallucination powerful enough to affect even photographic plates" (233), and even Ben, writing just ten days after the event, feels confused and skeptical and is tempted toward his customary naturalistic understanding: "What really did I feel? People are grotesquely suggestible, to facilitate sexual congress and tribal solidarity" (233). This reaction is, in fact, consistent with Neo-orthodoxy: if God is Wholly Other, then any attempt to reduce him to human understanding will always be in error, subject to human fallibility.

The reviewers who responded to *Toward the End of Time* with hostility were reacting, I think, against the very notion of fallibility: Birkerts's desire for Ben's suffering to be redemptive seems based in the therapeutic idea that one can and should purge one's self of fear, selfishness, and anger and become a kinder, more considerate, productive member of society. Birkerts's claims to the contrary, Ben does actually undergo changes during the course of the novel: immediately following his description of his encounter with the torus, he feels "an icicle poke of pain in a nether recess of myself, a dark and inaccessible underside I have always preferred to pretend is not there" (233-34), which leads, eventually, to his prostate surgery; this unwilling confrontation with aspects of himself that he would ordinarily ignore suggests, at least symbolically, that Ben is acquiring a deeper self-knowledge. After his operation, he grieves for the death of the children in his woods and feels responsible for his failure to protect them; he seems to regret his callous treatment of Deirdre, recalling "her searing wish — I felt it now, at last — to be sheltered" (295); he describes himself, after returning home from the hospital, in terms of returning to childhood, suggesting some sort of rebirth (266); and he seems more likely to praise, thinking, at one point, "What bliss life is" (299). His impotence and incontinence render him unable to resort to the easy humanism of animal health that he has fled to throughout his life. He writes that after dreaming about having an erection, "I awake and peek inside my soaked Depends," only to discover that his penis "is as red and flaccid as a rooster's comb" (291). Wallace concludes that Updike wants us to feel sorry for Ben in this condition; it seems to me that Updike would allow our response to be somewhat more complex, any empathy we might feel for Ben tempered by the recognition that, given his values and habits, this turn of events feels supremely right, both judgment and punishment for his past actions. Certainly Ben's response to the sights he sees in the Depends suggests remorse for his past: "How could so superfluous an appendage ever have served as the hub of my universe? The foolishness of life hits me, stunningly, as the last plausible shreds of my dream dissolve" (291).

As Birkerts has rightly pointed out, however, these redemptive signs are not the only realities in Ben's life. He remains spiteful, cynical, jealous, hostile toward Gloria, enormously self-involved, and nostalgic for the days when he could, in his words, "shoot semen into a woman's wincing face like bullets of milk" (296). The discontinuity between Ben's repentance and his hardness of heart suggests that Updike is less interested in portraying the holiness of a saint or the depravity of a sinner than he is in depicting that more densely populated territory occupied by people pierced by longings for both extremes but wholly committed to neither. Ben, in Updike's view, is not the grotesque aberration that reviewers despised; he seems instead to be intended to be a figure who, like the characters in myths and legends, ultimately transcends time and place. Myths endure because they reflect human desires and fears that persevere from one era to another. John B. Vickery argues that Graves's White Goddess is a representation of

> both the natural and psychological worlds in which man must live subject to forces other than his own untrammeled will . . . an extended metaphor for the vicissitudes and exaltation that come to man from the external world of nature and society and from the internal world of his own metabolism and psyche. (Vickery, x)

In this symbolic economy, Ben's desire for, fear of, and anger at Gloria are of a piece with his pleasure in physical life, both his own and that around him, and his revulsion at either's decay. He loves many things, yet his need for transcendence makes him feel confined by what he loves; he violates, as the reviewers noted, some of our most cherished ethical norms, but the merely ethical cannot contain him, because he has the need for God, who lies at the end of no human way. Like his house, Ben has "no back, but two fronts" (*End of Time,* 7); he is a Janus who looks, with longing, in two directions at once. He is always both spiritual and secular, rational and mythical, believer and non-believer, conqueror of the earth and slave to the forces of decay and desire; he is Updike's Everyman. The reviewers who had no sympathy for Ben and felt disappointed that there was no point in the novel at which he woke up and began to solve his problems have not only missed Updike's point that there is no simple solution to the problem of being human; they also appear to have never peered deeply into mythology, theology, or the contradictions within their own lives.

PART 2

UPDIKE AND THE CHRISTIAN RELIGION

An Umbrella Blowing Inside Out

Paradoxical Theology and American Culture in the Novels of John Updike

KYLE A. PASEWARK

The fictional figure upon whom John Updike has expended more ink and paper than any other, the sympathetically disreputable Harry "Rabbit" Angstrom, has, Updike writes, "no taste for the dark, tangled, visceral aspect of Christianity, the *going through* quality of it, the passage *into* death and suffering that redeems and inverts these things, like an umbrella blowing inside out. He lacks the mindful will to walk the straight line of a paradox." Similarly, he thinks that Judaism "must be a great religion . . . once you get past the circumcision." Like Updike himself, Rabbit "has always loved that feeling, of being inside when it rains. . . . Things that touch and yet not."[1]

We might suspect that the failures of Rabbit Angstrom and others of Updike's fictional constructions are related to their incapacity in the face of paradox. That is true, as we will see, but to begin there might lead to a judgment about Updike's characters that does not affect the way we understand ourselves and our culture. Updike's fiction is, after all, addressed to readers. Fiction implicates its readers and the culture in

1. *Rabbit, Run,* 237/203; *Rabbit at Rest,* 430/1440; *Rabbit Is Rich,* 117/726. For Updike's own joy in "being out of the rain, but *just* out," see *Self-Consciousness,* 34.

which it appears. The theological and cultural question of this essay asks less about Updike or his characters than it does about *us:* What does Updike's fiction say about religion, culture, and intuitions of divine presence in this time, in this place, which Updike describes as "this great roughly rectangular country severed from Christ by the breadth of the sea" (*Self-Consciousness,* 103)? If what Updike presents to us is paradoxical, then the initial question is, How should we read the paradoxical?

Updike's emphasis on paradox invites us to think about an alternative way to read his fiction, namely, as the presentation of paradoxes that *arrest* readers. Only in decayed art such as Soviet realism, or, sad to say, some Christian theology, is meaning reduced to a single thrust. Moreover, Updike's penchant for paradox and his intensification of Kierkegaard's indirect communication further expand the range of meanings present in his fiction.[2] This understanding implies that Updike's contribution to the argumentative disciplines of religious and cultural criticism is possibilities rather than conclusions. Distinct from most so-called "Christian fiction," like that of C. S. Lewis, Updike's words are not evidently directed through fictional characters toward a single conclusion. Rather, we will have to do what any responsible thinker should do anyway: sift through the possibilities, follow threads, see where they lead, and evaluate them argumentatively. Updike's fiction does not deliver a claim to be true: rather, it engages us in the demand to think truly. But *we* must do it; Updike will not do it for us. We cannot simply receive a revelatory or authoritative message; we must help discern and create it.

This imposes burdens on the interpreter. To approach Updike's work as demanding its reader to think truly means that to proceed immediately upon finishing a work of Updike to facile praise or condemnation of his characters — and even more, of Updike himself — on the basis of our own moral, religious, or epistemological positions is out of place.[3] Rather, Updike dislodges and challenges our normal ways of

2. Some of the literature concerning Kierkegaard's influence on Updike's fiction includes George Hunt's *John Updike and the Three Great Secret Things,* Ralph Wood's *The Comedy of Redemption,* and John Stephen Martin's article, "Rabbit's Faith: Grace and the Transformation of the Heart."

3. Unfortunately, this attempt to compare Updike or his work to *assumed* positions is common, ranging from paeans to Updike's unconventional characters to condemnation of them. Less frequent, however, are attempts to take Updike's work as a *challenge* to rethink previously held positions.

being, depriving us, as Tolstoy did in *The Death of Ivan Ilych*, of the quiet but arrogant certainty that living correctly is sufficient for living well (Tolstoy, 145). We, as much as Updike or his characters, are cast from the innocent garden of our moral and cultural certainties. It is true that theologians, cultural critics, and virtually anyone else will come to conclusions regarding the possibilities Updike presents through paradox; it is also true that we must rethink ourselves and our culture in the process.

I will emphasize a particular point of entry into Updike's work, namely, what he has to say about one of the most pressing problems in American culture, and therefore American Christianity and other religions as well: the problem of freedom. Paradox may be the only fruitful approach to this question, for the American vision of freedom is itself paradoxical. If we are not to lose the vision of a more powerful freedom than we now have, any "answer" to the questions of freedom will retain a paradoxical character. Thus, there are methodological limitations to which we must conform. We must hew to the course of paradox if we are not to distort the messages that Updike's fiction sends to constructive cultural and religious thought. We proceed, therefore, with remarks about paradox in general, in Updike's fiction, and in Christian traditions.

I

As usually formulated, reason operates non-paradoxically. Analytic reason often takes paradox to be contradiction or intellectual slovenliness. In the execution of non-paradoxical reason, however, we run aground frequently. It is more convenient to have our umbrellas rightside out, but it seems rarely to work that way. We plan feverishly, carefully, and minutely. One of the perplexing features of human existence is that those plans almost never seem to work quite the way they were conceived. Hannah Arendt noted that "nothing happens more frequently than the totally unexpected." But calculative reason omits, as it must, the unexpected from its calculations and then coronates itself as reason entire. But, Arendt continues, because "the event constitutes the very texture of reality within the realm of human affairs, where the 'wholly improbable happens regularly,' it is highly unrealistic not to reckon with it" (Arendt, 300).

Americans, however, seem particularly lacking in taste for such paradoxes. We think in political and personal dualities rather than dialectics, of interference with our best-laid plans as nothing but obstruction, of direct routes rather than winding roads. The contemporary dearth of philosophies of history and unwillingness to explore the theological category of providence in any depth indicate our resistance to or incompetence for paradox. When our modern confidence in the unambiguous progress of history was shattered, we were left with nothing to say.[4] We want straight lines but not paradoxical ones. Our pragmatic temperament asks for clarity and purity. However, all that we thought banished returns. Good, well-educated, liberal, and free-willed people find themselves acting, for whatever reason, in ill-mannered, ignorant, illiberal ways that seem somehow not matters of "choice." Seekers of purity usually turn out to be the most fanatic perpetrators of evil (as our politics are demonstrating robustly in 1999), and in general, the more clarity we demand of the world, the muddier it seems to become. Perhaps this is because paradox is not finally irrational or anti-rational but that which simultaneously shatters reason and makes it necessary.

II

Updike's penchant for paradox is indubitable. How else to describe the world of *Roger's Version?* Roger, a jaded but conservative divinity school professor who has lost his faith, is the strongest supporter of the doctoral project of an evangelical who wants to prove the existence of the unchangeable, primitive God by means of the most recent and advanced computer technology. Roger supports the project because he believes that if it is approved the student will lose his faith — and Roger is right. How else but paradox to account for the erotic effect of Tom Marshfield's ascetic desert retreat in *A Month of Sundays?* What else but paradox is Clarence Wilmot's final sermon in *In the Beauty of the Lilies?* Clarence, who has lost his faith but believes more strongly than ever in the rigid Princeton interpretation of divine election (he knows only that he is not elect), preaches that we can choose our own election in direct contradiction to what he knows inwardly to be true. The congregation

4. On this point, see Langdon Gilkey's *Reaping the Whirlwind: A Christian Interpretation of History*, 9-10.

affirms, against its pastor, the classic doctrine but for the next year advises Clarence that he must recover his own faith (49-108). In case we miss the stiletto thrusts of paradox after paradox, Updike twists one toward the heart: Clarence received a "revelation . . . of God's non-existence" (104). What else but paradox explains Clark, Clarence's great-grandson, who recovers faith and is accounted a hero, although it is he who sets off the murderous charge to a Waco-like confrontation between the authorities and Clark's Temple of True and Actual Faith (448-88)? Paradox is the fabric of Updike's fiction, and if one had to choose a single message it would be that paradox is the stuff of life, that the twists and turns of paradox are the only straight lines offered.

Updike's emphasis on paradox inherits an influential line of Christian theology, represented in exemplary ways by Augustine of Hippo, Martin Luther, John Calvin, Søren Kierkegaard, Karl Barth, and, though Updike is not inclined to acknowledge it, Paul Tillich and Reinhold Niebuhr. Moreover, although Updike has an uneven reputation among feminists, paradox seems to be undergoing a rebirth in feminist thought as well. The pre-twentieth-century masters of paradox in Christian theology had a common emphasis on the paradoxical character — and terror — of ordinary human life. Augustine's singular genius was his recognition that a final religious devotion to aspects of the world — whether the self in his *Confessions* or a political structure in *The City of God* — destroyed precisely what one intended to worship. Luther intensified these Augustinian paradoxes by carrying them into the worship of God. Luther's most pious statement — "a kingdom awaits the godly, even though they themselves neither seek it nor think of it. . . . What is more, if they [acted] for the sake of obtaining the Kingdom, they would never obtain it" (Luther, 33:152) — lies on the precipice of atheism (an atheism for the sake of God's will), though it would take the West several hundred years to take that plunge. Calvin's theology of election folds terror and comfort into a single doctrine; comfort cannot be had without terror. Luther's bold "I am willing to be damned for the glory of God" is equally Calvin's. But Calvin also knew that only a doctrine of election could finally conquer terror; only if we lack freedom to produce our final salvific meaning is freedom on earth possible.[5] Unlike Augustine, Luther, and Calvin,

5. This is why, for both Luther and Calvin, the relatively good work is possible only if the elect have *knowledge* of their salvation.

who were driven to paradox, Kierkegaard took pleasure in it. For quite un-Nietzschean reasons, Kierkegaard possesses a Nietzschean elation in asserting that a life of comfort is convincing evidence of God's hatred, whereas a flood of divine love causes only pain, misery, and heartache.[6]

Updike has commerce with each of these great paradoxists. We already alluded to the substantial body of work treating Updike's relation to Kierkegaard and the importance of the paradox of indirect communication. With respect to Augustine, Updike achieves his own paradox. In "Augustine's Concubine," Updike suggests that what has often been taken as one of Augustine's greatest acts of piety, giving up (or rather expelling) his unnamed mistress for the sake of celibacy, was instead his greatest blasphemy. The mistress, it turns out, was more faithful to God than her lover (*Problems,* 132-40). For its part, the Calvinist paradox of election is the soil of *In the Beauty of the Lilies* and is also vital, we will see, to the treatment of freedom's paradox in Updike's novels. Luther's paradox, mediated by Barth, of the simultaneously hidden and present God appears in Roger Lambert's insistence that God be a living God rather than a mere fact that we could take or leave at our pleasure (*Roger's Version,* 219).

This plethora of possible, challenging meanings present in art generally, and in Updike's indirect communication especially, means that it is insufficient simply to look at the novels as if one were a mere observer. The conversation between art and its recipient calls for an explicit account of the experience of reading. Moreover, reflecting on the reading of Updike's novels tells us more about those works themselves and the culture that they engage. Paradox is present not only on the printed page but also in the experience of reading. One can better appreciate the strangely conflicted effects of Updike's fiction when one finds that others' encounters with Updike are as offbeat as one's own. A philosopher at a liberal arts college once remarked to me that "I used to believe that Updike had nothing to say, and then I thought, 'Then why have I been reading him for thirty years?'"[7] With respect to content, Updike confronts us with characters who are concerned with no

6. For particularly stark versions of this claim, see Søren Kierkegaard, *Kierkegaard's Attack on "Christendom," 1854-1855.*

7. The judgment that he had nothing to say was leveled at Updike's work very early, and he comments in *Self-Consciousness* about how odd that criticism seemed to him (103).

two things as much as sex and religion, which often turn out to be the same thing. And yet I know of no one who is consistently aroused to warm comforts of faith or hot flashes of libido while reading Updike's work. Those of us with moralistic impulses continually disappoint ourselves in finding the really romantic, beautiful trysts less inviting than the seamier, less responsible ones.

Our moral worldview is also confounded. When teaching the Rabbit novels, I was greeted with the predictable reaction of horror, disapproval, even outright hatred of Rabbit for his shameful conduct at the funeral of his infant daughter (*Rabbit, Run,* 292-307/252-64). His shocking treatment of his wife, Janice, generated the amazement that ought to — but usually does not — attend Adam's conduct in the Garden, the model of Rabbit's betrayal. Students fumed that Rabbit needed to "grow up," be more loving, less selfish, to think of others for a change. They wanted Harry to be a quiet, placid, and responsible lover, without self-aggrandizing aspiration and its accompanying self-obsession, and even cruelty. Of course, at the beginning of *Rabbit Redux,* he is all that and more. He is moral, responsible, without illusions of grandeur, the perfect American father, a husband tolerant of his wife's missteps, self-sacrificial to the core (*Rabbit Redux,* 3-31/269-93) — and students, to a person, disliked him even more. My reaction was the same. His weakness was contemptible, his lack of drive and vision despicable, and we castigated him for the acceptance of destiny — an acceptance that we had all urged upon him earlier and, by the way, would urge again. Similarly, we are repulsed by the egoism of Tom Marshfield, who is convinced that the woman who cleans his room during his imposed ascetic exile secretly wants to bed him. But I felt better about the world when it turned out to be true; solace seemed more available (*Month of Sundays,* 205-28). One paradox of reading Updike's fiction is that seemingly decent readers often prefer indecency, whereas decency itself, which we hope the world may embrace, seems weak, enervated, even impious. It is, I think, at this point, the confrontation between the work and the reader, that one can see most clearly Updike's diagnosis of American culture and religion; it is also in this confrontation that many of us can look inwardly and outwardly and see its truth.

III

Updike's fixation with the sexual and religious speaks also to what really constitutes the heart of contemporary American religiosity: the God of freedom. In fact, the American dream of freedom constitutes the "immovable mover" of many of his major characters — "immovable" because the American interpretation of freedom is never questioned, "mover" because the response to the "grace" of freedom animates much of the action. That a conception of freedom should drive the American characters of an American novelist is not surprising; after all, the religion of freedom is really the great American civil religion.

Rudolf Otto, in his groundbreaking book *The Idea of the Holy*, argued that for an experience to elicit worship, what is experienced must be apprehended as an awesome power to which we are inescapably subject. The paradox of religious experience — indeed, of any vital religion — is that awe is felt as both repelling and attractive; in the very constitution of religion, the believer is frozen between two desires, obedience and escape. This is not so distant from the claim of Otto's contemporary, Max Weber, who suggested in his book *The Sociology of Religion* that the social founding of religions often arises from attachment to a charismatic figure, a theme to which I will return. Contemporary American culture, however, skirts the "tremendum," that awe-inspiring and also terrifying aspect of the holy. Rather, we opt for an unambiguous — and thus certainly non-paradoxical — deification of freedom. Updike's work goes a long way toward reconnecting us with Otto's insight; if we are to have freedom as does God, or even a god, we would be well-advised to attend to its terrors as well as its promise.

There can be little doubt that our American civil religion is freedom. The rhetoric of freedom comes in many forms. We invoke freedom itself, of course, but also choice, rights, opinion, space, the individual, and so on — moons circling the rock of freedom. It is fortunate that there are so many avatars of freedom because freedom is busy — politically, economically, socially, and personally. On the single day of November 6, 1997, *The New York Times* reported the following: the overwhelming passage in the House of Representatives of a bill including a 28-point "Taxpayer Bill of Rights"; Oregon voters' reaffirmation of an assisted-suicide law hailed by one of its supporters as a victory that overcame "the political machinery of those who oppose choice"; up the road, the defeat of a Washington state handgun safety bill, opposed by the National Rifle Association as an "invasion of privacy and a ploy to infringe on the constitutional right of U.S. citizens to bear arms"; and testimony in the Murrah Federal Building bombing case that Terry Nichols carried an anti-government article which declared that "The enemies of freedom" must know that "we will physically fight! They must know we will not shrink from spilling *their* blood." Finally, the paper reported that the defeat, two days before, of an initiative to abandon affirmative-action policies in Houston was due largely to the fact that "affirmative action supporters kept its opponents from seizing the high ground of equal opportunity and civil rights."

Freedom was not exhausted nor even winded; it is accustomed to a crushing workload. Like singer icon Madonna, it seems not to fear overexposure. The rhetoric of freedom is the mantra of American life. As Arthur Schlesinger, Jr., put it in his Clinton-invoked book, *The Vital Center,* freedom is a "fighting faith," even though it is hard to tell whose side the god of freedom is on: on the right (against government, as in the taxpayer bill of rights, Nichols's photocopy, and the defeat of the handgun law), or the left (Houston's affirmative action program and Oregon's suicide law)? What is clear is that political victory today cannot be won without our being persuaded that a program will increase freedom and choice, and that its opponents are oppressive thieves of freedom.

Before freedom, all other gods — the God of Christianity, Judaism, Islam, the Buddha, Shiva, the spiritualities of the New Age, and appropriations of Native American religions — fall silent or complicit. We too, they say, are on the side of the new triune God — Freedom Almighty, its Only Begotten Child Rights, and the Spirit of Choice. Civil wars are fought in freedom's name, as the bitter contest between the Christian Coalition and the American Civil Liberties Union shows. The Coalition's 1994 *Contract with the American Family* lacks entirely the scriptural citations one expects. Instead, it asserts a variety of rights and freedoms that the Coalition expected its allies to pass in the form of coercive law. Three of the Coalition's first four initiatives were: "Restoring Religious Equality: A constitutional amendment to protect the religious liberties of Americans in public places"; "Promoting School Choice"; and "Protecting Parental Rights: Enactment of a Parental Rights Act and defeat of the

U.N. Convention on the Rights of the Child." On the other end of the spectrum, in a 1998 mailing, Ira Glasser, executive director of the ACLU, reduces the *entirety* of moral contest to "Freedom vs. authoritarianism. That's what the struggle over competing visions of morality is *all* about."

These latter examples go beyond political rhetoric. Instead, they reflect a desire to be insulated *from* politics, even if one must use political means to become reclusive. The Declaration of Independence was a political document. However, its status as "American Scripture," as Pauline Maier calls it in the title of her book, is less something political than a philosophy of life. Equality, life, liberty, and the pursuit of happiness are now personal, not political; the political ramifications of those lofty terms are ignored. The Declaration's real force today is as a *personal* validation. American freedom is anti-political. Its expression in millennial America extends to — indeed, is more fundamentally based in — the economic, social, and personal arenas. The market, of course, tells us not only about things monetary but also about our personal and social devotions. Sometimes marketplace iconography of freedom is plausible, if unsupported. Witness the unconscious but near-ubiquitous linkage of "democracy" with "free markets." At other times, the images of freedom are comically makeshift. The slogan for Kellogg's Corn Flakes: "Let freedom pour!"; for Goodyear tires: "Serious freedom." If you are dilettantish about freedom — or darkly repressive — you will drive to the store on Michelins to buy Cheerios. One can only imagine that high-priced advertising firms produce commercials with such language because they believe it will strike consumers' spiritual center.

And the marketers are right, because, particularly under the guise of choice, rights, and independence, freedom is the god of the home hearth as well. Mary Ann Glendon's *Rights-Talk* amply demonstrates the reduction of our discussion of the good to contests over rights. We hear incessant demands, from the daytime talk-show circuits to our own homes — and from our own mouths — to more or less clichéd versions of "my own personal space," desires for independence, "getting away from it all," and so on. A 1989 poll asked American teenagers (adults now) what, if anything, "made America special." A whopping 63 percent answered "freedom" (*Democracy's Next Generation,* 14, 67-75). Freedom is the trump-card of every claim, from Kellogg's trivia to Nichols's disease to the pathetic outburst of Richard Thornton, spouse of one victim of Karla Faye Tucker, who minutes after Tucker's execution said, "I want to say to every victim in the world, demand this. Demand this. This is your right."[8]

IV

Still, the paradoxical — indeed, self-contradictory — character of American freedom is not clear. We might find it distasteful without thinking it paradoxical. Many of Updike's major characters, particularly in the Rabbit novels and *In the Beauty of the Lilies,* however, are more consistent and dedicated — religious — executors of the myth of freedom than the rest of us. Although we prize freedom, we compromise with its assumed opposite, responsibility, though as good Americans we resent the need to compromise. We are, in other words, imperfect and guilty worshipers. Updike's characters, however, answer the question, What would happen if one took the paeans to freedom with ultimate, religious seriousness? What if we worshiped, with our whole mind and whole heart, at the altar of freedom? What would happen is precisely what does happen in Updike's work: as seekers of freedom, his major characters ask for nothing more than to be alone but still require others, and though they begin by demanding freedom, they become ugly dominators of others and ultimately self-destructive as well.

Contemporary American culture is supported by the mythos of individual autonomy, which is both an end and a means. As a means, autonomy is directed toward achievement: we are to act to improve ourselves, and no dream is out of reach to those who apply themselves. On the other hand, freedom is also the goal of the process: the culture of rights is essentially a culture dedicated to personal freedom, unhindered by others.

Herein lies one paradox: the dream of achievement is social in character. In order to be aware that one has accomplished what one should, one must be recognized by others. Augustine's analysis of pride as socially produced remains instructive. However, precisely the desired recognition depends on those others that the dream of free-

8. *New York Times,* February 4, 1998, A17 (Chicago edition).

dom needs to escape in order to be free. This paradox explains Rabbit's series of escapes and returns. He must run to escape the clutches of the "net" of responsibilities that hold him (*Rabbit, Run,* 24/23), but he must return because he requires recognition, a place he is known. Theodore Kaczynski is a violent version of Rabbit: he could not give up his need for recognition, any more than could Thoreau, that now-revered figure who was virtually ignored by his nineteenth-century contemporaries. Each required not only that he be free of others, but also that others know, admire, and even imitate his freedom, which stands in stark opposition to their original visions of freedom. The prospect or fact of anonymity is pure horror for Rabbit; for Essie and her son, Clark, in *In the Beauty of the Lilies;* periodically for Bech; and for the biographer of James Buchanan — that nearly anonymous President who lacks even the distinction of being "most anonymous" — in *Memories of the Ford Administration.* In a culture in which freedom is religion, in which the experience of powerful and final meaning comes in autonomy itself, it seems we cannot leave behind the Weberian notion of charisma — only now we are our own leaders.

That is half the problem. The other half is that, in order that we and others know that we have maximized our freedom, our culture of achievement requires that each one of us reach for the top. The proof of having reached for the top is, of course, only the fact of one's standing there. This vision used to make exceptions for the "retarded," but the "challenged" are no longer exempt. The American form of elevated accomplishment requires that others remain below the self, that they become those whom one can touch but must not be touched by. The measure of redemption in our religion of freedom is the distance between ourselves and the crowd, the degree and frequency of our ecstatic elevation above others and our own everyday lives. The forms of freedom and ecstasy *are* our religion. This is one reason why sex is such an obsession for Updike's men. Updike's intercourse is generally an elation and escape from lives that are uninteresting and deadening to those living them. To have achieved what we are promised that we can achieve demands conquest of others and of one's own monotony. It demands the achievement of purity, but that achievement — because it *is* the distance between the isolated religious moment and profane time — renders the remainder of our ordinary lives meaningless. Our meaning and religious fulfillment come in and during the extraordinary, exceptional event.

Updike's main characters lack a meaningful relation to ordinary life. His ministers, for their part, generally either reemphasize the insistence on achievements and activity that we cannot fulfill (Eccles) or separate heaven and earth so that religion refers only to a realm above us from which we are infinitely separated except in rare moments of clarity (Kruppenbach). What his central characters lack is a religious relation to ordinary life, an ecstasy of the ordinary. Consequently, their attempts to achieve grace, to be found worthy by God and others, rely on deception and manipulation, on falsifying and distorting love. Rabbit also cannot tolerate women having affections that are not directed at him, while at the same time he must steal women's affections from others.

Finally, the freedom Updike's characters seek is apolitical. Even where we might expect political content in Updike's novels, there is none. Political life is a mere backdrop to what the novel's figures think really important. Ben Turnbull spends an extraordinarily small amount of his time thinking about the politics of the Sino-American nuclear exchange in *Toward the End of Time.* Even as Updike whimsically works Ben and Gloria into participating in building a new order under, eventually, the reestablished national government led by Federal Express (which emerges in response to anarchic "freedom"), there is no political *thinking* or discussion in the Turnbull household. The passing of Ben's male culture leaves him feeling displaced, but only that. In *Rabbit Redux,* Skeeter's claim to be "black Jesus" has surprisingly little to do with American racial turmoil, while Rabbit's casual patriotism backgrounds Rabbit's rediscovered religious intensity, but no more. Of all the tumults of the 1960s, Rabbit and Janice participate in only the most personal — sexual adventurism and drugs. The vapor trail of apartheid was the Angstroms' bedroom romp with fifteen Krugerrand; of the hostages in Iran, conversion to silver (*Rabbit Is Rich,* 215-19 and 365-76/816-19 and 952-62). Nelson, for his part, arrives at Kent State years after the National Guard left. This lack of political consciousness is not a weakness in Updike's work but an expression of his characters' deepest American contemporaneousness.[9] For them, too, life, liberty, and happiness are personal, not social.

9. For a criticism of Updike's work as insufficiently political, see Raymond A. Mazurek, "'Bringing the Corners Forward': Ideology and Representation in Updike's Rabbit Trilogy."

We are depicted more accurately than not by Updike's characters. They act on our own deepest yearnings; the difference is only that we flinch before the demands of this kind of freedom, while they do not. But they are us, extended and consistent. The shift in our understanding of Weber's "charisma" is instructive, including each of the elements of the mythology of freedom. Whereas "charisma" could — and should — refer primarily to the vision that the prophet communicates, we now mean by "charisma" an unnamable and mystical power by which the charismatic one brings others under his or her hypnotic spell. Jesse of the Temple of True and Actual Faith, the leader of the commune in *S.*, and, in the end, S. herself are charismatic because they are able to make their adherents *feel* import and meaning despite the emptiness of their vision. Moreover, these charismatic figures grow in stature just because they are unaffected by what happens to others. Jesse *gains* status because he is aloof from all others. These charismatics are inside when it rains, and their umbrellas protect them when they venture out. When ecstatic fulfillment comes only in interruptions of the ordinary, it hardly matters what causes the break; nor, in the end, does it matter that feeling free is often the product of authoritarian control. Freedom devours itself. Updike is right to say, "A cultural emphasis on individual freedom makes choosing evil a lively option" ("The Persistence of Evil," 65). When charisma becomes power over others' feelings, and only that, the vision of freedom has reached its true demonic height and depth.

V

We do not expect a resolution of the ambiguity or demonism of freedom in the same characters that manifest that very demonism. Religious fanatics seldom provide answers to their own dilemmas; rather, such devotion to an idea blinds rather than illuminates. As we have seen, Updike's characters are quite insensible of the damage they cause themselves and those around them. But to live in the orbit of such devotion often produces insight into its poison. If Rabbit does not understand the horror of his religion, those who are affected by him, and, indeed, continue to love him, do. We should look, in other words, to Updike's minor characters for a way out of the American dilemma of freedom, not to his heroes.

Indeed, pointing us to the minor characters is another way to subvert the myth of freedom. Just as freedom in its libertarian form becomes domination, so the major characters dominate Updike's novels. If we look for a solution to the problem of dominating freedom, we should look exactly to those who do not dominate the literary page but are content to live in the shadows of attention. Were the grand vision of American freedom attacked by another constantly looming figure, we would have a conflict between two heroes both struggling for adherence to their vision, and we would have gotten nowhere in the effort to undermine the elevation of the hero.

If we are to discover visions other than the dominant mythos of freedom in Updike's work, then, we should look not to the grand, major characters but to the less imposing ones. It is true: some of them present a vision without external force or domination. In the Rabbit series, this is the case with Thelma Harrison, Janice, and finally Nelson. Each of these discovers a religious relation to ordinary existence, and their power arises from their ability to use the occasional and extraordinary moments of life — sex, forgiveness, grace, even death — to baptize the ordinary, to make living and not the escape from it religious and ecstatic. Still, the measure to which Updike has taken the pulse of American conceptions of meaning is indicated by the fact that, in the extensive secondary literature on the Rabbit series, Thelma Harrison is usually dismissed as inconsequential, no one has given sustained attention to Janice Angstrom, and Nelson is nearly invisible.[10] We read Updike on the basis of our own religious predilections, and those characters who see a way to a different conception of meaning, a fulfillment that is both beyond and within the texture of everyday life — in traditional Christian terms, a meaning that is both transcendent and immanent — a religion that requires the health and beauty of others, are routinely ignored or pitied by interpreters. The degree to which the typical reaction to these novels is satisfied with praising Rabbit as a prophet of freedom or decrying him for being a boor is the degree to which Updike points to our problem without providing a solution. It is the degree to which, in short, Updike is an artistic theologian and

10. A particularly clear instance of noting Thelma's character only in order to dismiss her is Kent D. Smith's *Faith: Reflections on Experience, Theology, and Fiction.* Most sources, however, do not get even that far. See my essay "The Troubles with Harry: Freedom, America and God in John Updike's *Rabbit* Novels" for an extended argument about the inviting religious vision of Thelma Harrison.

not an argumentative one. We must discern the destinies, religions, and meanings of his creations: we must harvest the import of his prose from the failures, successes, collapses, and triumphs of his characters. Paradoxically, the triumphs are rarely triumphant, the successes rarely meaningful or enduring; we should attend carefully to those characters who seem to really discover meaning and happiness; we should ask what produced such meaning, how the characters came to it, and under what circumstances. They were freed, true, but perhaps because they did not worship activist freedom.

An argumentative Christian theologian might be expected to say something about the ability of his or her own religious community to bring about the conditions for a baptism of the ordinary. Unfortunately, there is not a great deal positive to say. I think Updike is centrally accurate in his depiction of the degree to which American Christianity has abdicated a mission to relate heaven and earth and to provide resources for making ordinary life ecstatic. For the purposes of improving this life, which was the core concern of the Hebrew Scriptures and the Christian Testament, and of most significant theologians from Augustine through to the mid-twentieth century, contemporary American Christian life seems almost bankrupt. God does not, it seems, touch the faded fabric of mundane existence. The question of the meaning of transcendence for this existence is nearly absent. The separation between heaven and earth is nearly complete, except in conservative religious circles, which for their part demand the achievement of grace more strongly than did any Pelagian, and more harshly than did Updike's insipid Rev. Jack Eccles.

Still, the Christian tradition has some resources. In addition, our culture, in which the Christian inheritance still plays some often unconscious part, has resources as well. To note literary resources seems consonant with the vein we are mining. It seems to me that the novels of Anne Tyler present a series of models for the ecstatic relation to the ordinary, though without the penetrating analysis of freedom's paradoxes present in Updike's work. Tyler is interested in what Updike calls "nothing breaking through but normal healthy happiness" (*Rabbit Is Rich,* 179/783). How to find our way from Updike's agonistic relation to freedom (and his guilty relation to happiness) to Tyler's ecstasy of the ordinary, or to the philosopher J. Glenn Gray's hope in *The Warriors: Reflections on Men in Battle* that we can unite "power with gentleness," is far from obvious. But if we follow the artistic theologian's characters through to their conclusion, the argumentative theologian becomes aware that this *is* the task.

Whether we can pursue that task in traditional theological categories is not clear. Instead, we may be forced to affirm one paradox set in motion by the Reformation — that of worshiping God most reverently by forgetting God. But even if that is our course, we may yet find hope in Flannery O'Connor's comment about Hazel Motes, that "[his] integrity lies" in his *not* being able to "get rid of the ragged figure who moves from tree to tree in the back of his mind." She continues, "Does one's integrity ever lie in what he is not able to do? I think that usually it does, for free will does not mean one will, but many wills conflicting in one man. Freedom cannot be conceived simply. It is a mystery" (O'Connor, 5).

As we approach a millennium that will not be apocalyptic but the unexceptional passage of one day into another, the religious question for our culture is not whether we can find meaning in an extraordinary, cataclysmic end of or escape from time but whether we can find ecstatic, religious meaning in unremarkable passages of time. Can we tolerate a conception of freedom that is not paradoxical in conception but frighteningly so in effect, delivering exactly the opposite of what it promises? Can we have a freedom that promises greatness to all but, ruthlessly executed, necessarily leaves most of us with guilt, not for anything we do or fail to do, but for simply being unexceptional? A freedom that insists that we touch others without allowing ourselves to be touched and infects the connections between ourselves and others? A conception that demands that we be inside when it rains, or possessed of an umbrella-like shell that protects us from all that is outside us? A freedom that is, in Rabbit's conception, being "clean," having "nothing touching you that is not yourself (/your element)" (*Rabbit, Run*, 143/123)?

If we answer No to this view and what it drives us to, then what will religions have to say? If they are not simply to capitulate to the culture in which they operate, they will have to find a way to found religion in a power and awe of the ordinary, a charisma of gentleness. We will have to find ways to make ordinary life ecstatic and ordinary guilt a medium of forgiving redemption. But this forgiveness will have to come from elsewhere and arise from the passive voice of being forgiven rather than the activity of re-creating the self in its primal innocence or achieving forgiveness, as Jack Eccles would have had it. It will require, in other words, that we allow ourselves to be touched and that freedom be understood as receptive as well as active. Freedom will have to become paradoxical and therefore straight. When the breath of the Spirit has not blown, when we are too protected and too dry, withering inside and out, let us retain these hopes — that we will be touched from beyond by the divine through others in this world, that we will find intimations of the sacred and ecstasy in the ordinary, that we will be exposed when it rains, outside with umbrellas blown inside out so that heaven's rains may saturate the parched heart of freedom.

What Is Goodness?

The Influence of Updike's Lutheran Roots

DARRELL JODOCK

Although John Updike now belongs to an Episcopal congregation, he has often mentioned the Lutheran Church he attended while growing up in Pennsylvania. Are there indications that his outlook on life was influenced by the distinctive characteristics of Lutheranism? And may an answer to this question assist the person who interprets and evaluates Updike's writing?

One could investigate the role of religion in Updike's writing, the influence of his Christianity, or his relationship to Protestantism. These would all be important topics that, in one way or another, touch on our theme, "What is goodness?", but they are not my primary concern. Mine is a narrower question — namely, his relationship to that one branch of Protestant Christianity known as Lutheranism.

It would be impossible in the space of one essay to include the numerous citations required to demonstrate that significant differences do in fact separate Lutherans from other Protestants. However, this constraint is not a serious obstacle, because the claim turns out to be relatively uncontroversial, even if not always recognized or understood. We will simply assume *that* they differ. *How* they differ will become clearer as we proceed. For now, let us say only that differences occur in their respective understandings of the place of morality, divine immanence/transcendence, God's role in the world, and the life of faith.

The question to occupy this essay will thus be whether Updike's outlook reflects a Lutheran or a non-Lutheran form of Protestant Christianity. The essay will argue that at points where Lutherans disagree with the dominant form of American Protestantism, Updike sides with the Lutheran outlook. The point is not that a Lutheran outlook is better or that he is praiseworthy for following it. My claim is simply this: when Updike's theological/philosophical outlook is apprehended correctly, one's understanding of his work is enhanced. Apprehending that outlook correctly is, moreover, an essential step on the way toward any significant evaluation of his work.

The various Protestant denominations can be grouped into several "families." For the sake of simplicity, comparisons here will focus on only one other family: those Protestant groups with their roots in England, Scotland, Switzerland, and the Netherlands — the Presbyterian, the Congregational, the Dutch Reformed, and even, in a somewhat more ambiguous way, the Episcopal tradition. Ignoring differences within this family and fully recognizing that they do not follow John Calvin at every point, I will, for purposes of shorthand, simply lump them together and call them "Calvinist." I focus on the Calvinist tradition because it has so greatly influenced American culture. In fact, in the minds of most Americans, to be a Protestant is equivalent to being a Calvinist. To be sure, the Quakers and the Mennonites and the Baptists all played their role in the early years of our nation and continue to do so, but from the Calvinist Puritans America drew its covenant theology, its image of itself as a "new Israel" and a nation "set on a hill" to be a moral example to the world, its particular piety regarding the Bible, its "godly law" tradition, and its images of the virtuous life. Even those Americans not belonging to one of these denominations have often been heavily influenced by a Calvinist outlook — if in no other way than by that unique mixture of Puritan and Deist themes known as American civil religion.

Thus our starting point is an assertion that the Lutheran tradition differs in identifiable ways from the historically (in the United States) far more pervasive and influential Calvinist tradition. The presence of recognizable differences, however, does not imply the absence of significant similarities. Rather, the disagreements between the Calvinists and the Lutherans occur within the context of a good deal of commonality. Even if separate "families," Lutherans and Calvinists are "first cousins." Among other things, both affirm justification by grace through faith, the priesthood of all believers, a sense of vocation, a strong sense of the communal dimension of life, and the freedom to interpret the Bible without being governed by the church's tradition or its magisterium.

The question of Updike's relation to Lutheranism could be meaningful even if Updike himself did not acknowledge a distinction between Calvinist and Lutheran forms of Protestant Christianity, but he does recognize it, and his awareness of the distinction further supports its importance. During an interview in 1976, Jeff Campbell reminded Updike that Michael Novak had linked him with an alert, open, human, sensual Calvinism and then asked, "He [Novak] says Calvinism, but from my point of view I see you as much more Lutheran than Calvinist. Does that distinction make any sense to you?" Updike replied:

> It makes a lot of sense to me and I agree with you. I was raised as a Lutheran. Now to an extent all Protestant churches would look alike to a Catholic like Novak. . . . In the county I was from, the Lutheran and Reformed churches existed on the same block, but they were distinctly different churches. The Calvinist church just gives off a different vibe. I do think that in some way the personalities and fundamental emphases of the two great founders show through still. Lutheranism is comparatively world-accepting; it's a little closer to Catholicism than Calvinism. I don't feel much affinity with the New England Puritan ethos insofar as it still persists. No, I would call myself a Lutheran by upbringing, and my work contains some of the ambiguities of the Lutheran position, which would have a certain radical otherworldly emphasis and yet an odd retention of a lot of Catholic forms and a rather rich ambivalence toward the world itself. (Plath, ed., 94)

As his response reveals, Updike himself regards the Lutheran and the Calvinist traditions to be "distinctly different," identifies himself with the Lutheran, and describes it as "comparatively world-accepting" and exhibiting a "rich ambivalence toward the world."

My claim is that in those key areas where the Lutheran tradition diverges from the Calvinist, Updike's outlook reflects the Lutheran pattern of thought. Not only does Updike acknowledge this similarity, he often traces its source specifically to his Lutheran upbringing. I contend, furthermore, that understanding his proclivity toward a more Lutheran way of viewing life will prevent interpreters from expecting what he is not prepared to deliver.

I

As background for what follows, I want to begin by identifying a few of the characteristics of the Lutheran tradition. With these in mind, observations can be made about its differences from the Calvinist tradition.

1. The Lutheran tradition is not moralistic. That is, it does not think right behavior determines a person's value or status before God, and it does not emphasize, formulate, or inculcate detailed moral guidelines. Although it recommends that humans follow certain basic ethical principles, it finds little reason to construct codes of conduct. A person's basic orientation is more important. Is one oriented toward self or toward God? Is one self-centered or inclined to assist others? And in its consideration of motives and actions, the Lutheran tradition recognizes the *profound ambiguity of our moral life,* even in persons who are rightly oriented toward God and their neighbors.

The Calvinist tradition may not be moralistic, but it gives relatively greater prominence to moral teachings and to the "godly behavior" expected from believers. It also tends to emphasize "godly laws" and public morality. In its (often commendable) effort to uphold public morality, little attention is given to moral ambiguity. Calvinism is relatively more confident that believers, with the guidance of the Bible, can identify the right pattern of behavior for society and for an individual's life.

2. The Lutheran tradition focuses its attention on the *character of the God-human relationship*. The word "faith," which is so central to its vocabulary, signifies involvement in a trusting relationship, not the acceptance of a set of teachings. Creeds and doctrines are helpful and important, but subscription to them is not as fundamental as is a person's orientation — in faith toward God and in service toward other human beings. Trust is more essential than correct knowledge.

3. For Lutherans, God's radical adoption of sinful persons by grace leads to a *radical freedom* for the adopted one — a freedom *from* coercive requirements and a freedom *for* service to one's neighbor.

4. If "having a sense of humor" means not taking things *too* seriously, the Lutheran tradition includes a *sense of humor.* It does not, for example, take the Bible as ultra-seriously as do some other Protestants. On its view, the Bible is not literally the recorded speech of God but a collection of diverse voices that witness in various ways to the one God. The "Word of God," moreover, is properly a "living voice," a spoken rather than a written text. Luther could even call James an "epistle of straw" and joke about replacing it in the canon with the writings of his colleague Melanchthon. Similarly, for Luther, sin involves a sober preoccupation with the self. Because faith does not take the self too seriously, Luther could urge the usually cautious Melanchthon to "sin boldly." And the Lutheran tradition does not take church structures or ecclesiastical authority too seriously, asserting from the beginning that uniformity of ceremonies is not necessary for church unity. (See "The Augsburg Confession," article 7.)

The Calvinist tradition, more so than the Lutheran, tends to emphasize the divine origin and divinely inspired unity of the Bible and tends to find there the definitive pattern for church polity, public morality, and individual ethical behavior. It has fostered serious self-examination of the kind practiced by the Puritans, thus giving more attention to measuring one's own spiritual health than Luther thought wise.

5. The Lutheran tradition underscores and affirms the *presence and activity of God in the world.* God is present "in, with, and under" nature and human beings. This implies an emphasis on the immanence of God, on God always at hand and always at work. The Lutheran understanding of the world is based on the metaphor of incarnation. Just as in Jesus the divine joined the human without overwhelming or displacing the human, so God is able routinely to work "in, with, and under" any other aspect of the created world. As Updike remarked to Campbell, Lutheranism is "comparatively world-accepting." The Calvinist tradition, as we will see, has emphasized the transcendence of God and a clear and radical distinction between what is finite and what is infinite.

6. The Lutheran tradition exhibits a *fondness for paradox.* In Wisconsin in 1912, for example, one group of Lutherans "settled" a long-standing controversy by affirming *both* predestination *and* free will, thus holding together in paradox what the Calvinist tradition has tended to resolve either into a consistent predestination, as at the

Synod of Dort (1618-1619), or, in other times and places, into an Arminian emphasis on the role of human decision in accepting or rejecting God's offer of grace. The Lutheran fondness for paradox extends to other topics as well, affirming, for instance, that God is "both hidden and revealed" and that a believer is "simultaneously justified and a sinner."

II

With these features of Lutheranism in mind, let us turn to John Updike and consider first the subject of moral ambiguity.

While discussing *Couples* and the scene in which lightning strikes the church where Piet once worshiped, Ralph Wood writes, "This celebrated incident points up the moral passivity of Updike's work: his reluctance to find fault and assess blame, his conviction that our lives are shaped by forces too vast for mere mortals to master" (*Comedy of Redemption,* 190). This criticism assumes that Christian writing *should* give moral instruction; it expects something that Updike, because of his Lutheran orientation, is not prepared to deliver. As Updike has said about the Rabbit Angstrom tetralogy,

> The religious faith that a useful truth will be imprinted by a perfect artistic submission underlies these Rabbit novels. . . . Rather than arrive at a verdict and directive, I sought to present sides of an unresolvable tension intrinsic to being human. Readers who expect novelists to reward and punish and satirize their characters from a superior standpoint will be disappointed. (*Rabbit Angstrom,* xiii)

As Wood correctly discerns, the literary resolution in an Updike novel does not usually include a resolution of its moral issues. It is also correct that Updike is reluctant to "find fault and assess blame" in any overt way. But all of this does not indicate "moral passivity." Instead, it signals Updike's recognition of profound moral ambiguity in humans, even redeemed Christian believers.

Both Updike's characters and his plot developments typically exhibit moral ambiguity. In 1968 he told an interviewer, Sally Reston, "I guess I hope to show in fiction that goodness and evil are mixed" (Plath, ed., 20). In another interview in 1980 he said to Charlie Reilly,

"This kind of moral ambivalence, I guess, does interest me and makes my heroes somewhat unattractive to a lot of people. But it's the kind of hero I come up with again and again: a person who combines good and the absence of it in an interesting, sometimes comical, way" (Plath, ed., 128-29). As Donald Greiner has observed about Updike's treatment of sex,

> for Updike erotic experience is morally ambiguous. Rabbit [in *Rabbit, Run*] and Jerry [in *Marry Me*] try to combat the shrinking of their spirits within marriage by pursuing the mystery of Other in the guise of women. . . . they turn transgression into an opportunity for creativity. Because eroticism — even adultery — unifies the physical and the spiritual, the transgression may be both ethically wrong and spiritually right. The ambiguity of adultery is the key. (*Adultery,* 114)

Seldom are Updike's characters models of exemplary behavior. Even after four volumes, "Rabbit" Angstrom is hardly a saint! Equally seldom are they diabolical embodiments of evil, although, to be sure, they may exhibit evil by indulging in "an exaggerated sense of self" to the extent of harming others (Detweiler, *Breaking the Fall,* 108). In other words, Updike's characters are mixed: they are good and bad, self-centered and value-oriented, isolated and involved. Yet Updike's fiction is not nihilistic or despairing. As he has said, he "feels a tenderness toward [his] characters" and loves them too much to be satirical at their expense (*Picked-Up Pieces,* 501); he has not given up on them. Their faults are neither judged harshly nor overtly punished. Opportunities for moral behavior and for a deeper, richer engagement with others keep opening up. His characters are not abandoned to evil or to sainthood. Moreover, the absence of judgment does not reflect a lack of moral standards. Morality does matter. When asked by Jan Nunley if, when he writes about characters like Tom Marshfield and Roger Lambert, "there's still something in there that wants people to do what they say they're going to do," Updike replied, "Yeah . . . I do hold them to a higher standard, as I hold myself" (Plath, ed., 257). In Updike's writing there may be no simplistic scheme of retribution within which good behavior is regularly rewarded and immorality regularly punished, but lives are either more humane or less so, depending on the ethical decisions his characters make.

Updike has viewed his writing as a moral conversation with the reader. As he told Eric Rhode in 1969,

> all my books . . . are meant to be moral debates with the reader, and if they seem pointless — I'm speaking hopefully — it's because the reader has not been engaged in the debate. The question is usually, "What is a good man?" or "What is goodness?" and in all my books an act is inspected. Take Harry Angstrom in *Rabbit, Run:* There is a case to be made for running away from your wife. In the late fifties beatniks were preaching transcontinental travelling as the answer to man's disquiet. And I was just trying to say: "Yes, there is certainly that, but then there are all these other people who seem to get hurt." That distinction is meant to be a moral dilemma. (Plath, ed., 50)

Wood accuses Updike of "ethical quietism" (*Comedy of Redemption*, 190), but Updike's moral dilemmas are not designed to produce quietism. His writings stop short of resolving moral issues because the dilemma is expected to be sorted out existentially. The actual resolution needs to occur *in* the reader. What the fiction does is to describe as accurately as possible the moral ambiguities of human existence. As Lutherans could say, it "holds a mirror" up to humanity so that individuals can see themselves truthfully, thereby reducing the self-deception to which all humans are particularly prone. The intended result of such "mirroring" is for the individual to make an existential "leap," as Søren Kierkegaard would express it, or to "turn around," as Luther would say — using the literal meaning of the biblical word "repentance" — so that, under the aegis of a new relationship, a "new person" begins to emerge. So, in addition to encouraging moral resolution, there is also a religious openness: *Rabbit, Run* ends, Updike writes, "on an ecstatic, open note that was meant to stay open, as testimony to our heart's stubborn amoral quest for something once called grace" (*Rabbit Angstrom*, xii). When speaking with Willi Winkler in 1985, Updike put it this way:

> I grew up Lutheran, but my parents were not especially religious. I decided then not to give it up. . . . But because of that, I came to the decision to write about the imperfect world — a world that is fallen. That's why many people find my books so depressing. But for me it isn't depressing to say that the world is imperfect. Here the work begins: One confesses this imperfectness more or less happily and starts to think about what one is to do with the world in this condition. (Plath, ed., 174)

Only with a Lutheran "sense of humor" does someone confess "this imperfectness more or less happily"! Updike can do so because "*We are rewarded unexpectedly.* The muddled and inconsequent surface of things now and then parts to yield us a gift" (*Olinger Stories,* vii).

In order to perform this function of "mirroring" an imperfect world, moral resolution *within* the text is not required. For example, Ben Turnbull in *Toward the End of Time* lives in his retirement with the consequences of his prior choices. He finds little companionship with his wife, is largely cut off from his children, has sex with a prostitute, fondles a fourteen-year-old girl in his backyard, becomes discouraged with his golf companions, is largely cut off from his former colleagues at work, and remains passive in the face of violence. The character almost never gets outside himself. Were he viewed as a positive example, the author's outlook would also have to be characterized as extremely narcissistic. But the novel does not present Ben Turnbull as a moral example; instead, it leaves its reader with a question: Do I want to become like Ben? Is my life leading in that direction? In order to engage his readers in moral deliberation, it is not incumbent upon John Updike to present a positive moral model, nor does he need to point out, explicitly and moralistically, the failures of Ben Turnbull's life; the mirror is enough. The portrait creates the "space" needed for ethical reflection and existential decision.

As indicated above, the Lutheran tradition, for better or worse, has been non-moralistic. According to its diagnosis of the human condition, the fundamental problem is not human behavior in the sense that changing behavior *alone* will accomplish much. John Updike himself suggested as much when he told Sally Reston that "Lutherans believe doctrine — faith — is important, but not deeds, because we are all mired in sin" (Plath, ed., 20). Suzanne Henning Uphaus explains that "Updike is always suspicious of ethical action, believing that it hides an impoverished spirit. . . . Updike's novels suggest that involvement in ethical action is a barrier to faith rather than a means to its fulfillment" (Uphaus, 6-7). According to Luther, the fundamental problem is the orientation of the human being, who, apart from grace, is "curved in upon oneself." The remedy for this problem is a combination of "law," the "mirroring" that reveals one's real condition, and "gospel," the communication of God's unilateral, unmerited acceptance of a person, yielding a reconciled relationship. Humans need reorientation in order to be free to exercise the wisdom needed for ethical decision making amid conflicted circumstances — a wisdom that does not merely follow rules but finds innovative ways to serve justice and enhance the well-being of others (*Luther's Works,* 45:128).

Perhaps more needs to be said at this point. Calvinism has often viewed the consequence of faith to be "godly living," and thinkers influenced by Calvinism have often assumed that their responsibility includes giving instruction regarding such "godly living." This instruction may take the form of recommended general religious practices but often also includes specified moral behavior. Apart from revelation, Calvin said, humans are "blinder than moles" (*Institutes,* 2.2.18); they need moral instruction. Not only do they need grace, they also need knowledge: true knowledge of God and of human nature. In Calvinism believers are expected to please God, and they need to know how to do that. By contrast, Luther did not emphasize lack of knowledge. Humans are already knowledgeable; they have simply been so "curved in upon themselves" that they have misapplied what they know. They are disoriented, and they use their reason to serve themselves rather than God and their neighbor. Consequently the essence of faith is a restored relationship and a reoriented self. Once reoriented, the person is free to love, and, as Luther would repeatedly say, one does not need to tell lovers how to treat each other. Thus, Luther placed emphasis neither on knowledge nor on the need for ethical instruction. And even more significantly, the consequence of faith is not behavior aimed at pleasing God but behavior aimed at serving the neighbor. Faith-active-in-love entails a self-forgetting and, in a sense, even God-forgetting preoccupation with the needs of another person and efforts to assist that person. Note, for example, how Updike employs a similar criterion when, in the passage previously quoted about *Rabbit, Run,* he says, "but then there are all those other people who seem to get hurt." The issue is not whether rules get broken; the basic question — both for him and for a Lutheran approach to ethics — is whether people get hurt.

III

Another feature of the Lutheran tradition is that its attention is focused on the character of God-human and human-to-human relationships. What is crucial for humans is not necessarily what they believe to be true about the attributes of God but what kind of relationship they have with God. As students of Luther's life have so often pointed out, his central question was "how can I find a *gracious* God?" and his scholarly and religious breakthrough came when he realized that God is an active agent, initiating a reconciled relationship with humans. Moreover, a particular teaching — for example, that we cannot save ourselves — may strike persons differently. To the person outside of faith it is bad news, while to the believer the exact same words are a source of comfort. That is, even the existential meaning of a doctrinal statement is affected by the kind of relationship a person has with God. The character of the relationship makes all the difference in the world — at least from the vantage point of the individual himself or herself.

Given this, what should one say about John Updike's seeming preoccupation with isolated individuals? Is this an expression of his own narcissism, as some have said? (see Wallace, "John Updike"). I think not. For one thing, in order to stimulate an existential decision about ultimate loyalties and about morality, a good deal of attention must be focused on the character who is experiencing the dilemmas. A view "from the inside" is what the reader facing an existential decision has in common with a character in Updike's fiction. If the conflicts were to remain external, there would be no dilemmas, and the intended effect could not be achieved. Second, the dilemmas of the characters come to light in their personal relationships. Although aspects of nature are described in detail and often are important to Updike's stories, contending with/conquering the natural world (climbing mountains, hunting whales, traversing the wilderness, and the like) is not a central theme in his writing, as it has been for some other American novelists. The strengths and weaknesses of Updike's characters are revealed in their relationships with other persons. When Tom Marshfield at the end of *A Month of Sundays* succeeds in seducing Ms. Prynne (*Month of Sundays*, 227-28), it is clear that not many of the hoped-for changes have occurred; the reader then knows how to assess his prior journal entries. On the other hand, in *Roger's Version* something positive does occur in Roger's relationship with Verna. At first his attraction to her is primarily carnal. However, near the end of the novel, when he lets her go back to Ohio, be reconciled with her parents, and put her life together, he seems genuinely to care about her. At dinner during their last meeting, he says, "My goodness, I loved her, not expecting to" (*Roger's Version,* 310). Unlike what happens earlier in the story and unlike Tom Marshfield's behavior, Roger makes no effort to have sex with her. The moral growth that is evident in this relationship, however, does not make Roger or his life exemplary. Roger goes back to his wife, but, despite the fact that her affair with Dale Kohler has ended, she is "irritable and abstracted" and "sleeps more than usual." No magic change or happy ending there! She instead explains to Roger that she is going to church "to annoy you" (328-29). Apart from the humor of that comment, it is evident that she and Roger continue to love "one another in our sorry way" (309). In Updike's writing, the relationships are revealing. Portraying narcissism is not the same as endorsing it. We are back to "mirroring" again.

Like Updike, Luther emphasized the interior view. The phrase that Lutherans have used to capture this perspective is *coram Deo* — literally "before God," but in the sense of being in the presence of God, or face-to-face with God. *Coram Deo* is a first-person encounter with God rather than a third-person description of God or the God-human relationship. For Luther, only theological thinking done from the point of view of the human face-to-face with God could be genuinely helpful for the religious life of any human being. *Coram Deo* thinking shows clearly what is at stake for the participant, theologically and religiously. Because it tends to create the illusion that the human being can exercise control of his or her relation with God, any third-person description is potentially misleading.

Luther understood the relationship of one human being to another from a similar perspective. Appropriate behavior focuses on the needs of the other. Following a prescribed pattern is not what makes it loving or morally commendable. The value of an ethical act is revealed *"coram"* the other person. Thus, a preoccupation with the interior view is not necessarily out of tune with the priority of the interpersonal but is rather very much in keeping with Luther's theme of "thinking in the presence of the other."

IV

One of John Updike's most explicit affirmations of the Lutheran tradition can be found in the following passage:

> During that same adolescence, I reluctantly perceived of the Christian religion I had been born into that almost no one believed it, believed it really. . . . I decided I nevertheless *would* believe. I found a few authors, a very few — Chesterton, Eliot, Unamuno, Kierkegaard, Karl Barth — who helped me believe. . . . I rarely read them now; my life is mostly lived. God is the God of the living, though His priests and executors, to keep order and to force the world into a convenient mould, will always want to make Him the God of the dead, the God who chastises life and forbids and says No. What I felt, in that basement Sunday school of Grace Lutheran Church in Shillington [Pennsylvania], was a clumsy attempt to extend a Yes, a blessing, and I accepted that blessing, offering in return only a nickel a week and my art, my poor little art.
>
> Imitation is praise. Description expresses love. I early arrived at these self-justifying inklings. Having accepted that old Shillington blessing, I have felt free to describe life as accurately as I could, with especial attention to human erosions and betrayals. What small faith I have has given me what artistic courage I have. My theory was that God already knows everything and cannot be shocked. And only truth is useful. Only truth can be built upon. From a higher inhuman point of view, only truth, however harsh, is holy. (*Self-Consciousness,* 230-31)

What comes through here is how God's radical Yes leads to a radical human freedom moved by courage.

In this passage, Updike identifies himself as a believer — indeed, as a believer in a more profound sense than many of the people he knew in his youth. He credits, among others, Søren Kierkegaard, the nineteenth-century Danish Lutheran philosopher who emphasized the radical commitment of faith and the "otherness" of God, and Karl Barth, the twentieth-century Swiss theologian, with helping him believe. Like the ministrations of midwives, however, their assistance is over. He remains neither a disciple nor a student of their theologies. A theologian in the Calvinist tradition, Karl Barth was part of a "Neo-orthodox" recovery of Reformation themes. Like Kierkegaard he emphasized the "otherness" of God. In Barth's theology Christ was central, and he endeavored to work out an entire system of thought based on the humanity and divinity of Christ. The primary author of the Barmen Declaration in 1934, he opposed Nazism as a form of idolatry that challenged the lordship of Christ. Regarding Barth's influence on him in 1960-61 Updike says: "Barth was with resounding definiteness and learning saying what I needed to hear, which was that it really *was* so, that there was something within us that would not die, and that we live by faith alone — more or less; he doesn't just say that, but what he does say joined with my Lutheran heritage and enabled me to go on" (Plath, ed., 102). With Barth's help he renewed his faith but continued to understand it in a Lutheran way. His faith became a lived reality, an existential reality, characterized by an affirmation of the "Yes," the gracious blessing of the God who is God of the living. On the basis of that blessing he has felt "free" to "describe life as accurately as I could." From his freedom has come "artistic courage" — presumably to tell the truth, even about the "betrayals" and "erosions" of life. And this truth is not only useful; it is "holy."

Although Updike borrows from Karl Barth the language of "Yes" and "No" to express what Luther called the "gospel" and the "law," the passage is thoroughly Lutheran in outlook. According to that outlook, the fundamental human problem is estrangement from God, and thereby from each other and from nature. This estrangement is overcome by a free act of grace wherein God takes the initiative, comes close to human beings, and restores their brokenness. The consequence is a profound human freedom, including freedom *from* coercion, freedom *for* service, and freedom *to* tell the truth. Included in this truth telling is a profound awareness of the ambiguity of human existence. In humans the glories and perversities are so intertwined as to require paradoxical and dialectical description. Moreover, truth telling is "useful." Its purpose is to strip away pretension and produce a self-recognition that opens people to God and to each other, enabling them to support the dignity of others and do justice in society, even when these activities involve cost to themselves. In this sense truth telling is "holy"; it simultaneously serves God's purposes and uplifts creation.

Initially it may seem that the insight Updike describes in the above passage is generically Protestant rather than distinctively Lutheran. However, despite references to Barth, Eliot, and others, Updike himself identifies the source of his insight to be his Lutheran Sunday school. And a closer examination reveals that the consequence — namely, artistic courage — is more in keeping with the Lutheran than with the Calvinist tradition. For Calvin, revelation supplies the knowledge of God that humans lack, and the God thus revealed is for him a transcendent being, standing above it all, very much in control of what happens in the world. During the early history of Calvinism, church buildings were devoid of art and church services lacked music (other than metrical Psalms) because of the fear that art and music would distract from revelation; they called attention to the human and ran the risk of idolatry.

Luther's understanding was different. For him, too, God was unlike humans, but God's immanent activity received greater emphasis. The power of God was "essentially present at all places, even the tiniest tree leaf" (*Luther's Works*, 37:57). Anything could be a "mask" of God. Just as the body and blood of Christ were really present "in, with, and under" the bread and wine in the Eucharist, so God was present "in, with, and under" anything in the world. Christ, who partook of the omnipresence of the divine, could even be bodily present "in stone, in fire, in water, or even in a rope" (*Luther's Works*, 37:342). The whole world was sacramental.

Luther composed music and wrote hymns for the church. He felt that human agency was no impediment to divine presence and activity. Similarly, he allowed statues and paintings to continue to adorn church buildings and risked an unauthorized return to Wittenberg from his protective exile at the Wartburg castle in order to rebuff the enthusiastic crowds that had begun to destroy them. Operating with the "incarnational principle," Lutherans detect God's presence in the world — an ambiguous presence, perhaps, but a presence nonetheless. From this point of view, a truthful account of the world is thus not distracting but revealing. What comes through when John Updike calls "holy" his act of describing "life as accurately as I could" is precisely this incarnational principle. During an interview with Jan Nunley he called it a form of praise:

> Any act of description is, to some extent, an act of praise, so that even when the event is unpleasant or horrifying or spiritually stunning, the very attempt to describe it is, in some way, part of that Old Testament injunction to give praise. The Old Testament God repeatedly says he wants praise, and I translate that to mean that the world wants describing, the world wants to be observed and "hymned." So there's a kind of hymning undercurrent that I feel in my work. (Plath, ed., 253)

Description becomes praise only when God is understood to be present in the world being described.

Working out this incarnational principle is what leads to the Lutheran fondness for paradox. As I have already indicated, Calvinists tend to portray God as "above the fray," very much in charge of what is occurring, and orchestrating it in such a way that good will eventuate. In this outlook even what seems to defy God's purposes is used by God to serve that greater good. Believers who hold this view usually find it to be a source of comfort and security. However bizarre and discomforting one's experiences may be, believers can be confident of life's meaningfulness on some more ultimate level. For Luther, God does not stand above the conflict but enters into it, getting bloodied and dirtied in the process. Confidence comes not from some expectation about the outcome but from trust in the benevolent purposes and comforting presence of the God who is active. Whereas the world of the Calvinist is ultimately orderly, the world of the Lutheran is fundamentally conflicted. Faith is more of a wager or a hope than certainty about an orderly world. The comfort it offers is divine companionship rather than the security of a predictably beneficial outcome.

According to Luther, such a God can be described only via the use of paradox. The God who enters into creation is a powerful creator but appears as a poor, weak infant in a manger in Bethlehem, born to a powerless Jewish girl. The God who enters history to overcome evil appears himself to be overcome as he cries out in agony on the cross. Such a God is "both hidden and revealed." God is in fact most hidden precisely at those points where God is most clearly revealed. In the face of defeat, God is present. Amid the worst kind of evil, God is at work. The proper work of this God is to show mercy, but the mercy often appears under the cloak of wrath. More than anything, God is a living presence, too much alive to be boxed in by human expectations and human propositions.

When Ralph Wood says that the "ethical quietism" he finds in Updike derives "from an overly transcendent sense of God's otherness" (*Comedy of Redemption*, 190), he has picked up on only one side of the paradox and "flattened out" the tensions inherent in it. Let me make several comments about Wood's interpretation and Updike's view of God.

First, yes, contemporary Americans are especially prone to experience God's absence, but it is not the absence of distance, of an overly transcendent God; it is the absence involving what Luther would call the "hiddenness" of a God who is *both* hidden and revealed. What is experienced existentially as the absence of God results from the characters' self-absorption. God remains available and active, immanent and omnipresent, but not recognized. For Updike, God's presence can be seen, not as characters withdraw from life, but as they enter into it. Sex, which has so many complex dimensions in Updike's writings, can be an avenue into life and thus even into an experience of the presence of God.

Second, Wood misunderstands Updike when he says, "Updike takes refuge in an abstract monotheism that makes him ambivalent about every moral reality" (*Comedy of Redemption,* 190). Updike's ambivalence comes not from "abstract monotheism" but from his Lutheran awareness of the paradoxical character of the presence of God. God can be present even amid behavior that God does not endorse.

Third, Wood himself correctly recognizes that "Updike has no patience with the merely 'nice' Deity worshipped in most of our churches, the friendly Fellow with whom we can 'empathize'" (*Comedy of Redemption,* 191). In the passage to which Wood here refers, Updike says, "I've never really understood theologies which would absolve God of earthquakes and typhoons, of children starving . . . and this God is above the nice god, above the god we can worship and empathize with" (*Picked-Up Pieces,* 504).

Further, Wood also recognizes the Lutheran theme of God's graciousness in, for example, the short story "Pigeon Feathers."

> Like Luther inspecting the solitary kernel of grain, David [Kern] examines but a single feather from one of the pigeons he has slain. He is overwhelmed by the gratuitous beauty contained in the plumage of these dead birds. It convinces him, as neither creed nor church can, that only a gracious Host could lay so sumptuous a feast for the eyes. (*Comedy of Redemption,* 195)

In Updike's story, Kern is convinced "that the God who had lavished such craft on these worthless birds would not destroy His whole creation by refusing to let David die forever" (*Pigeon Feathers,* 150). Wood understands that "Updike shares Luther's humbled gratitude before everything created. Whether they be human fabrications like window sashes and telephone poles, or natural creations such as horse chestnut trees and green hedges, all things *made* bespeak their maker" (*Comedy of Redemption,* 193).

Finally, however, what Wood does *not* do is to put his two quite divergent observations together and recognize that Updike's God, like Luther's, is tension-filled and paradoxical, not an expression of "abstract monotheism."

V

Not only must God be described in paradoxes, but paradox must also be used to describe the life of the believer. According to Luther, the human who believes is "simultaneously justified [= right with God] and a sinner." Paradoxically, a person may be closer to faith when in despair than when feeling confident. The believer, both Luther and Kierkegaard emphasized, is called to love the neighbor with such abandon as to lose herself; but in so losing herself, that believer simultaneously (and paradoxically) finds her true self. The believer is called to "die," but in dying to find life. In *Rabbit at Rest*, such a dying to self is exactly what would have been necessary in order for Rabbit Angstrom to have gone to meet with his wife, son, and daughter-in-law; such a dying could have been redemptive. Instead, he again "ran," this time to Florida, where death of a different kind — first the death of isolation and then physical death — awaited him.

Paradox also carries over into morality. Luther was very cautious about the self, very impressed with its capacity for self-deception and self-aggrandizement. Because believers are still sinners, his caution included the life of faith. The relationship with God implied in "justification by grace through faith" involves receptivity to God's gifts: the gift of acceptance, the gift of forgiveness, the gift of freedom. But the human always wants to take credit for what happens and so tries to find ways to transform gifts into accomplishments. Likewise, the relationship with others implied by justification is one of servanthood. Just as God's gifting is spontaneous, so the believer's gifting to others is to be spontaneous and uncalculating. Yet humans again are tempted to transform their gifting into accomplishments. They look over their shoulder to see if their acts are making God smile with parental approval — thereby subtly transforming other-directed acts into self-enhancing behavior.

This caution about the resilience of human self-centeredness results in a view of the moral life that is highly ambiguous. The "best" of human acts are marred by conflicted and conflicting motives, while some of what meets with greater societal disapproval may issue from a generous concern for the dignity of another.

Updike is similarly fond of paradox. For example, with regard to art, consider the rest of the passage in which he calls a truthful description "holy":

> Yet fiction, like life, is a dirty business; discretion and good taste play small part in it. Hardly a story appears in print without offending or wounding some living model. . . . Parents, wives, children — the nearer and dearer they are, the more mercilessly they are served up. So my art, like my religion, has a shabby side. (*Self-Consciousness*, 231)

The role of sex is another example of paradox. In Updike, sex is simultaneously a way to be in contact with the mystery of life celebrated by religion and also an expression of the embodied naturalness of humans. "According to Updike, sex is the closest to a religious experience that the physical world provides, so the protagonist often searches for spiritual satisfaction in sexual encounters" (Uphaus, 6). In *Roger's Version,* Dale's quest for intellectual signs of God gets sidetracked by his sexual involvement with Esther, but it is not merely a diversion. Sex draws him into the reality of living, into the immediacy of human relationships rather than the "colder" world of computers. Even an affair with a married woman is on some level humanizing; yet sex is not redemptive, for he is not sure if he has been used by Esther. When the affair ends, he is merely depressed. For Updike, even the use of explicit detail regarding the human anatomy and sexual activity is not (automatically at least) a detraction from the dignity of life. Sex is simultaneously a way for participants to be in contact with life — life that is God-given and gracious — and a mirror that reveals their flawed character, which distorts and destroys that life.

As another example of Updike's fondness for paradox, consider his short story "Leaves." There the "net effect" of the shadows' pattern is "its intricate simultaneous suggestions of shelter and openness, warmth and breeze" (*Music School*, 53). The "shelter and openness" of the leaves mirror the conflicted character of Updike's characters, caught as they are between domestic responsibility and freedom. In that same story the description of the leaves is followed by another paradox regarding humans: "Can our spirits really enter Time's haven of mortality and sink composedly among the mulching leaves? No: we stand at the intersection of two kingdoms, and there is no advance and no retreat, only a sharpening of the edge where we stand" (54). Humans are not the center of the world but live at the juncture of the heavenly and the animal realms where they experience the tensions and exhibit the paradoxes inherent in that duality.

The various kinds of paradox intertwine; they reflect a fundamental duality in the human situation.

VI

Another place where Updike's indebtedness to Luther surfaces is in his attitude toward governments. They are to be respected, but they are flawed. Their actions are as ambiguous as anything else that is human. So are attempts to overthrow them.

Luther distinguished between the "two rules" of God — sometimes, less accurately, called the "two kingdoms" of God. The basic idea is that God rules in two ways. God's "proper work" is to show mercy and open the door for humans to have a restored relationship with him. The means used to accomplish this objective is the spoken word, the "good news." However, because of human sin, God also has to rule in another way. God protects people from being harmed by others, keeps order, and fosters justice through governments, police and court systems, and authority structures in all areas of life: schools, families, corporations, hospitals, and even the institutional embodiments of the church. In this, God's "alien work," coercion is sometimes used. The authority structures of society and the humans who design and operate them exercise control over people in their community, limiting their behavior so that it does not harm others. On Luther's reading, the Bible does not endorse any particular kind of political system or any particular set of laws, but it does affirm God's desire that *some* system be in place to protect human life. The standard whereby that system is judged is not some ideal pattern but whether the government in question serves and protects the community. If it does, it deserves support.

One consequence of Luther's distinction between two rules of the same God was that he did not want any political program to be labeled "Christian." Those who support such programs always have a vested interest in their outcome and are thereby advocating their own interests over against someone else's. He did not object to Christians taking political stands, participating in politics, and advocating political programs; he objected only to "baptizing" such programs with the name "Christian" (*Luther's Works,* 46:23-34). Politics was part of the second rule of God, not the first.

Luther says (*Luther's Works,* 45:93-94) that a person who exhibits genuinely Christian behavior (if such a person exists — the point is theoretical) does not need authority structures because he or she loves others and does nothing to hurt them. But such a genuine Christian still submits to authority structures *because* the community needs them. For the same reason, that Christian can also hold office, despite the entanglements with coercion that office-holding entails.

In his own sixteenth-century setting, the purpose of Luther's distinction was twofold. On the one hand, he objected to some civil authorities, especially Roman Catholics, who claimed the right to coerce belief or religious practice. In so doing they overstepped the bounds of the authority given to temporal rulers, mistakenly using the coercive methods of the second rule of God to try to effect the first sort of governance and to accomplish what only the Word of God can do. On the other hand, Luther also objected to the anarchists of his day who wanted to disband governments, and he disagreed with the ancestors of the Amish and the Hutterites who taught that believers should not hold office or serve in the army. To his way of thinking, these Protestants were extending the mercy of the first rule into the second form of governance.

Updike's indebtedness to Luther's teaching regarding the "two rules" is evident in his reaction to the Vietnam war. Called upon to join writers publicly opposed to the war, he refused. In a chapter in *Self-Consciousness,* "On Not Being a Dove," Updike offers an explanation for that refusal — one that is autobiographical, sociological, political, and religious. It balances many competing observations about his friends, himself, and the nation. He admits that "it pained and embarrassed me to be out of step with my editorial and literary colleagues . . . and with many of my dearest Ipswich friends, including my wife" (*Self-Consciousness,* 117). Clearly his refusal must have come from deeply felt convictions.

One factor was that he saw in the anti-war protesters a streak of American perfectionism that he did not think appropriate. (He exempted Kurt Vonnegut and others who spoke from personal experience.)

> A dark Augustinian idea lurked within my tangled position: a plea that Vietnam — this wretched unfashionable war led by clumsy Presidents from the West and fought by the nineteen-year-old sons of the poor — could not be disowned by a favored enlightened few hiding behind college deferments, fleeing to chaste cool countries, snootily pouring pig blood into draft files, writing deeply offended Notes and Comments, and otherwise pretending that our great nation hadn't had bloody hands from the start, that every generation didn't have its war, that bloody hands didn't go with having hands at all. A plea, in short, for the doctrine of Original Sin and its obscure consolations. (135-36)

What is evident here is that, despite the rhetorical flourishes that sound as if they are coming from the far right, Updike is not glorifying war. Unlike so many who opposed the protesters, he is not a super patriot. He is not whitewashing the authorities whom he is reluctant to oppose. Original sin affects them too. The ambiguity he sees is but an expression of that original sin emphasized by the fifth-century Christian philosopher so influential for Luther, Hobbes, and the framers of our Constitution with their "checks and balances": Augustine of Hippo. The depth of Updike's perception that the world is fallen is evident when he continues, "If a dirty war was being fought in Indochina, what was so unusual? What was worth protesting, decrying, getting self-righteous about? That was what the world was — a dirty war, somewhere or other, all the time" (151). He saw himself reacting to a theological animus: "down dirty sex and the bloody mess of war and the desperate effort of faith all belonged to a dark necessary underside of reality that I felt should not be merely ignored, or risen above, or disdained. These shameful things were intrinsic to life" (135).

Such a reaction would be pessimism pure and simple were it not balanced by the love for the world that we have already seen in Updike. As he has said, he describes the world with candor in order to change it. So this is not ultimately a form of quietism that gives up on the world. It is instead a recognition of the moral ambiguity of all political movements — both those that supported the policies of the Johnson administration and those that sought to overthrow it. That the issue is ambiguity, not pessimism, is evident in Updike's willingness to be self-critical. However much the social station of the protesters affected their anti-war sentiments (120), equally so did his own social station affect his reaction to the war (137). He had, he says with some irony,

> voted for Lyndon Johnson, and thus had earned my American right not to make a political decision for another four years. If he and his advisers (transferred intact, most of them, from Kennedy's Camelot) had somehow got us into this mess, they would somehow get us out, and it was a citizen's plain duty to hold his breath and hope for the best, not parade around spouting pious unction and crocodile tears. (119-20)

But — and here comes his self-criticism — "Had I," he wonders, "in fact *too* successfully found a place for myself out of harm's way?" (149). A person who takes himself and his political program too seriously does not raise such questions!

In 1525 Luther acknowledged that many of the demands of the peasants were just, and he urged the princes to negotiate with them (*Luther's Works*, 46:42-43), but when rebellion broke out he felt that it was the princes' duty to restore order. In the following quotation, Updike sets that advice alongside the tradition of revolution.

> I was, as an American Protestant, the beneficiary of a number of revolts — Luther's, which dumped the Pope; Cromwell's, which dumped the monarchy; and Sam Adams's, which dumped the British — and saw no need for any more. I was, furthermore, a Christian, and Christ said, "Render unto Caesar those things which are Caesar's." I was, by upbringing, a Lutheran, and Luther had told the "murdering and thieving hordes" [*"die räuberischen und mörderischen Rotten"*] of rebellious peasants to cease their radical turmoil and submit to their Christian princes. (*Self-Consciousness*, 129-30)

He is heir to both traditions, but in the end the Lutheran strand triumphs. Updike's reaction to the anti-war protest was much like Luther's to the peasants. Rebellion was inappropriate. He concluded that "the pacifism invoked in the anti-Vietnam protest was hypocritical and spurious. Under the banner of a peace movement, rather, war was being waged by a privileged few upon the administration and the American majority that had elected it" (131). What ultimately prevails is Updike's deep awareness of sin. The world in which we live is not ideal.

Once again Updike has employed a Lutheran approach to the issue. I do not mean that everyone using Lutheran principles would automatically arrive at his position on the war, but the considerations he uses to explain his position are rooted in the Lutheran tradition. These considerations include a reluctance to label the anti-war protest "Christian" or to see it as unambiguously right, a reluctance to privilege pacifism as the only Christian option, a view of the world that expects conflict and sees the need for using power to control it, a readiness to participate (at least via voting) and accept responsibility for the actions of the candidate one supports, and a readiness to be self-critical. Although he is not confident that authorities are always right (128-29), he is inclined to give them the benefit of a doubt and so credits "the Johnson administration with good faith and some good sense" (114). What is missing is any sense of righteous outrage at the conduct of the government. There is a weariness and a sadness at the outcome of its policies, yes, but not outrage. Evidently he had never expected its actions to be either genuinely Christian or 100 percent moral! American perfectionism was not his starting point. Also missing is any inclination to join a moral crusade. The issues are in his mind too complex and thorny to be solved by the hatchet-action of a crusade. A scalpel is needed instead. "My disposition to take contrary positions and to seek for nuances within the normal ill-suited me for the national debate" (146). The civil fury was too distressing and the polarities too confining. What is striking is that Updike invoked religious ideas to explain his position, religious ideas deeply indebted to Lutheran theology.

VII

A more complicated issue is Updike's relationship to Luther's emphasis on Christ as the source of hope. As we have seen, Updike affirms the graciousness of God, a graciousness that Luther saw so well expressed in Christ. However, unlike Luther, who regarded his calling to be "to preach Christ," Updike sees his own vocation to be description. Description has more to do with the first article of the Christian creed than the second, more to do with creation than redemption. "I think," he said in an interview in 1978, "that the first item of morality for a writer is to try to be accurate, to tell the truth as you know it, and not to get onto a preacher's platform" (Plath, ed., 120). Or in an even more telling statement from 1993, "I'm not trying to force a message upon the reader, but I am trying to give human behavior theological scrutiny" (249). What he tries to describe is an American society that has claimed to be redemptive but is in fact "severed from Christ." Note Updike's response to a criticism that he wrote too well but had nothing to say:

> I, who seemed to myself full of things to say, who had all of Shillington to say, Shillington and Pennsylvania and the whole mass of middling, hidden, troubled America to say, and who had seen and heard things in my two childhood homes, as my parents' giant faces revolved and spoke, achieving utterance under some terrible pressure of American disappointment, that would take a lifetime to sort out, particularize, and extol with the proper dark beauty. *In the beauty of the lilies Christ was born across the sea* — this odd and uplifting line from among the many odd lines of "The Battle Hymn of the Republic" seemed to me, as I set out, to summarize what I had to say about America, to offer itself as the title of a continental *magnum opus* of which all my books, no matter how many, would be mere installments, mere starts at the hymning of this giant, roughly rectangular country severed from Christ by the breadth of the sea. (*Self-Consciousness,* 103)

The lived social reality that he sets out to describe exhibits a deep "disappointment"; it is "severed from Christ by the breadth of the sea"! His job is more fundamental than delivering an overtly sermonic message about Christ: it is to describe and thereby to "mirror" the reality, trusting that such a description is not only holy but also useful, that showing people the "disappointment" they try to deny may open them to the "leap" or "reorientation" that brings life. His hope for such a reorientation is built on a profound sense that God's grace is itself ready to break through. To return to the foreword to the *Olinger Stories* quoted earlier, "The muddled and inconsequent surface of things now and then parts to yield us a gift."

VIII

Updike's outlook, as reflected in his novels and his own comments about his writing, has retained characteristics that reflect a distinctively Lutheran understanding of Christianity. Because of that outlook, reviewers should not expect to find moral instruction or an unambiguous resolution of moral issues. They should not expect a clear, nonconflicted message about a transcendent God. Nor should they be surprised that sex is understood to be an appropriate topic for theological scrutiny, because any aspect of the world is at one and the same time potentially sacramental and potentially distorted by self-centered behavior. They should not be surprised that the disappointments of an America built as it has been on a triumphalistic civil religion are the subject of description. Nor should they be surprised that the vehicle chosen is a narrative description of persons who in their own flawed ways either love or fail to love, either build up or harm one another. Critics ought not to expect the outlook of a Lutheran to be anything other than Lutheran.

Writing as a Reader of Karl Barth

What Kind of Religious Writer Is John Updike Not?

STEPHEN H. WEBB

Karl Barth is universally acknowledged as one of the most brilliant theologians of the twentieth century, and yet he is also probably the least read and most misunderstood of all modern theologians. Although his reputation in North America continues to grow, especially among evangelicals, his influence in American theological circles has never been clear. Indeed, the name of Karl Barth for many is enough to conjure an image of rigid scholasticism and narrow dogmatism — accusations that actually characterize more accurately some of his followers than Barth himself.

Some of the problems of reading him are purely practical, and some are ideological. His first book, a commentary on *The Epistle to the Romans* (1922), was an explosive work that broke with the liberalism that dominated German theology at that time. It is an immensely complicated and dense text that combines the bleakness of existentialism and the fragmentary aesthetic of expressionism to demonstrate the unknowability of God. Barth wanted the act of reading it to be as much a trial and tribulation as the act of faith itself.

Barth later grew suspicious of such theological pyrotechnics and left behind his youthful provocations in order to pursue a neo-orthodoxy, even though many of his critics doubted how *neo* it was. The result was the *Church Dogmatics,* which represents Barth's lifelong project of grounding theology in the uniqueness of Jesus Christ and God's gift of grace to the church. It is so long (4 volumes in 13 books), however, that many people prefer to criticize it without having read it at all.

Barth began as a theological rebel who rejected the easygoing complacencies of liberalism on the basis of a heroic existentialism. He ended his career as an equally rebellious traditionalist who taught that theology could exist only on the basis of the language used by the church. What remained constant in his thought is a stubborn rejection of modernity and a persistent attempt to recover the otherness and the majesty of God.

Is it not, then, surprising that one of America's greatest writers has devoted himself, especially early in his career, to a long and passionate reading of Karl Barth? John Updike is known for the daring of his prose, the way he can describe anything and everything, each sentence a tribute to the miraculous capacity of language to capture even the most intricate and complex (as well as intimate and indecent) experience. It is as if Updike wants to test whether language can be a sufficiently subtle instrument to satisfy our science-driven demand for the empirical and perceptible — a palpable sense of the real.

Many postmodern writers push language in playful and ironic directions in order to challenge the notion of what is real. Updike, by contrast, wagers that the most supple and delicate of technical linguistic innovations are necessary, not as a way of drawing attention to the artificiality of all human making, but as a way of honoring the world as it is.[1] How, then, do we get from Barth, the theological traditionalist who staked everything on the capacity of God to speak a true Word in Jesus Christ, to Updike, who drenches the world with words, a productive outpouring that gives life to the old-fashioned hope that literature can still operate descriptively, not just ironically?[2]

1. Postmodern fiction is obsessed with the problems inherent in language and writing; such fiction, then, is not confident about the referential or descriptive power of language. Updike's most deliberately postmodern novels are *A Month of Sundays,* where the narrator is a writer in search of an audience, and the Bech books (*Bech: A Book, Beck Is Back, Bech at Bay*), where Updike creates a writer who explores the act of writing itself.

2. Although Updike can be very ironic in his prose, his irony is stable, rather than unstable, in that he questions but does not completely deny the very promise

The evidence of Updike's loyalty to Barth is plentiful. Updike once said that reading Barth saved his life,[3] and he repays that debt not only in essays about Barth but also by portraying Barthian characters. There is Marshfield in *A Month of Sundays*, Kruppenbach from *Rabbit, Run*, and a very Barthian sermon on gender in *Of the Farm*. In his autobiographical poem, "Midpoint," he writes, "Praise *Barth*, who told how saving Faith can flow/From Terror's oscillating Yes and No" (*Collected Poems*, 96). In another poem, "Die Neuen Heiligen," he writes, after stanzas on Kierkegaard and Kafka, "Karl Barth, more healthy,/and married, and Swiss,/lived longer, yet took/small comfort from this;/ *Nein!* he cried, rooting/in utter despair/the Credo that Culture/left up in the air" (323). At times he seems most drawn to the early, existentialist Barth, rather than the later Barth of the *Church Dogmatics;* and indeed, Updike can praise Kierkegaard with the same enthusiasm as Barth. But Updike is also aware that the later Barth does something different than the old theological trick of trying to develop an existential anthropology in order to show people how much they need God.

Perhaps Updike is drawn to Barth because both men are reacting to the situation of being a Christian in a non-Christian age.[4] My sense is that Updike avoids a certain kind of religious fiction in precisely the same way that Barth wanted to avoid a certain kind of theological apologetics. In other words, Updike follows Barth in being a bit skeptical about certain strategies of appealing to the religious sensibilities of his readers. Barth did not make direct arguments for the truth of Christianity. Even in his early period, he revealed the power of God only by showing the absence of God in the world, thereby making a negative case for theism. In his later work, he focused on God's capacity to reveal God's self, but he did not infer from this characterization of God that good Christian men and women were therefore somehow better than the rest of humanity or that the church was an institution that is

---

of language to communicate something real. Barth, too, called upon theologians to have an ironic attitude toward the world, but his irony is grounded in a trust in the hidden but effective providence of God. Both Updike and Barth, then, use but also limit irony in ways that distinguish them from the postmodern tendency to make irony the fundamental trope of uncertainty and indeterminacy.

3. *Time*, 26 April 1968, p. 74.

4. It is possible that Updike was also attracted to Barth in part because Barth was so unfashionable and yet so intellectually challenging. See *Self-Consciousness*, 141-42.

set apart. God reveals God's self, but the world is still the world, utterly fallen and full of the trivialities and tragedies of human existence. The fact of God's revelation, Barth argues, enables the theologian to accept the world for what it is, without romanticizing human nature or turning cynically against human foibles. The world is God's gift, and God accepts humanity even as God sees us truly, as the godless creatures that try nonetheless to play God.

The theologian thus cannot appeal to some presumed religious sensibility that all people are thought to share, because there is no unambiguous natural evidence of God's presence in the world. For Barth, theologians need to be ironic in their attempts to persuade others of the truth of the gospel. Any direct attempt to argue that humans need God is bound to flatter humanity by either praising our natural capacity for an awareness of God or rationalizing our sinful state as the necessary precondition for turning to God. Barth thought that theologians should be neither optimists nor pessimists about human nature. Instead, they should try to see the world both for what it is and for what it can become, and thus accept the world as the good but fallen place for God to carry out our redemption.

This might sound as if Barth is sacrificing the truth of Christianity to his reservations about the ability of theologians to make a persuasive case for it. Not at all. Indeed, Barth could reject all Christian apologetics because he thought that opposition to the church is only apparent and not real. The Lord of the church, after all, is universal and one. This truth admittedly cannot make much sense to the world on its own terms. The theologian should accept the self-description of the modern world in all its utter secularity, while retaining only the right to stake out theology's own language, a language that is, in the end, utterly inclusive, comprehensive, and final. By giving the world its freedom from the obligation to be religious, Barth has cunningly maintained theology's centrality all the more.

The best way to persuade readers about the viability of Christianity is not to try to persuade them at all. Barth thought that the best apologetics was a good dogmatics — in other words, that theologians should not confuse the two realms of the divine and the mundane by trying to prove God's presence in the world. The Christian is the one who can let the world be the world, rather than trying to offer religious interpretations of various worldly events and features. To try to argue that God is one more knowable object in the world risks turning God into a finite object that can be debated and analyzed, which does not do justice to God's infinite otherness. Such arguments also inevitably confuse one aspect of the world with God, thus turning something finite into an idol. Granting God's uniqueness — that is, treating only God as God and not confusing God with the world — ironically lets the Christian take the world for what it is, a good gift of God, but not God's own self. Nothing in the world is sacred and inviolable, although anything, seen in the right light, can be a channel of God's grace.

Barth's theology could thus sound stubbornly traditional and strikingly modern at the same time. Updike, I want to argue, shows us what fiction would look like based on this same set of theological principles. Updike, too, does not think that he can persuade his readers that Christianity is true, and he does not try to initiate his readers into a spiritual journey. He does not try to create characters whose very limitations drive them into the arms of God. He does not try, in other words, to defend God by condemning humanity. In this way, one can correlate the kind of theology that Barth did not like with the kind of religious fiction that Updike does not write. Barth was suspicious of Christian art, and so is Updike: "My art is Christian only in that my faith urges me to tell the truth, however painful and inconvenient, and holds out the hope that the truth — reality — is good. Good or no, only the truth is useful" (Plath, ed., 104). It should be no surprise, therefore, that a Christian writer imbued with Barth's theology would end up being one of the best practitioners of realistic fiction today. Just as Barth rejected modern trends in theology as faddish and thought that the most radical thing a theologian could do would be to ground theology in the church, Updike follows the apparently traditional but really radical path of a descriptive prose that exercises the human freedom of creativity without thereby negating the reality of worldly constraints on that freedom.

Updike's apparently inexhaustible capacity to explore the physical details of the world parallels Barth's seemingly endless *Church Dogmatics*, which, too, cannot say enough about the goodness of God's creation. There is a joyful drive in much of Updike's embellished descriptions of things, as if he cannot describe the world enough to satiate his hunger for it or to stave off the thought of death.[5] His prose is

5. This preoccupation with death is one way in which Updike is not in agreement with Barth's theology. Updike frequently has expressed a quite literal fear

incarnational in the sense of Barth's interpretation of Christology: God has entered the world and revealed God's self in Jesus Christ, but the world is not thereby divinized. The world is still the world, in all of its flaws and faults, and yet we can see the world differently, because God has loved it so.

Updike's fiction, like Barth's theology, is unapologetically religious.[6] Updike is not out to indict the world, to convict it of its sins and trespasses. He does not resent the world's secularity, and his analysis of the infinite complexities involved in every act of memory or reflection is never bitter or condescending. Updike does not condemn his characters, like Flannery O'Connor, and he does not have a penchant for apocalyptic endings. He does not destroy the fictitious worlds he has created. Yet he also does not see the world as full of grace, which would risk turning every story into a parable for divine salvation. Many critics of Updike want stronger endings, more violence, and clearer messages in his work, faulting him for a surfeit of style over substance. They want him to try to convert his readers by exercising his authorial prerogative of either damning or redeeming his characters. Instead, Updike maximizes the freedom of his readers, just as God maximizes our own freedom. He has an ironic and wistful sensibility, a providential vision of the ways in which good and evil intermix, how human nature is inherently ambiguous, and yet how the light of God's grace can still illuminate even the shadows of our existence.

His treatment of sexuality is a good example of how he affirms the world in all of its earthiness but also sees the limits of human desires, without thereby treating sexuality as an allegory of religious longing. He can take sex so seriously precisely because he is not trying to give the world a religious interpretation. He lets the world be the world, which also, as a happy by-product, lets God be God.

In one short story, Updike even goes so far as to parody the use of sex as an analogy for religion. The narrator in "Lifeguard" is for nine

---

of death, and thus he has a very literal interpretation of the Christian doctrine of resurrection. On this issue, he is unlike Barth, who tended toward the opaque when he talked about the afterlife, afraid of playing to humanity's natural and selfish desires and preferring instead to confront humanity with the paradox of the cross.

6. My phrase "unapologetically religious" is adapted from William C. Placher's wonderful title, *Unapologetic Theology.*

months a year a student of divinity, studying Barth among others, but "for the remaining quarter of the solar revolution, I rest my eyes on a sheet of brilliant sand printed with the runes of naked human bodies. That there is no discrepancy between my studies, that the texts of the flesh complement those of the mind, is the easy burden of my sermon" (*Pigeon Feathers*, 212-13). The lifeguard compares sexual lust to the spiritual spelunking that his professors require of him. He also compares seduction to conversion. He has all of these thoughts while watching from high above "Protestantism's errant herd" (219), gathered on Sunday mornings at the beach rather than in churches.

Can the beach be the paradise all these formerly church-going people have been seeking all along? Is this where Christianity ends in America? The lifeguard's final thought is that what he really desires is to save someone, literally. He listens for "the call for help, the call, a call, it saddens me to confess, that I have yet to hear" (220). The story ends with impotence and absence, calling into question the "easy burden" of the lifeguard's sermon on the power of the flesh.

A Month of Sundays also pushes the analogy between sex and religion to its very limits. The prodigal minister, Tom Marshfield, is a Barthian because his father was a liberal: "I did not become a Barthian in blank recoil, but in positive love of Barth's voice, his wholly masculine, wholly informed, wholly unfrightened prose. In his prose thorns become edible, as for the giraffe. In Barth I heard, at the age of eighteen, the voice my father should have had" (*Month of Sundays*, 24-25). Marshfield tries to find in sex the same kind of hard and resounding affirmations that he found in Barth's theology. He is able to find some sort of salvation not in otherworldly pursuits but in entering more fully into the messiness of this world, just as God did.

Marshfield is perhaps Updike's most Lutheran creation, a man who sins boldly and seeks God in the paradoxes of faith. Yet the ending of the novel is ambiguous: sex is both a sacrament for Marshfield and a symptom of his own narcissism and pride. Marshfield can pursue the mystical only through the physical, which leads him back to the very beginning of all his problems. What is most striking about Marshfield's final sexual act is that his partner, Ms. Prynne (his ideal reader, for whom he is writing this book), remains mysterious and unknowable. He bids her to come to him with an apocalyptic longing ("Even so, come," he writes to her [226]), and when she finally does, he feels like he has been brought to an edge, over which he should gratefully slip. This sexual experience has forced Marshfield outside of himself so that he might see his life afresh and begin it anew. Nevertheless, Updike resists portraying sexual ecstasy as simply a sacramental avenue for religious rejuvenation. We are left to judge for ourselves whether Marshfield will turn his life around or whether he will continue to fall victim to his own confused desires.

Sexuality is humanity's newest (or oldest?) attempt to build false idols and worship in false temples, but it is also a part of God's good creation, so that there is something holy even in the midst of all of our mad scrambling after physical pleasure. For example, in Updike's most sexually explicit novel, *Couples,* he clearly sees sexuality as a false substitute for religion, but he is also tenderhearted about the anxiety that drives his characters into each other's arms (and bodies!). After all, lightning (an act of God) destroys a picturesque New England church near the end of that novel, leaving sex alone as a means of exploring the sublime wonder of something mysteriously other.

Sex is the modern altar of choice, but can it really replace the church? What does Updike think about the church? At first glance, his own bemused and disconcerting reflections on his own and others' churchgoing might seem to be at odds with Barth's insistence that all theology is grounded in the church. Yet Barth also could be very leery about the habits of piety that the church cultivates. In fact, Barth always insisted that the church remains a human institution, and as such it cannot live up to the many expectations people have for it. Not only that, the church is also the site of humanity's highest spiritual strivings, which are full of pride and self-righteousness, so that the church stands under the judgment of God. The church cannot be justified, except that it is the place where all human attempts to justify their own activities come to an end with God's preemptive justification of everything human. The church is the shape that God's grace takes, so that its persistence in history attests to the power of the word that is spoken there.

Updike also finds the church to be an oddly compelling place. In *Of the Farm,* the narrator, Joey, likes going to church in order to witness "the strange courtesy, paid the universe, of Christian belief" (148). The story is about a farm that Joey's mother allows to remain fallow, but precisely due to its uselessness the farm is full of memory and power. Churches too, Updike seems to be saying, are a strange mixture of the useless and the fecund. Precisely because they are so out of step with modern concerns, they can still hold us with the power of something other.

Barth was hesitant in his theology to try to explain how or why people become Christians. He did not want to offer a theory of conversion because that would reduce this mystery to some human achievement, replacing the unpredictable movement of the Holy Spirit with the all too predictable science of psychology. Updike, too, seems struck in much of his work by the inexplicable draw of religion and our inability to understand why some people feel this pull more than others. In a short story, "The Deacon," he portrays a man named Miles who goes to church without knowing why. At least it is better, Miles supposes, than spending nights away from home drinking in bars. Miles does not really consider himself religious — which is significant because Barth always made the distinction between trying to be religious and being grasped by the Word of God.

Every few years, Miles changes jobs and towns and finds a new church to attend, but with his latest move he decides to start staying at home on Sunday mornings. His wife, who never goes to church with him, knows that something is missing, and she encourages him to find a new church again. He does, and one winter night he attends a committee meeting to which no one else comes. Miles has time to survey the "souvenirs of the church's past" (*Museums and Women*, 48), seeing the church both as a second home, intimate and reassuring, and as an antique store, filled with the relics of a forgotten past. The wooden structure withstands the storm, which is some comfort, but its emptiness — "an emptiness where many others have been" (48) — reminds Miles of death. The church is a tomb with many hidden treasures and an ark providing protection from the storm. To be religious is to be both discarded and salvaged. The metaphors are mixed, but the message is clear: being alone in a church is a good place to think about death.

Updike's long reading of Barth has clearly influenced his fiction, in terms of both style and content. Indeed, given Barth's distinctive theological vision, it should be no wonder that Updike, one of the only great contemporary American writers who identifies with mainline Protestantism, is drawn to Barth and not to liberal theology. The real question is whether liberal theology has sufficient moral and intellectual weight to excite and sustain the literary imagination. That is the very question that is raised in *Roger's Version*. This novel shows that the temptation of the Barthian position is a cynicism toward the world, but that the liberal project of trying to infer God's existence from the worldly evidence is even more easily exhausted and dissipated.

Roger, who teaches courses on heresy at a divinity school because he lost his Methodist parish due to a sex scandal, is experiencing the spiritual fatigue of middle age. He looks at his second wife from a wry distance, knowing that she is bored with him, and he is attracted to his niece, Verna, who is living in poverty with her fatherless baby daughter nearby. Halfway through the novel he meditates on Tertullian's argument concerning the soul's dependence on the body, which leads Tertullian to affirm the resurrection of the flesh. Roger has become weary of religion (he is not in the distribution but the quality control line of the religion business, he says at one point), but he still has a taste for mystery, as well as a realistic acceptance of the ways in which sexuality expresses mystery for us today.

Sexual experience parallels the transcendence and mystery of religious passion, but sex is also degraded by being overly hyped and thus turned into one more commodity in a consumer society. Sex mimics but cannot replace religious passion. Roger is therefore still inclined to be enticed by the traditional theological texts and arguments about God. Indeed, Roger keeps his real theological passion, Karl Barth, to himself, because mentioning Barth in a seminary classroom would only cause the students to titter: "Barth, in this liberal seminary dominated by gracefully lapsed Unitarians and Quakers, was like sex in junior high school" (*Roger's Version,* 27). In contrast to the lightweight Tillich, Roger is attracted to Barth's style, "the superb iron of Barth's paragraphs, his magnificent seamless integrity and energy in this realm of prose — the specifically Christian — usually conspicuous for intellectual limpness and dishonesty" (40).[7] Barth represents a theological virility that is strong enough to say No to the human desire to play God, a No that paradoxically liberates humanity to let the flesh be flesh, a blessing of existence that nonetheless cannot carry the full weight of the divine.

Into Roger's life steps Dale Kohler, a computer whiz who wants to use science to prove the existence of God. Roger has a very Barthian reaction to this, as could be predicted from the epigraph to the book from Barth's *The Humanity of God:* "What if the result of the new hymn

7. For a careful analysis of Barth's style, see Webb, *Re-Figuring Theology.*

to the majesty of God should be a new confirmation of the hopelessness of all human activity?" The god who stands at the end of any human effort, according to Barth, cannot be God. Roger is disdainful of Dale's theological Pelagianism, the idea that we can win salvation by relying on what we know about God, but he is more sympathetic to Dale's sexual exploits. Indeed, Roger sees (or perhaps just imagines — the novel is ambiguous), in graphic detail, Dale carrying out an affair with his wife. When my students read *Roger's Version,* they are amazed that a theologian could watch (or imagine), let alone enjoy watching, his wife having sex with another man. Nonetheless, Roger argues that God was not embarrassed to become human, so by implication we also should not be ashamed of our embodiment. "Without some huge effort of swallowing shame such as Tertullian outlines, there is no way around matter" (170). Voyeurism is a sign of both Roger's religious cynicism, his weariness with so much human effort squandered on justifying and divinizing trivial human desires, and his religious freedom, his ability to transcend his own situation and see it for what it is, but without being judgmental or condemning. The phrase "swallowing shame" is significant here given Roger's detailed vision of his wife performing oral sex on Dale. Roger is resigned to the fact that the flesh has its own laws, and there is very little we can do about that. I can never quite persuade students that Roger is fully affirming the human world of lust and love while still placing it in the context of a divine mystery that redeems all of our passions, no matter how distorted or perverse.

I am glad for this failure, because I am convinced that Roger represents a self-critical moment in Updike's appropriation of Barth. Is Roger a voyeur because he does not really believe in the presence of God in the world, and thus is reduced to spying on sex as a way of replacing some sense of God's presence, or is he a voyeur because he is free from the world and thus can grant others their freedom while still maintaining a sense of God's majesty? Does Roger use Barthian theology to validate his licentious behavior with his niece? At one point he does say that his proof for the existence of God is the enormous silence and distance of God that allows us both to explore our freedom and still to worship the divine (281). Roger feels impotent about controlling the sexual desires of others, as well as his own (he does consummate his lust for his niece). Our pursuit of otherness through sex knows no limits or boundaries, he seems to acknowledge, yet we cannot force the issue of knowing God.

There is one otherness that is removed from all of this heavy panting and petting, an otherness worth guarding and protecting, even as Roger lets his other desires unfurl and sprawl.

In the end, sexual lust does have its limits. Roger is worried about the possibility of getting a venereal disease from Verna, and he knows he has committed the heresy of deliberately sinning in order to experience all the more God's forgiveness. Dale is spent from his affair, and he gives up his project of proving God's existence. Dale has sought the sacred through reason and the flesh, but neither computers nor Esther's body could properly contain his spiritual longing. Indeed, Dale appears to be losing his faith at the end of the novel because it could not withstand its collision with the bare reality of lust and flesh. Roger keeps his, because his faith is in something removed from all human effort, but it is also a faith that loves even the laws of the flesh. Roger knows that sex cannot save him, so his affair with Verna does not have the drama of Dale's relationship with Esther. By contrast, Esther is reinvigorated by their affair, but Dale has invested too much in it, and now he feels lost.

Roger, however, is not unchanged. For all of his confidence and cynicism and his talk about not being embarrassed about the flesh, he needs to be drawn back into the world, away from his Barthian isolation. He, too, needs salvation, and he needs the restoration of his marriage. He has used his passion for Barth as a way of standing apart from the world, even as he has preached a worldly faith. His affair with his niece has helped somewhat, but even more importantly, after her departure from their lives she leaves behind her daughter in their keeping. Moreover, Roger's wife decides, at the very end of the novel, to go to church, just to annoy him. He gets what he wants, but he also gets what he needs, people in his life who will tie him more closely to the finite world than before, a world he so far has spent too much time just imagining.

It is true that in his later novels Updike does not dramatize Barthian themes as directly as in his earlier ones. Indeed, he admits that he does not read Barth much anymore, although this is because he feels as if he has absorbed Barth, not because he no longer agrees with him (*Self-Consciousness*, 230-31). I would argue, however, that *In the Beauty of the Lilies* is in many ways his most Barthian novel, demonstrating that Updike can use Barth indirectly, as the theological foundation of an utterly worldly vision.

In the Beauty of the Lilies is not his first tale about the decline of religion. Most of his books explore the religious emptiness of contemporary America, and there is this line in *The Centaur:* "Priest, teacher, artist: the classic degeneration" (269). The Rabbit books are all about the loss of religion: Rabbit Angstrom is driven by a sense of guilt and unease but lacks the theological framework to make sense of his situation. Indeed, as that series progresses, religion plays a diminishing role, so that Updike is describing what is missing in Rabbit's life by a rhetoric of omission, a strategy that says a lot through what it does not say.

In the Beauty of the Lilies is both a literal description of the fall of religion and a kind of allegory about the tragic inevitability of religion's fate in the modern world. Indeed, the novel offers a panoramic investigation of the pathetic consequences of the transformation of a theocentric into a humanocentric world. The book constitutes an argument, then. Both diffuse and focused, this novel demonstrates how the cinema (rather than sex, as in his earlier novels) is America's true and most original idolatry.

Clarence Wilmot, who is loosely based on Updike's own grandfather, loses his faith not because of the atheist philosophers he reads but because of the nineteenth-century theologians who try and fail to certify revelation through historical argument. He suddenly realizes that he sees the universe as empty and absurd — which it is, of course, but from a Barthian perspective this is no reason to lose one's faith. In his student days, Clarence could balance himself above "the chilly Baltic Sea of Higher Criticism" (*In the Beauty of the Lilies,* 15), but when the vitality of faith leaves him, he is plunged into unbelief. A meeting with the moderator of his presbytery, a smug liberal minister who tries to convince him that he need not believe anything in order to remain a servant of the church, only leads him further into despair. After leaving the church, he becomes an encyclopedia salesman, finding in the distribution of undigested knowledge a fitting fate for a former minister. He ends his days in the comfort of movie theaters. Clarence does not know a God worth loving, and the other characters in the book will be haunted by this failure.

Clarence's son, Teddy, lives under a vague sense of shame at having lost this religious heritage, and, on one reading, he chooses passivity and cowardice as a response. The closest thing Teddy has to a religious experience is his realization that he should leave his New York

City career and return home to marry his high school sweetheart, Emily. He becomes a postman, a quiet job of making rounds that gives him the structure he needs. Teddy is a quiet character, and Updike's prose in this section of the novel grants his ordinary life a remarkable grace. The ordinary is made sublime as only Updike can transfigure the everyday with the subtle magic of metaphor. If there is a hero in this work, it is Teddy, and how Updike conjures his mild existence as serene and true is one of the wonders of the book.

The story of Teddy is surely meant to recall Kierkegaard's *Fear and Trembling,* a book Updike knows well. Kierkegaard argues that a tax collector could be a knight of faith and nobody would know it. For Kierkegaard, the knight of faith has given up the world, but not with a spectacular display of self-denial. The knight of faith is not infinitely resigned from the finite, because he lives as if the finite has been given back to him, at the very moment that he sacrifices it to God. For Kierkegaard, such a subtle movement of the Holy Spirit is absolutely unobservable. To live in the world but not of it, to embrace the world but also to deny it, is a paradox, a monstrous contradiction that, if achieved, would necessarily be invisible. Teddy seems to achieve precisely this trick, although Updike respects Teddy's privacy and the fundamental anonymity of all knights of faith, so that we really don't know Teddy's inner life sufficiently to judge it. Yet by portraying Teddy's life as mysteriously graced in an utterly ordinary way, Updike has come close to making Kierkegaard's invisible paradox visible.

The sense of living a special if uneventful life is passed on in a distorted way to Teddy's daughter, Essie. She has an exalted sense of herself. How could God not love her, she keeps asking of the world, since she is so very lovable? There must be a God, precisely to love her as she deserves. Of course, such self-love can never be fulfilling, because it cannot recognize the source of love in true otherness, so Essie's fate is an unhappy one. Essie pursues a career in the movies as the one place where her sense of specialness can be most dramatically validated. The movies not only reinforce her need to feel sacred and unique, but they also give countless movie-goers the sense of entering another world, where stars walk like saints upon the earth, aglow and set apart. As he did with sex in his earlier novels, Updike explores Hollywood with a mixture of fascination and mistrust, compassion and skepticism that is consistent with his vision of the world as both good and fallen.

Clark, Essie's son, is raised in such an empty environment that only a new god can save him. He joins a cult, with predictable results. However, as his fanatical world is collapsing in bullets and fire, he makes a heroic decision to save the children of the cult, a tough decision that echoes Clarence's fateful decision to leave the ministry of the established, mainline Protestant tradition, with all of its rights and benefits. This full circle of stubborn honesty unites the family, even as this family history demonstrates the slow and steady descent of religion in America.

Some readers have expressed dismay that the book is not more of a sermon. What are we to do, in the light of these various transformations of godlessness? Updike is making an argument about what the middle class in America has done to religion, the Puritan heritage that once spoke of a God powerful enough to maintain our attention, soothe our fears, and humble our egos. But Updike does not seem to be offering us any easy answers. For just that reason, this is a book whose thesis Barth, I think, would have liked very much. Religion inevitably offers more than it can deliver, and people can transform religion into various dreams of their own making. What persists is our freedom to make honest and difficult decisions, to turn away from flaccid forms of religious belief and to salvage what is left of the religious shambles we have made.

Barth did have his own taste in fiction. In a rare and revealing comment on literature in 1944, he defends a strict realism:

> I expect him [the modern novelist] to show me man as he always is in the man of today, my contemporary — and vice versa, to show me my contemporary in man as he always is. I expect the novel to give evidence in every page that its author not only knows this man properly and sees right through him, from the depths of his heart to his outward manners and mode of speaking, but also treats him honestly, i.e. loves him as he is and as he is not, without regret or contempt. Furthermore, it should tell me what its author finds special in this man — that and no more. In other words, it should have no plans for educating me, but should leave me to reflect (or not) on the basis of the portrait with which I am presented. Finally, its form should correspond to the portrait of the man whom it presents; its form should be necessary, strict and impressive to the extent that I do not forget the man I have been shown in his temporal and timeless aspects. I should be able to live with him, and indeed perhaps have to live with him again and again. (Busch, 313)

Much of this description could be quite simply applied to the work of John Updike, even though there is no evidence that Barth ever read Updike.[8] In fact, Barth was not an avid reader of novels. He was, however, a great lover of music, and he would often begin his days listening to Mozart. In Updike's foreword to a collection of essays by Barth about Mozart, Updike writes, "Karl Barth's insistence upon the otherness of God seemed to free him to be exceptionally (for a theologian) appreciative and indulgent of this world, the world at hand" (Barth, *Wolfgang Amadeus Mozart*, 7). Barth could be a very difficult theologian in his criticisms of the limitations of liberalism (think of his "Nein!" to Brunner about natural theology), so one might think that he would be attracted to the bombastic turbulence of a Beethoven rather than the playful serenity of a Mozart. Yet Barth heard in Mozart the palpable texture of divine comedy, God's resounding Yes that makes possible all of our very human No's.

Mozart's music is not the personal confession of romanticism, nor is it an orderliness that prematurely assimilates discordant elements in an organic whole. Instead, as Updike suggests, Mozart "sweeps into his magnificent lightness everything problematical, painful, and dark" (11). One of the things that Barth liked about Mozart is that he did not burden his listeners with his own creative labors. The listener is free to participate in this infinite play, without worrying about becoming self-conscious about the rules of its composition. This is true of much of Updike's fiction, which is never as confessional as that of his contemporaries, like Roth and Bellow. Indeed, much of what Barth says about Mozart could be applied to Updike, whose own prodigious energy seems, at times, equally innocent and playful, not tragic and yet saturated with an understanding of the ambiguity of life. Mozart's music is too full of notes, as it has been said, just as Updike's prose is too full of metaphors. It is that very restless fecundity that keeps both artists from appearing to be facile romantics.

Updike, too, is trying to find a countless number of ways to say Yes to life, a variety of Yes's that is as complex as creation itself. Writers of fiction, who are granted an almost religious power to create the world anew with every story, are frequently too tempted to play God

8. The one reference Barth makes to Updike is in a letter in which he requests a copy of the review Updike wrote of his book on Anselm. See Barth, *Karl Barth, Letters*, 139.

by judging their characters from the perspective of an omniscient narrative voice. This temptation to play God is, Barth always insisted, at the very heart of the religious life, and only a religion that accepts us as we are, without humiliating us or divinizing us, can check such a destructive impulse. Updike, too, suspects that religion, with its pride and its absolutes, causes the very same problems that it tries to solve. Updike thus sets out to show that God's grace sustains us in the very midst of our most petty and trivial desires and ambitions.

His message might be less dramatic than the art of those who want to tell us where the world went wrong and how we can be saved from it all. But he holds his literary mirror close to life as we actually live it. The resulting drama sometimes seems incomplete and uneasy, as if the divine Yes is muffled in all of our all-too-human noises. Yet the lightness of Updike's touch gives that Yes the last word. In *A Month of Sundays,* Marshfield surely speaks for Updike when he discusses what is at stake theologically when something is described. Marshfield observes that, for many writers, intuiting an object means describing its isolation and emptiness. "Whereas for me, puttying a window sash, bending my face close in, awakens a plain suspicion that someone in the immediate vicinity immensely, discreetly cares. God" (*Month of Sundays,* 25). We do not have to hear it, but what else could Updike be saying — or, better put, listening to — as he blesses with each sentence the very frailty of human nature, and casts our shadows into the light.

The World and the Void

Creatio ex Nihilo and Homoeroticism in Updike's *Rabbit Is Rich*

MARSHALL BOSWELL

For all their concern with middle-class mores and contemporary American history, John Updike's four novels about Harry "Rabbit" Angstrom nevertheless comprise a thorough and cogent articulation of their author's complex theological vision. This vision, a unique compound of Søren Kierkegaard's existentialist philosophy and Karl Barth's Neo-orthodox theology, not only informs Rabbit's approach to human experience but also functions as one of the tetralogy's chief organizing rubrics. Yet whereas theological concerns saturate *Rabbit, Run* and *Rabbit Redux,* the third installment in the series, *Rabbit Is Rich,* seems relatively God-free. Midway through the novel, Rabbit himself remarks that a "stony truce" has arisen between himself and God. Do not be fooled by the placid surface, however, for *Rabbit Is Rich* represents one of Updike's most provocative theological explorations. In fact, the title character of this award-winning novel arrives at spiritual redemption by embracing both homoeroticism and sodomy. The novel features not only a homosexual minister but also an episode of anal intercourse that, in its language and in its position in the completed tetralogy, positively rewrites earlier sexual episodes in the series that many of Updike's more astute readers have already interpreted in theological terms. In *Rabbit Is Rich,* John Updike boldly conceives theology from the belly of blasphemy.

Updike's blasphemous theology is fundamentally dialectical in structure. Borrowing freely from Søren Kierkegaard's existentialism and Karl Barth's fiercely orthodox thinking, Updike has developed a unique metaphysical vision founded upon the unresolved tension produced by the existence of a divine "something" and an equally divine "nothing." For both Updike and Barth, the "something" represents all of God's willed creation, while the "nothing" represents all that which God has not willed. Nothingness becomes the implied negation of all that God has created. Yet since God also created the world from nothing, he must, by extension, exist in that nothing as well, since it is the place from which he set his creation into motion. Hence the something and the nothing, the world and the void, become two sides of a single vision of divinely sanctioned creation.

Born into a Lutheran family, Updike perhaps finds in Barth's dialectic a fruitful parallel to Luther's doctrine of the "left hand of God," that destructive and irrational side of God's almighty power that creation carries, as it were, in its very womb. Updike has often expressed his peculiar fascination with this negative aspect of God. In a 1968 interview with Charles Samuels, he declared his belief that "there's a fierce God above the kind God," and that the "God who throws the lightning bolt" is the "ultimate power," the supreme entity who supercedes the "nice god . . . we can worship and empathize with" (Plath, ed., 33). Just so, it is this "fierce God" who emerges from the void, from the nothing, a realm that operates in Updike's vision not only as a necessary corollary to the "something" of creation but also as a consoling absolute in and of itself, a paradoxical origin that, beginning with *Rabbit Redux,* has moved closer and closer to the center of his own eschatological vision. In this latter regard, Updike reveals his debt not only to Kierkegaard but also to the existentialist theologians and philosophers who followed in Kierkegaard's wake, specifically Paul Tillich, Albert Camus, and, especially, Martin Heidegger, all three of whom have been the subject, at one point or another, of Updike's critical pen.[1] While Updike never wholly abandons his Lutheran roots,

1. Updike (unfavorably) reviewed Camus's first novel, *Happy Death,* in a 1972 issue of *The New Yorker.* That review has been reprinted in *Picked-Up Pieces* under its original title, "In Praise of the Blind, Black God" (279-87). His 1966 review of

he is nevertheless a child of World War II who came of age intellectually in the cool, late modernist ambience of the 1950s. Ever enthralled by paradox and tension-producing contradiction, Updike over the decades has fashioned himself into a Barthian believer with an existentialist's high esteem for the void.

George Hunt, to whom the following discussion is indebted, finds helpful formulations of Updike's vision of that void, of that nothing, first, in the novelist's introduction to Frank Sheed's *Soundings in Satanism,* and, second, in Karl Barth's writings on what he calls the "divine No," theories that form the core of Updike's own thinking on these same matters. In the *Soundings* introduction, Updike argues that Satan, or the devil, is simply the "name" given to a "nothingness" necessarily posited by God's "something" — that is, God's creation: "A potent 'nothingness' was unavoidably conjured up by God's creating *something.* The existence of something demands the existence of *something else*" (*Picked-Up Pieces,* 89). The "nothing" *is* that something else: it is a "metaphysical possibility, if not necessity," that has a positive, even active content. The presence of a something necessarily implies the possibility of a corresponding nothing. Where there is order, there must also be disorder. God's light has a shadow, just as his will has limits. And beyond that will lies all that he did not will — Dachau, Belsen, Belgrade. Beneath God's shadow lurks nightmare and death.

These latter ideas Updike derives directly from Barth, for indeed a great portion of the *Soundings* introduction consists of a lengthy quotation from Barth's *Church Dogmatics,* a useful gloss of which is provided by Hunt. For our purposes, however, we will turn to the *Dogmatics in Outline.* There, Barth succinctly affirms that "creaturely reality" is always a "*creatio ex nihilo,* a creation out of nothing." Why? Because the world is not a mere pantheistic manifestation of God but rather a distinct creation summoned into existence *by* God. If God "alone is real and essential and free," then heaven and earth, humankind and the universe "are something else, and this something else is not God, though it exists through God" (*Dogmatics in Outline,* 55). In other words, when God creates "something," there must originally have been a "nothing" beforehand. Barth deals with evil in the same teas-

---

Heidegger's brief tract, *Discourse on Thinking,* can be found in the same volume, tellingly placed in the "Religious Notes" section, alongside reviews of works by Norman Pettit, Paul Tillich, and Karl Barth (126-27).

ing, paradoxical way. In a metaphor Updike calls "frightening," Barth describes evil as "the reality behind God's back" (57).[2] It is a "repudiated and excluded thing" that nevertheless exists by the necessity of God's will. Barth's argument runs as follows: If God's will represents all that God has made — the whole of which, as Genesis insists, is "good" — then evil represents all that God "did not will." Or to quote Barth directly: "The whole realm that we term evil — death, sin, the Devil and hell — is *not* God's creation, but rather what was excluded by God's creation, that to which God said 'No.'" The "being" of evil — that is, of nothingness — has definite ontological validity, but only insofar as it is "the power of the being which arises out of the weight of the divine 'No.'" (57; Barth's emphasis). Thus Barth allows evil to exist as part of God's creation without making it a *positive* part of God's will. Rather, it is the necessary "something else."

Updike first develops this dialectical vision in *Rabbit, Run,* in which Harry has a dream of "lovely life eclipsed by lovely death" that articulates this Barthian conception of the divine Yes and No, of the "something" and the "nothing." In the dream, Rabbit sees "two perfect disks, identical in size but the one a dense white and the other slightly transparent, move toward one another slowly." The bright disk symbolizes the sun and life, while the transparent disk symbolizes the moon and death. Though the "sun" is "stronger," the "moon" manages to cover the "sun" so that "just one circle is before his eyes, pale and pure" (*Rabbit, Run,* 282/242). Life, the dream suggests, is an eclipsing of death — and vice versa. For every something, a nothing. *Both* life *and* death, however, are characterized by Rabbit as "lovely," just as Updike insists, in the *Soundings* introduction, that the nothing "thrives in proportion" to God's something: "The world always topples. A century of progressivism bears the fruit of Hitler; our own supertechnology breeds witches and warlocks from the loins of engineers" (*Picked-Up Pieces,* 90). This dialectical vision represents what Updike elsewhere in *Rabbit, Run* calls "the dark, tangled, visceral aspect of Christianity, the *going through* quality of it, the passage *into* death and suffering that redeems and inverts these things, like an umbrella blowing inside out" (237/203). The nothing is there, to be sure, but it is redeemed by the something that lies at its back. Thus redeemed, it becomes part of God's creation, though not of

2. Updike refers to this passage in the *Soundings* introduction, though he admits that he was unable to locate its actual source.

his will. Updike's God is also, dialectically, the angel of death. And although, as the narrator observes, Rabbit "has no taste" for this aspect of Christianity, he nevertheless must confront it head on.

Throughout the subsequent novels of the tetralogy, Updike charts Rabbit's steady and on-going confrontation with the death-dealing aspect of this fierce God. In *Rabbit Redux,* Harry engages in a number of intense dialogues with an African-American militant named Skeeter in which this twofold quality of creation gets applied to America's involvement in Vietnam. In *Rabbit at Rest,* as the title clearly declares, Rabbit quite literally confronts that nothing head-on, specifically by dying. Nevertheless, God seems to have been pushed to the margins of the tetralogy's third installment, *Rabbit Is Rich.* Whereas *Rabbit, Run* presented Rabbit with a character such as Reverend Eccles to challenge him in his Kierkegaardian faith, and whereas *Rabbit Redux* offered up the powerful figure of Skeeter to overturn all of Rabbit's most cherished assumptions about white justice and the God-sanctioned American dream, *Rabbit Is Rich* gives Harry no more challenging partner than his whining son, Nelson, who declares at one point that he has more faith in the veracity of the "Amityville Horror" phenomenon of the late 1970s than he does in Harry's subjective, Kierkegaardian God (161/766). Comparatively speaking, the Harry of *Rabbit Is Rich* is blithely secular. His wealth largely accounts for his new attitude: now that he is fat and prosperous, he has more or less lost his interest in the unseen world that lies beyond death. What's more, he has begun to realize that his past relationship with God and that unseen world has been, to say the least, traumatic. Midway through the novel the narrator remarks, "He doesn't want to think about the invisible anyway; every time in his life he's made a move toward it somebody has gotten killed" (162/767). All that remains of his relationship with God is a sort of metaphysical "calling card left in the pit of the stomach, a bit of lead true as a plumb bob pulling Harry down toward all those leaden dead in the hollow earth below" (231/830).

In part because of statements like these, the critics have by and large taken Rabbit at his word and assumed that theology does not play a major role in the overall thematic theater of *Rabbit Is Rich.* Generally assumed to be the economic section of the tetralogy, the novel is primarily treated as a critique of consumerism, in which money has become Rabbit's "new God." Robert Detweiler's assessment is fairly representative of the critical consensus. According to him, "Consumerism is in fact the main topic of this novel, in conjunction with sex, just as *A Month of Sundays* links sex and religion and *The Coup* blends sex and politics. It is fitting," he adds, "that *Consumer Reports* has become Rabbit's Bible" (Detweiler, *John Updike,* 175). Yet although it is certainly true that religion is not a central concern of *Rabbit Is Rich,* the metaphysical realm still occupies a large role in the novel. Updike uses this third installment of his tetralogy to explore even further the ramifications of the divinely sanctioned nothing to which Eccles and Skeeter introduced Rabbit in the two previous sections. This nothing assumes in *Rabbit Is Rich* an even more central place in Harry's overall religious vision than it has previously. Far from being an anomaly in the tetralogy's four-part structure, the novel in fact constitutes a crucial step in Updike's ongoing explication of his balanced, dialectical theology.

The first place to begin exploring this unique perspective on Barth's divine "No" is the novel's lone minister figure, the Reverend Archie Campbell, whom Rabbit derisively refers to as "Soupy." The nickname not only derives from Campbell's Soup but also serves as an oblique reference to what the Angstroms assume to be Campbell's homosexuality. Though not many readers have made the connection, Reverend Campbell is a reincarnation of Reverend Eccles from *Rabbit, Run.* Like Eccles, he is a liberal, largely earth-bound Protestant clergyman informed by a tolerant, lax, and primarily bourgeois value system. Also like Eccles, he does not attempt to serve as an exemplar of faith, or a "burning" witness of the unseen world, as the Barthian Kruppenbach advised in *Rabbit, Run.* Rather, he performs the rites and duties of the church the way Harry performs the duties of an automobile salesman. In a prenuptial meeting at the Angstroms' house intended to square away Nelson and Pru's wedding arrangements, he displays absolutely no concern about Nelson's profession of atheism. Rather, he lets himself be "brought around" to performing the proposed shotgun wedding, since, in his view, his job basically involves the pronunciation of sacred words. His is a service industry, primarily. With regard to Nelson's wedding, Rabbit notes that Campbell simply "has what they want: a church wedding, a service acceptable in the eyes of the Grace Stuhls of the world," Grace Stuhl being a gossipy crony of Ma Springer (*Rabbit Is Rich,* 200/802). The now successful Rabbit even admires in Campbell this solid sense of vocational pride. "Laugh at ministers all you want," Rabbit thinks during the wedding ceremony, "they have the words we need to hear, the ones the dead have spoken" (243/841). Of course, this view squares with

Rabbit's new "stony silence" with God, as well as with his sense of religion simply as something that makes his mother-in-law "feel better."

As a reprise of the blandly ineffectual Eccles, Campbell would seem to serve as little more than a barometer of Rabbit's new attitude. By gauging Rabbit's acceptance of this reincarnation of his old theological antagonist, we can chart his gradual transformation from youthful mystic to nominalist bourgeois. Yet Campbell's purpose in the novel is considerably more complex than that, and the key to his significance lies precisely in his homosexuality. Perhaps one reason the book's past readers have generally downplayed Campbell's centrality is because, by and large, they have not explored how the Reverend's homosexuality figures into the novel's overall symbolic terrain. Such downplaying is understandable considering how apparently insignificant his homosexuality is to the novel's plot. With the publication of *Rabbit Angstrom,* however, this assessment should change. For what these same readers had no way of knowing is that Campbell's homosexuality represents yet another link to Reverend Eccles. They had no way of knowing this because Updike cut a scene announcing Eccles's own homosexuality from the original edition of *Rabbit Redux.*

To be sure, at one point in *Rabbit, Run,* Harry speculates briefly that "Eccles is known as a fag,"[3] yet nothing comes of this observation in the novel that contains it, so readers have understandably let the remark go without much comment. And because hardly any mention at all is made of Eccles in the 1971 text of *Rabbit Redux,* he has occasioned little critical attention outside considerations of *Rabbit, Run.* In the version of *Rabbit Redux* that appears in *Rabbit Angstrom,* however, the cut scene has been restored. In his introduction, Updike comments only in passing on his rationale for the restoration, saying simply that the Reverend's "'outing' seemed to deserve a place in the full report" (*Rabbit Angstrom,* xxiii). As we shall see, the real reason for reinserting the cut scene relates to its importance in explaining the role of Eccles's 1970s counterpart, Archie Campbell. So illuminating is Eccles's own "outing" that one can almost imagine Updike, during the composition of *Rabbit Is Rich,* wishing he had not cut the scene.

3. The 1960 Knopf edition of *Rabbit, Run* on page 129 does not contain this comment. It was part of a sentence deleted from Updike's original manuscript on advice from Knopf's lawyer. The *Rabbit Angstrom* edition contains the whole sentence: "The thought flits through his brain that Eccles is known as a fag and he has become the new pet" (111).

In the now restored episode,[4] Eccles turns up on the same bus Harry rides home from work. Dressed in a pink shirt, he sits down beside Harry "with a stagey sigh" (*Rabbit Angstrom*, 436). During their brief conversation, Eccles reveals that he has not only lost his wife but has also quit the ministry, both events attributable to what he vaguely refers to as his "indiscretions." Now he works variously as a camp counselor and a P.R. agent for a theater troupe. Although his homosexuality is never commented upon directly, the attentive Rabbit senses something different about the new Eccles, particularly the "hungry way" he says, "I can be my own *man*." In the former minister's eyes "there is something new, a hardened yet startled something" (437). To Rabbit's way of thinking, Eccles has somehow "become burlier, more himself" (438).

One thing that has brought him out is the 1960s in general, his advocacy of which seems to have been the main purpose of the scene. "I think a very exciting thing is happening in Western consciousness," he tells Rabbit. "At long last, we're coming out of Plato's cave" (439). Before leaving Rabbit, moreover, he proclaims, "I think these are *mar*velous times to be alive in, and I'd *love* to share my good news with you at your leisure" (440). Eccles seems to feel at home in the sixties because the tenor of the times has given him the courage not only to "become burlier, more himself," but also to affirm his own faithless, earth-bound do-goodism. After freely admitting to Rabbit that he probably never really believed in what he preached, he goes on to characterize his belief system, both then and now, in terms that pit him squarely within the countercultural ethos of free love: "I believed . . . in certain kinds of human interrelation. I still do. If people want to call what happens in certain relationships Christ, I raise no objection. But it's not the word *I* choose anymore" (438). Examined in isolation, the scene neither adds to nor detracts from the overriding message of *Rabbit Redux.* Although Eccles's embracing of the sixties lends credence to Rabbit's rejection of the same, the novel does not need this scene in order to make its point.

On the other hand, its restoration within the scope of the "full report" makes a fairly strong impact. If nothing else, it invites us to pay more attention to Campbell's homosexuality. Whenever an element from a previous Rabbit novel reappears in its successor, that element

4. See *Rabbit Angstrom*, 436-40. The corresponding spot in *Rabbit Redux* from which the scene was excised appears on p. 199 of the original 1971 Knopf edition. It would have followed the paragraph ending with *"Amen"* (Updike's italics).

generally returns in a dialectically opposite manner. So seems to be the case with this issue of homosexual ministers. Whereas in *Rabbit Redux* Eccles's homosexuality is presented negatively as part of the novel's widespread critique of the 1960s, in *Rabbit Is Rich* that homosexuality returns in a positive light. In addition to his admiration of Campbell's professional poise, Rabbit in a way also envies the minister's gayness.

> Campbell taps out the bowl of his pipe with a finicky calm that conveys to Harry the advantages to being queer: the world is just a gag to this guy. He walks on water; the mud of women and making babies never dirties his shoes. You got to take off your hat: nothing touches him. That's real religion. (*Rabbit Is Rich,* 202/803)

Rarely does Harry give even the slightest bit of credence to conventional notions of theologically sanctioned morality. As the narrator of *Rabbit at Rest* directly affirms, "Rabbit never had much use for old-fashioned ethics" (*Rabbit at Rest,* 400/1413). His attitude toward the Reverend's sexuality is no exception. Rather than view Campbell's homosexuality as a sin, for instance, he sees it as a way to *avoid* sin. His sexual activity does not involve the planting of "seed" into the fertile "mud" of the female womb, nor does it lead to the production of fallen human beings, each of whom is stained from birth with the taint of original sin. Instead, he practices a sterile and therefore *innocent* sexuality free of the burden of ontological guilt. In this regard, the gay Campbell is the perfect minister, an outsider to the heterosexual world of guilt-making activity and a suitable messenger of the otherwise unattainable sinless path.

The passage above also contains a subtle pun that directs us to an additional, and considerably more significant, feature of Campbell's homosexuality. When Rabbit reflects that "nothing touches him," Updike intends the first word of the clause to serve as both an indefinite pronoun and a noun. In other words, the "nothing" does in fact touch this serenely innocent man of the cloth. Here, too, Campbell's homosexuality is a factor, for in *Rabbit Is Rich,* that "nothing" is intricately and consistently associated with, of all things, the anal cavity. As many previous critics have (sometimes squeamishly) noted, *Rabbit Is Rich* is strangely preoccupied with anal activity. Judie Newman writes, "Rarely in a novel, with the possible exception of *Tender is the Night* or *Portnoy's Complaint,* have so many major events taken place in bathrooms" (*John Updike,* 62). She goes on to assert that the "scatological emphasis is relentless," citing for evidence both the repeated use of the word "shit" and "Harry's fascination with homosexual practices." No mere gesture of provocation on Updike's part, this "scatological emphasis" serves as part of a complex metaphorical network linking money with feces, the anus with the void, and the void with the divine nothing hinted at by Skeeter in the previous installment. It is this "nothing" that touches Campbell, and it is this same "nothing" that is beginning to get a handle on Harry.

Updike connects the novel's scatological and theological preoccupations through a deft linking of the anal cavity with the grave. He prepares the way for this striking piece of symbolism through his extensive use of a "tunnel," or chute, motif. The "tunnel" image appears most overtly in the episodes devoted to Rabbit's jogging. These scenes differ from their *Rabbit, Run* counterparts by their association not so much with *angst* as with a concern for health. The year is, after all, 1979, when the fitness boom was just crashing down on America. Although Rabbit's running obviously ties into the novel's overarching entropy theme — the book is set, again, during the late seventies' "energy crisis" — it also resonates with that theme's related issue, the persistent pressure exerted by the buried dead. Each time Rabbit runs, for instance, he contemplates the dead, who "stare upwards" at him as he imagines himself "treading on them all," with this audience of buried loved ones "cheering him on" (*Rabbit Is Rich*, 141/748). Significantly, in the second of these jogging excursions the narrator describes Rabbit entering "a tunnel" under which the dead pine needles form "a carpet" (141/748).

The tunnel is not just a passageway to death, however, for earlier in the novel Rabbit considers the life of his possible daughter Annabelle Byer as a "bloody tunnel of growing and living, of staying alive" (34/651). This tunnel image is in turn amended to a reverie concerning the "secret message carried by genes," a message Rabbit has elsewhere conceived as pushing through "those narrow (/DNA) coils" (86/698). From these coordinate points we can begin to map the meaning behind the tunnel motif: it is a symbol for the passage of life, the "bloody tunnel of growing and living," at one end of which lies sinful conception and at the other end of which lies the void that awaits us beyond death. Updike informs us about this concluding destination in a golf-playing sequence that directly echoes Rabbit's metaphysically enhanced golf game, twenty years earlier, with Reverend Eccles. On a day much concerned with anxiety and athletic grace, and one characterized by a nagging "feeling he should be somewhere else," Rabbit imagines "the fairways as chutes to nowhere" (178/782).

In sum, the "tunnels" or "chutes" that appear and reappear in *Rabbit Is Rich* serve not only as unsettling refashioning of Bunyan's Road of Life but also as telescoped figures for the novel's complex linking of themes such as original sin, heredity, and death. By introducing this motif in the golf-playing sequence, Updike also connects this novel's exploration of immortality to that of *Rabbit, Run.* In that earlier novel, Harry perceived the game as a window into that "unseen world" whose existence he sensed so keenly. The "something behind all this" that Rabbit once imagined was calling out to him made its most forceful appearance on the golf course, via a perfect swing that inspired Rabbit to shout, "That's *it!*" (*Rabbit, Run,* 134/116). Now that the unseen world is revealed to be "nowhere," this latter golf-playing episode, coupled with its employment of the tunnel motif, also functions as a continuation of the divine "No" explored in *Rabbit Redux.*

Indeed, in this third installment of the Angstrom saga, the "something" beyond the quotidian real has become a "nothing," while the God who sanctions that unseen world has become, for Rabbit, exclusively the "nobody" who hovered over his home before the fire that, in *Rabbit Redux,* took Jill's life. Nobody, or perhaps No-body, is the Creator who produced the world from nothing and whom Skeeter imagined as Chaos personified. For Rabbit, this God is the same "gentleman" who has withdrawn from his life, leaving only a "calling card . . . in the pit of the stomach," and it is this same Nobody who absorbs the dead into the void that is his domain. That Rabbit's God has in fact become "Nobody" is made clear in a brief, deceptively quotidian exchange between Janice and Harry concerning their role in creating Nelson's problems. First, Rabbit speculates, "You sometimes wonder . . . how badly you yourself fucked up a kid like that," to which Janice sensibly remarks, "We did what we could." Then she adds, "We're not God." "Nobody is," Rabbit responds (*Rabbit Is Rich,* 312/904). His comeback — with which, significantly, Updike ends the chapter — works as both an offhand response to Janice's clichéd homily and a subtle announcement of this novel's conception of the Creator. In other words, Rabbit and Janice are not God. Nobody is God.

In this more than in any other aspect of its resonant and complex conception, *Rabbit Is Rich* functions as a continuation of the dark, nihilistic vision spelled out in *Rabbit Redux.* In both cases, the void being posited is associated with the kingdom of death, and yet at the same time Updike is careful to insist that this kingdom is also God's kingdom. Where the Christian nihilism of *Rabbit Is Rich* differs from that of its bitter, unsettling predecessor is in its almost buoyant attitude. Once again, an element from a past Rabbit novel has reappeared in its successor in an entirely new light. The nothing Rabbit encounters in his ripe middle age is not Skeeter's violent "world of hurt" but rather an almost comforting void similar to the "inner dwindling" that Rabbit now associates with freedom (*Rabbit Is Rich,* 97/708). Almost all the links of Updike's rich symbolic chain are now in place. The tomb connects to the anal cavity as well as to the tunnel images that serve as this novel's governing leitmotif. The anal cavity in turn becomes yet another tunnel, for both the tunnel and the anal cavity lead to a void associated with death. Finally, the tunnel leads to "nowhere," to the void, a vast nothing that, in Updike's dialectical vision, remains the province Nobody, the God of death and the progenitor of the *creatio ex nihilo.*

What's more, this kingdom of entropic death, this nowhere with its resident deity, Nobody, also has a spokesperson who is, in almost every way, Skeeter's polar opposite. That spokesperson is Archie Campbell, the soothing, professional minister in touch with the nothing. One night after returning from one of Reverend Campbell's prenuptial counseling sessions, Nelson caustically relates to his parents the substance of Campbell's teachings: "He keeps talking about the church being the be-riide of Ke-riist. I kept wanting to ask him, Whose little bride are you?" Then, in one of the novel's most spectacularly provocative moments of bland obscenity, Nelson supplies the unexpected answer. "I mean, it's ob*scene,*" he whines. "What does He do, fuck the church up the ass?" (*Rabbit Is Rich,* 213/813-14). Although Nelson is making a not very funny joke here, the joke nevertheless feeds into Updike's overriding theological speculations. With this passage, Updike in effect literalizes the homoerotic underpinnings of John Donne's "Batter My Heart, Three-Personed God; For You." In Campbell's "real religion," the religion of Nobody and his soothing empty Nowhere, the church is indeed a homosexual bride. Consequently, the consummation of this bride with its Christ is tantamount to a sort of divine sodomy, a conjoining that leads not to new life but to the empty void of Nowhere, Nobody's kingly realm.

All of this oblique and indirect material serves as background for

Rabbit's climactic, life-affirming act of sodomy with Thelma Harrison, a strikingly graphic episode (graphic even for Updike) that has left many past readers slightly bewildered. To be sure, regarded simply on its own, the scene is slightly bewildering (though it is no less effective because of that). It appears to be included primarily as part of what Updike describes elsewhere as the tetralogy's charting of Rabbit's increasingly baroque sexual life. He writes,

> In each novel — this much was a conscious decision — [Rabbit's] sexual experience is deepened, his lifelong journey into the bodies of women is advanced. Fellatio, buggery — the sexual specifics are important, for they mark the stages of a kind of somatic pilgrimage that, smile though we will, is consciously logged by most men and perhaps by more women than admit it. (*Odd Jobs,* 870)

What Updike does not say here — because he is in no way obliged to — is that this "somatic pilgrimage" is also, time and again, a metaphor for Rabbit's pilgrimage toward that unseen world, the world beyond life. He begins, in *Rabbit, Run,* expecting to find that something through intercourse with his lover in that novel, Ruth. Instead, he is tricked by Nature, who "leads you up like a mother and as soon as she gets her little price (/contribution) leaves you with nothing" (*Rabbit, Run,* 84-85/75). By *Rabbit Is Rich,* Harry is experienced enough in sexual matters to expect that nothing. As such, he is finally ready to embrace it. Anal intercourse makes that embrace possible.

The episode with Thelma is preceded by Rabbit's airplane ride to the Caribbean. Aloft, Harry can see, as he never could on land, how insignificant humans must look to God/Nobody. Earlier in the novel, while transporting his silver coins, he has a strange premonition of this insight: "now he can imagine how through God's eyes . . . he and Janice might look below: two ants trying to make it up the sides of a bathroom basin" (*Rabbit Is Rich,* 371/958). The "bathroom basin" is a particularly nice touch. Rabbit experiences another moment of God-like insight as he looks down from the plane window and sees "how easily the great shining shoulder of the ocean could shrug and immerse and erase all traces of men" (389/974). Immediately after making this observation, Rabbit feels the plane lift in altitude until "no white caps can be detected" and "immensity becomes nothingness" (389/974). Fittingly, the plane at this point becomes for Harry another tunnel leading to nowhere. With its "droning without and its party mutter and tinkle within," it seems, all at once, "all of the world there is." Rather than feel terror at this confinement, however, Rabbit experiences, of all things, God's presence:

> God, having shrunk in Harry's middle years to the size of a raisin lost under the car seat, is suddenly great again, everywhere like a radiant wind. Free: the dead and the living alike have been left five miles below in the haze that has annulled the earth like breath on a mirror. (390/975)

The God who "is suddenly great again" is clearly Nobody, in whose realm death and life are both annulled, as is the earth and all its guilt-making activity. The plane ride becomes for Rabbit a precursor to that final journey into the "eternal release from the hell of having to perform" (91/703), and it fills him not with fear and trembling but with a joy "that makes his heart pound."

More to the point, the plane ride is also a precursor to his tryst with Thelma Harrison, Ronnie's wife. Rabbit ends up with her through some typical late-seventies spouse-swapping. At first, he is disappointed to be assigned Thelma, for he has coveted Cindy Murkett all that summer, an infatuation born mostly from his financial envy of her husband, Webb. Rabbit even regards the swapping arrangements in financial terms, noting how Webb, more so than any of the other husbands involved, "has the treasure to barter" (407/990). His ending up with Thelma is a redeeming accident, then, for it forces him to accept his new sexual partner wholly on human, rather than financial, terms, something he has not done for some time now, even within the scope of his own marriage. His superficial mass-marketed fantasies about youth, money, and sexuality are first punctured by Thelma's unexpected allure, an allure he was unable to detect in the throes of his Murkett worship, for when she emerges from the bathroom he finds himself surprisingly stirred by her nakedness. Thelma continues to surprise him by her proclamations of love, of which Harry had been completely unaware. What she loves about him are precisely those qualities that Updike affirms about his hard-hearted hero — his selfishness, his faith in himself and others, his mystical ability to remind others of their specialness. "You're so grateful to be anywhere," she purrs, "you think that tacky club and that hideous house of Cindy's are heaven. It's wonderful. You're so glad to be alive" (418/1001). In making these confessions, Thelma, too, reminds Harry of *his* specialness. Thelma, it turns out, represents another of what Joyce Markle has termed Updike life-givers (Markle, 3).

This is particularly poignant considering that Thelma is dying from lupus. Accordingly, their love-making is not regenerative in the conventionally biological sense. For one thing, Thelma is menstruating. For another, they never perform heterosexual intercourse, opting instead for sodomy and masturbation. Late in the evening, they even micturate on one another. Thelma's movements are also surrounded by images of death, particularly in the way she "advances timidly, as if wading into water" (*Rabbit Is Rich,* 414/997). Ultimately, Thelma's close proximity to death makes her the third of Rabbit's three mistresses of the nothing, the first two being Ruth *(Rabbit, Run)* and Jill *(Rabbit Redux).* Yet of all these women, Thelma is the most redeeming. Not only is she the one mistress who sees Rabbit for what he is and loves him as such, but she is also the only one who embraces death in the way Updike advises as early as *Rabbit, Run,* where death and life are regarded as equally beautiful spheres that merely eclipse one another in repeated succession.

Thelma leads Rabbit to this serene acceptance of death through her selfless act of sodomy. Updike's description of Harry's entry is both memorably graphic and thematically important.

> It seems it won't go, but suddenly it does. The medicinal odor of displaced Vaseline reaches his nostrils. The grip is tight at the base but beyond, where a cunt is all velvety suction and caress, there is no sensation: a void, a pure black box, a casket of perfect nothingness. He is in that void, past her tight ring of muscle. (417/1000)

Here, finally, Harry experiences the "perfect nothingness" that will await him after death, a void figured as a "pure black box, a casket." This box is markedly different from the "velvety suction and caress" of the female vagina, with its deceptive promise of "something" and its consolation prize of "nothing." The "nothing" here is no consolation prize: it is the prize itself. With this act of anal intercourse, Harry has finally experienced the "underside" of sexuality, which is to say he now knows both the "something" and the "nothing" that sexual intercourse reveals to us. In the same way that Updike, taking his cue from

Karl Barth, insists that God's creation contains a dark side as well as a side of light, so, too, does he show us, in this unforgettable penultimate episode in the Caribbean, the dialectical nature of sex. This is the unexpected "lesson" that Thelma imparts to Harry: lovely death lies just beneath lovely life, and both are parts of God's creation.

And an oddly redeeming lesson it is, for after this encounter with the void hinted at by Thelma's "pure black box," Harry relocates, for the first time since the early part of *Rabbit, Run,* that elusive old spark from his days as a basketball hero:

> He dares confide to Thelma, because she has let him fuck her up the ass in proof of love, his sense of miracle at being himself, himself instead of somebody else, and his old inkling, now fading in the energy crunch, that there was something that wanted him to find it, that he was here on earth on a kind of assignment. (419/1001)

With this overt quotation from *Rabbit, Run* — "there was something that wanted him to find it" (127/111) — Updike places this scene squarely within the context of the tetralogy's ongoing examination of the interrelatedness of the divine something and the divine nothing. Ruth first introduces him to that nothing in *Rabbit, Run.* In *Rabbit Redux,* Skeeter continues this "education" by forcing Rabbit to acknowledge the fact that this nothing, and its association with death, is not only an integral part of God's creation but might also be "God's holy face." Thelma takes Rabbit even further into the nothing by showing him its curiously redeeming capacity. Indeed, as this passage and its *Run*-era echoes testify, Rabbit and Thelma's act of sodomy functions as a direct dialectical counterpart to Rabbit's ultimately disappointing sexual experience with Ruth. In that earlier episode, Rabbit sleeps with Ruth hoping to access the "something" that "wants him to find it." Instead, he comes to learn that sex "leaves you with nothing" (*Rabbit, Run,* 85/75). The Rabbit who meets up with Thelma is the benefactor of Ruth's and Skeeter's lessons, and as such he is better prepared to understand the nothing with which Nature leaves us. Thelma also demonstrates to Rabbit that this "pure black box" is almost indistinguishable from the "something" that Rabbit has been searching for his entire adult life. Having been introduced to this insight, Rabbit finds that he has regained that "old inkling" about the "something," and he has done so through Thelma's wholly selfless gift of the "nothingness" within her, a nothingness we all possess and whose messenger is no less than Reverend Campbell. While languishing in that void, Harry is in Campbell's domain. This is what Updike means by "fucking the church up the ass."

So resoundingly upbeat and apparently conclusive is Rabbit's Caribbean encounter with the nothing that it would seem to mark the end of the Angstrom saga. This perception is corroborated by the novel's coda-like detailing of Rabbit and Janice's happy move into their own home, complete with a sunken living room, just like Webb Murkett's. Because of these redeeming elements in the novel's denouement — so different from the deadly accidents beclouding the conclusions of the two previous novels — most of the critical work on *Rabbit Is Rich* has understandably treated the text as the obvious culmination of the Rabbit series. Unlike its predecessors, *Rabbit Is Rich* seems to wrap up nicely, with all its threads tied neatly into a bow. In fact, that upbeat ending merely balances out Rabbit's equally upbeat encounter with the nothing. Through the birth of Pru and Nelson's child, Rabbit understands how his eventual passage through the tunnel of death will represent merely the end of a journey that will be played out over and over again long after he is gone.

The baby, a girl, is christened Judy, another "J" name that links her to Rebecca June and Jill, Rabbit's two other "dead" daughters. In this novel of energy lost and found, Judy arrives on the last page as the long-awaited daughter Rabbit keeps looking for but can never keep. The language Updike uses to describe her echoes exactly the same language he used some twenty years ago to describe Rabbit's infant daughter, Becky:

> Oblong cocooned little visitor, the baby shows her profile blandly . . . the tiny stitchless seam of the closed eyelid aslant, lips bubbled forward beneath the whorled nose as if in delicate disdain, she knows she's good. You can feel in the curve of the cranium she's feminine, that shows from the first day. (*Rabbit Is Rich*, 467/1045)

Compare this passage with its sister passage from *Rabbit, Run:*

> In the suggestion of pressure behind the tranquil lid and in the tilt of the protruding upper lip he reads a delightful hint of disdain. She knows she's good. What he never expected, he can feel she's feminine, feels something both delicate and enduring in the arc of the long pink

> cranium, furred in bands with black licked swatches. (*Rabbit, Run*, 217/187)

The echoes are so precise as to demand comparison. Yet they also serve as a harbinger of more to come. Though Rabbit has finally got the daughter he once lost, that daughter still must go through the "bloody tunnel of growing" that will mar this goodness. What's more, that same daughter, as the book's final sentence tells us, is really "Another nail in his coffin" (*Rabbit Is Rich*, 467/1045). Rabbit's sense of a new beginning is fraught with this necessary knowledge of his own death, just as his introduction to the void that awaits him is haunted by that actual, fateful journey into the void itself. In its numerous direct references to *Rabbit, Run*, *Rabbit Is Rich* serves both as a long-deferred resolution of that book and as an opening to one more final chapter, a fourth installment, *Rabbit at Rest*, that will provide a similarly deferred resolution of the Angstrom saga as a whole.

Learning to Die

Work as Religious Discipline in Updike's Fiction

WESLEY A. KORT

The center of religious interest in John Updike's fiction, I believe, is the problem his narrators and characters have with their vocations, that is, with their jobs and responsibilities. Many of them expect work to be a way of connecting their own moral or spiritual potential with what lies outside themselves and of connecting themselves with something of greater significance to which their work can contribute. They have these expectations because they inherit, directly or indirectly, a Protestant belief in daily work as a religious vocation. This belief, however, has begun to wane because of disconnections between it and the kinds of work his narrators and characters find themselves doing and because the culture leads them to think of themselves as more important than the work they do or than that to which it contributes. Given these changes, the center of religious interest in Updike's fiction becomes the work it performs on the problem of work itself. The principal, religiously important product of that work is the construction of an understanding of work that stands between the Protestant doctrine of vocation and its cultural, narcissistic contrary. That understanding, I will argue, is one that warrants self-actualization in and through respect for the realities of other people's lives.

I

Updike's fictional history of twentieth-century America, *In the Beauty of the Lilies,* while it follows a family, primarily charts the changing character of work in American culture. The novel epitomizes Updike's fascination with work or vocation as the locus of religious behavior and meaning, and the history it narrates is the increasingly problematic status of work in American culture. In the novel American culture finally fails as a culture because it no longer relates people by means of their work to something beyond their own interests that is more important than themselves. Work, when it fails to give people something to live for, turns out to be only a way to die.

While the opening events of the novel — Mary Pickford's faint from exhaustion during the take of a film and the Reverend Clarence Wilmot's loss of Christian faith and vocation — seem unrelated to one another and to the meaning of work, they mark an exchange in American culture from a shared belief in religion's importance for understanding identity to a shared fascination for image-making. This exchange shifts cultural attention from the relation of persons with something more important than themselves to something that ultimately reflects their own self-projections.

Clarence Wilmot abandons his faith and vocation because Christian theology, he believes, particularly in its Old Princeton Presbyterian form, cannot adapt to the swiftly changing cultural situations of early twentieth-century America. Wilmot finds a growing gap between the theology of Charles Hodge and Benjamin Warfield and what he reads in the daily newspapers. This problem becomes acute when it moves to the question of work, as it does with the crisis created by a strike at the local mill. Not only does Christian theology have nothing to offer the conversations about this crisis but, at least in the Presbyterian form that Wilmot knows, it also sides with management against the workers because it has nothing substantial to say about factory work.

What Wilmot keeps, when he gives up his Christian faith and vocation, is the belief that work must be validated by a larger structure of meaning which houses it and which it serves. In a word, if work cannot derive its significance from a Christian account of the worker's world and relation to it, it needs something analogous to religion as a substitute for that earlier validation. Wilmot finds this alternative in his new job as encyclopedia salesman. Because the encyclopedias provide an encompassing and all-inclusive textual account of the world, Wilmot takes them as a substitute for Christian doctrine. He refers to the product he sells as "a commercially inspired attempt to play God, by creating in print a replica of Creation" (*In the Beauty of the Lilies,* 101). The only problem is that this alternative structure, somewhat like Presbyterianism, is a bit too static and proper, too exclusive in its promotion of what is respectable and legitimate. It informs but does not reveal. Consequently, Wilmot finds himself with increasing frequency in movie theaters where the "skirts of the supposedly safe, chaste, and eventless world" were lifted "to reveal an anatomy of passion and cruel inequity" (107). Encyclopedias provide an intellectual coherence, but movies provide the passionate connection with his world that Wilmot needs.

Wilmot's son Teddy fulfills the need for a meaningful context for work when, after some floundering, he enters the postal service. It is a job that, as his mother puts it, can "take him out of himself" (138), can relate him to something larger and more meaningful to which his work contributes. Teddy finds significance in mail delivery not only because he believes that he is "knitting together your society by carrying the mails" (204) but also because he still believes that the society and its communications relate him, by his work, to something more important than himself and his efforts.

When the third generation tries to address the question of work, it turns to another culturally unifying medium, film. Essie, in her movie career, takes her grandfather, the Presbyterian minister, as her inspiration because he "held a promise of lifting her up toward the heavenly realm where movie stars flickered and glowed" (270-71). While movies may hold some kind of transcendent status in the culture, the film industry seems to have lost the luster and integrity of the Mary Pickford era. To Essie work in the film industry feels a lot like prostitution.

This gradual loss of a value or meaning structure that allows work to connect persons to something larger and more important than themselves drives Essie's son Clark into an apocalyptic Christian community. He makes this move not only because his job in a Colorado ski resort seems vapid but also because the community's leader, Jessie, articulates a powerful and, apparently, attractive theology of Christian vocation: "'Except a seed dieth, it is not quickened into life.' First Corinthians, fifteen thirty-six. That's the whole Christian religion in a nutshell" (452-53). This theology of submitting the self to a larger good restores urgency to work, and Clark, who takes the name Esau, describes to his mother the difference between his and her attitudes toward work in these terms: while she has spent her life working for herself, he will be doing Jessie's work (456). The problem, of course, is that Jessie, the leader of the group, instead of viewing vocation in light of the Corinthian verse — that is, as a way of subordinating self to something more important — uses his position to secure self-attention.

The distance of the apocalyptic Temple of True and Actual Faith from the rest of American culture reveals distortions on both sides. The culture, in its loss of what Jessie presents as "the whole Christian religion in a nutshell," becomes a context in which work loses meaning and in which people are unrelated to anything outside themselves from which significance can be derived. But Jessie, isolated from the cultural contingencies, becomes himself not only the one for whom the members labor but also the one who commandeers multiple vocational roles, becoming a husband to all of the women and a father to all of their children. Christian vocation is not possible in American culture, but a Christianity that is isolated from the offices and responsibilities of ordinary life sponsors self-serving and finally narcissistic doctrines of vocation.

The apocalyptic tones of *In the Beauty of the Lilies* suggest the magnitude of the problem that American culture faces. The dissociation of religious belief from the culture has radically negative consequences because it prevents people in their daily work from having a relation to a structure of meaning that can impart to them a sense of purpose or direction, or from which they can derive significance. This problem has played a continuing and centering role in Updike's fiction from the beginning. No vocation, whether public (teacher, Christian minister, artist, carpenter) or private (husband, parent, child, sibling, or friend), is exempt from this loss of significance. All arenas of daily activity increasingly fail to impart a sense of purpose or significance because they are less and less contained by a structure of meaning to which a person is connected by means of work. The result is not only a trivializing of work but also an emptying of identity and a loss of confidence in American culture.

II

An earlier generational study of the growing problem of work is Updike's most complex novel, his Hawthorne-like romance *The Centaur.* What unifies its several layers is the uncertainty Peter Caldwell, the narrator, experiences about his own vocation as an artist and its relation to the vocations of his father, George Caldwell, as teacher and parent. As an adult in his canvas-cluttered New York City loft, Peter asks, *"Was it for this that my father gave up his life?"* (*The Centaur,* 270).

George Caldwell, whom Updike in an interview refers to as "a worker" (Plath, ed., 123),[1] is actually a man who is having trouble accepting his offices as teacher, husband, father, and son. Although recognized in his small eastern Pennsylvania town as a high school science teacher, he does not enjoy his work or believe that it is truly effective. He has become painfully aware of his own inadequacies, of student indifference or hostility, and of the principal's power. He is no more confident as a husband — he dislikes sex and resents his wife's decision to live outside of town in the country. He also resents his father who, although a Christian minister, died without faith and left his family in debt.

Despite these feelings, George avoids self-pity or self-preoccupation because he is a deeply charitable person. He shows respect for people, volunteers assistance with what Peter calls a "usual impulsive Christianity," and brings to conversations "a cavernous capacity for caring that dismayed strangers" (*The Centaur,* 82-83). To young Peter's chagrin, for example, George chooses to ignore the fact that a hitchhiker they pick up is homosexual, and George proceeds to engage the man in earnest conversation. A similar thing happens when they encounter a drunkard on the street. The man accuses George of wanting to pervert Peter, and George, rather than ignore the man or defend himself, engages him in conversation.

George seems to sum up the beliefs that sponsor his charity when he responds to the proverb his father-in-law often cites, "Time and tide wait for no man." The platitude implies that human beings are victims, and George finds that hard to accept. "'I was a minister's son,'" he says. "'I was brought up to believe, and I still believe it, that God

1. Updike immediately goes on to say of George as a worker, "It's bad to live in that kind of pressure, but it also dignifies a lot of your daily routines. It gives a purpose to your life. Survival becomes kind of sacred."

made Man as the last best thing in his Creation. If that's the case, who are this time and tide that are so almighty superior to us?'" (63). This Christian evaluation of human beings sponsors the high expectations of himself and other people that George brings to his responsibilities for and conversations with other people.

Although George sounds secure in the Christian belief that human beings are more important than natural forces, it soon becomes clear that this belief is assailed. For one thing, his father, from whom it is derived, died without faith, and George is afraid of losing his own. In addition, as a science teacher, George knows the distance between Christian and scientific descriptions of the relation of human beings to their world. In his lecture on the origins of human life George makes clear that in the scientific account human beings, rather than being the culminating consequence of a divine plan, hold an extremely tenuous and insignificant position relative to time and space. Finally, George is not as secure as his statement of belief makes him look because he has trouble getting through the day. Late, rushed, hampered by broken cars, snowstorms, and poverty, George seems more a victim of time and tide than "the last best thing" in God's creation.

All of this comes to focus in the question that is uppermost in George's mind, the question of death or of relinquishing life. Strangers find themselves "involved, willy-nilly, in a futile but urgent search for the truth" (83), for an answer to this question. His answer derives from three sources: scientific, mythological, and Christian. Drawing from a scientific source George contends that life evolves cooperatively and that it requires the surrender of individual members to the good of the whole (42). From the mythological source comes the force and significance of human decisions; the way to overcome victimization by death is to make a sacrificial decision to give one's life for the sake of another. That answer is embodied in the Greek myth of Chiron, which structures the novel, particularly Chiron's willingness to give life to Prometheus by his own sacrificial death.

The third, more Christian strand constituting an answer to the question of dying arises from scattered and unexpected encounters. For example, when George and Peter meet the drunkard who asks the question, "'*Are you ready to die?*'" (157), George is quick to press the man, "'Are *you* ready to die?'" "'What do *you* think the answer is?'" (158). Rather than answer, the drunkard turns on George and accuses him of perverting the boy, and George later says to Peter, "'That man brought me to my senses. We gotta get you into where it's warm. You're my pride and joy, kid; we gotta guard the silver'" (160). The man had directed George's attention away from the search for an answer to dying and had brought home to him the truth of his vocation as a father, the fact that he had an obligation to protect his son from and within a world marked by misunderstanding and distortion. Wanting to avoid the mistake of those who went West to find gold and in their frenzy ignored silver, George realizes that his search for an answer to dying jeopardizes his responsibilities as a father. While before he had seen his son only as a reason for not dying, he now sees him as a reason for living.

Another such moment occurs when George remembers something his father had said. They had walked past a tavern from which they heard laughter, and his father, unlike young George, was not offended by it. Instead, he said, half in jest, "'All joy belongs to the Lord.'" George took that "to heart," concluding that "Wherever in the filth and confusion and misery, a soul felt joy, there the Lord came and claimed it as his own . . . wherever a moment of joy was felt, there the Lord stole and added to His enduring domain" (296). Despite his resentment toward his father, George accepts this belief that common joys can relate human experiences to an "enduring domain."

George's complex answer to dying and to the meaning of his obligations in life allows him to make a decision. When he learns that he does not have a serious illness, he is elated, not because he will continue to live, but because his work can continue to support the little joys around him — his wife's joy in the land, his father-in-law's joy in the newspaper, and his son's joy in the future. His own offices of son, husband, father, teacher, and neighbor can be accepted because by giving himself to and in them he can sustain the joys of others and thereby contribute to that larger, enduring domain.

George's belief in the meaning of work stands as a transition between the Christian vocation of his father and the artistic vocation of his son. Since his boyhood, Peter has been pursuing his vocation by, as he puts it, trying to stretch himself "like a large transparent canvas" upon Nature "in the hope that . . . the imprint of a beautiful and useful truth would be taken" (293). At the time of Peter's narration, this attempt to arrest "time and tide" by framing them within his own sensitivity seems to have exhausted or failed him, and the resulting lack turns his attention to his father — *"Was it for this that my father gave up his life?"* (270). The narrative portrait is of George as "a worker," as a man who is not self-preoccupied but who charitably fulfills his responsibilities toward others. The concrete reality of his working father provides an alternative to the pattern of flight and self-preoccupation that Peter heretofore had been following.

It is crucial to recognize the transitional status of George's doctrine of vocation. Although containing Christian elements, it is an improvisation that begins to take on the qualities of a personal style. It makes George eccentric and memorable. In addition, the theology that supports the Christian element in his sense of work tends to divorce God from daily life as an arena of work. As George says to the Reverend March, God's mercy "never changes anything at all," and it is infinite primarily in the sense that it is "at an infinite distance" (253). A world separated from God and God's grace is a world that loses potential as a positive religious resource, and George can continue to understand his offices and work in it only by improvising a complex doctrine of vocation made up of scientific and classical as well as Christian ingredients.

Of the Farm, a companion piece to *The Centaur,* presents an even more sharply drawn sense of distance between the artist and his parents. The narrator visits his mother in her eastern Pennsylvania rural home with his recently wedded second wife. He comes to the farm from New York City, where he works in advertising, and his encounter with his mother, especially because of her integrity and resourcefulness, evokes from him the poetic language in which the story is told. Joey Robinson realizes, when he returns to his origins, how much of value in his background has slipped away from him in the course of his career and what a disappointment he has been to his mother: "My mother had wanted me to become a poet or, failing that, a teacher; in the end I had disappointed both her expectations" (*Of the Farm,* 80). Compared to his mother, Joey feels insubstantial and stands above the material he narrates with nothing more than the power of words. Although he reclaims some healing memories by his visit, especially the memory of his dead father and his youthful self, and is poetically empowered to narrate, he appears more derivative and tentative than the women around him, his mother and wife.

The problem Joey experiences is articulated by the pastor whose sermon he hears. The principal theological point is put this way: "We are all here farmers or the sons and daughters of farmers, so we know how the lowly earthworm aërates the soil. Likewise, language aërates the barren density of brute matter with the penetrations of the mind, of the spirit" (151). There are two ways in which this affirmation reveals Joey's problem. First, it suggests that words can do what, in the theological background from which the comment derives its force, should be done by the person. When words and persons are dissociated, as they are in Joey, especially given his work in advertising, then the narrator's or poet's work, as epitomized by Joey's expansive feelings of dominating his material, become self-serving. Second, the parent whom Joey, like Peter Caldwell, admires and celebrates is not brute or dead but very much alive. Rather than brought to life by words, she gives life to the narrator's words. The artist's parents, people who were both strong and sacrificial, are the ones who continue to carry the reality, with its potential force and meaning, upon which language depends, and who make available to Joey what the pastor later calls "the concrete reality of Christ" (152). The material gives rise to language as much as, if not more than, the language gives rise to the material.

III

The artists in Updike's fiction, who are often also narrators and who are also often close to the author, hold a potentially problematic position by virtue of their dissociation as workers from the practice and meaning of Christian vocation. What is crucial to an understanding of Updike's fiction is that his artists and narrators and, by implication, he himself, do not define themselves as religious exceptions to this general situation, as is the case, for example, in the fiction of Walker Percy. Updike identifies with those who suffer the problem rather than either standing in judgment on them or distinguishing his religiously identified characters (and thereby himself) from them. Suffering and contending with the problem of work comprise the religiously defined labor in which his characters, narrators, and, one may venture, Updike himself, are engaged.

It is in this light that Rabbit Angstrom and characters like him in Updike's fiction should be viewed. The narrator of *Rabbit, Run* leaves the reader in no doubt about why Harry has problems engaging the positions offered to him by his world; it's that he has "no taste for the dark, tangled visceral aspect of Christianity, the *going through* quality of it, the passage *into* death and suffering that redeems and inverts these things, like an umbrella blowing inside out" (*Rabbit, Run*, 237/

203). This would be harshly judgmental if it were not for the fact that Rabbit's inability to see his responsibilities and jobs as occasions to sacrifice self-interest for the sake of a larger significance is an inability created in him by the culture. And the novel's spokespersons for Christianity offer no viable alternative. The Reverend Eccles is an inadequate father to his children, as Lucy his wife says, and no pastor to his flock, as the Reverend Kruppenbach, a fierce Lutheran, points out. Kruppenbach represents an inadequacy contrary to that of the liberal Eccles by being irrelevant to the culture because of his dogged traditionalism and non-compassionate style.

Religion, epitomized by these complementary forms of ineffectiveness, is not the cause of the problem; religion simply is not able to address a culture that places no value on "the *going through*" qualities of living and that encourages flight into self-preoccupation and self-gratification. Rabbit was nurtured into this culture by playing basketball, in which the object was to get free for a perfect shot. In basketball, detachment and fulfillment were joined, and he looks for that combination all the time. Involvement, complexity, and the "dark, tangled" character of life are to be avoided or fled. The clinical word for the resulting state is narcissism, and Rabbit has it badly. In this he is similar to Peter Caldwell, Joey Robinson, Piet Hanema *(Couples),* and Jerry Conant *(Marry Me),* except that he has less in his past than they do that can help him understand the problem or offer a contrasting reality.

What makes Rabbit so engaging, despite his narcissism, is that Updike depicts him as energetic and inventively outrageous in the ways by which he makes the world conform to his own needs and interests. There is nothing in his world significant enough to draw him out of this orientation. The confinements of a forced marriage dominated by parents and in-laws and a series of blue-collar jobs that offer nothing to engage him mean that from the outset Rabbit is a person who is always working for the open shot, always wanting that basket with its "pretty skirt of net." The Toyota dealership at times offers a kind of separate peace, but only because it is separate. As the visiting executive says, "In U.S., Toyota company hope to make ireands [sic] of order in ocean of freedom" (*Rabbit at Rest,* 392/1406). But separation from American culture is not what Rabbit needs or, it seems, Updike wants. Toyota's goal is a business counterpart of the removal from American culture of religious sects. Work in such contexts becomes subordinate to advancing the institution and its leaders.

Rabbit seems to be aware that he has a problem, and at times he tries to find out what it is or to relate himself to something larger. Toward the end of his life he is reading history, for example, and he retains his interest in astronomy (44/1088 and 170/1204). Although he works at the problem, work itself as a point of connection between the self and a comprehensive structure of meaning is lost to him.

Janice retains or revives the old interest in work; she envies women out in the business world. But a Christian doctrine of vocation would be unavailable to her because she blames "patriarchal religions" for the cultural denigration of women. There is, therefore, no alternative to the gradual loss of meaningful work. At the end Rabbit is resigned to work as merely "earning his paycheck, filling his slot in the big picture, doing his bit, getting a little recognition" (451/1460). Without a "big picture" that confers meaning, however, work and religion die together; God "is like a friend you've had so long you've forgotten what you liked about Him" (450/1459).

IV

The center of religious interest in Updike's fiction, then, can be located in the work it does on the problem of work in a culture increasingly bereft of conditions that would support a Christian doctrine of vocation. Some of his characters can invoke memories and models of those who addressed their work as a religious discipline. Those examples of belief derive from traditional Protestantism, both Calvinist and Lutheran, which transferred the doctrine of work as discipline from monastic or clerical vocations to daily life. For Luther, work is the discipline by which the Christian learns to die to self-interest and in that dying is enabled to receive the gift of faith and of God's righteousness (Wingren, 30-60). For Calvin, daily work is the discipline by which the living knowledge of God, received in and through reading Scripture, is extended into and embodied in the larger world (Kort, 30-31). For both Luther and Calvin, daily work is or becomes a religious vocation. It does so because the Christian, by giving the self in and through work, dies to self-interest and experiences a new self arising in place of the old. It is this Protestant doctrine of work that stands behind or informs the many statements by narrators, preachers, and other characters in Updike's fiction about "the going through quality" of Christianity. Many of his characters are aware of this tradition, howbeit in attenuated form, and they address their offices and vocations with expectations that in and through them a new kind of relation will arise between their internal potential and external circumstances and between their individual initiatives and a larger context of meaning. They expect that their efforts and sacrifices will be transfigured into something new and something more. Problems arise when this transformation or exchange becomes questionable or is thwarted. This occurs because the culture gives characters offices and jobs that are too taxing, trivial, or abstract to function as religious disciplines and because the culture has shifted the locus of value from something outside the person to something actually or potentially within.

The conflict between the expectations created by the Protestant backgrounds of the characters and what they actually confront as offices and jobs in contemporary America forces them to recoil. This reaction opens up another kind of religiousness, an improvised aesthetic spirituality. It defines itself in opposition to narcissism as much as to the self-sacrifice of the traditional model. It is a discipline of aesthetic self-construction, and the reader finds it, as I have said, primarily in Peter Caldwell and Joey Robinson. It is a role created for and by many of Updike's narrators, such as the one in "The Blessed Man of Boston, My Grandmother's Thimble, and Fanning Island," who prays, "O Lord, bless these poor paragraphs, that would do in their vile ignorance Your work of resurrection" (*Pigeon Feathers,* 229).

Updike's artists and narrators produce, by their work on the problem of vocation, an alternative to both the Christian model and its narcissistic, cultural contrary. This alternative combines self-orientation with respect for the particular realities and contingencies of the actual world. It avoids the danger in the Christian option of enthrallment with and dependence on the past and the danger in the secular option of exploitation and narcissism. The compound created from elements of the Protestant past and the secular present is unsteady, but it works. Although it lacks the direct support of Christian doctrine, it is too dependent on it to acquiesce to cultural self-absorption. Most important, the work to which Updike puts himself, his narrators, and his characters, namely, the problem of work itself, allows his fiction to forge for the culture lively connections between religious belief and contemporary quandaries.

PART 3

UPDIKE AND AMERICAN RELIGION

Faith or Fiction

Updike and the American Renaissance

CHARLES BERRYMAN

At the height of the American Renaissance in the mid-nineteenth century, Nathaniel Hawthorne and Herman Melville often gave power to their fiction by challenging the Christian faith of their contemporaries. In a famous 1851 letter to Hawthorne, his new friend, Melville declared: "There is the grand truth about Nathaniel Hawthorne. He says No! in thunder" (*Writings,* 14:186). The distance between Hawthorne's craft of fiction and the certain faith of his Puritan ancestors is measured in his autobiographical introduction to *The Scarlet Letter.* Hawthorne is mindful that his forebear who came from England "with his Bible and his sword" would be apt to feel nothing but scorn for the vain and idle profession of a romance writer (*Centenary Edition,* 1:9). Hawthorne tests the value of his work against such inherited guilt by re-creating the Puritans in the pages of his fiction to explore and question their religious authority.

No writer in the twentieth century has been more fascinated by Hawthorne's interrogation of faith and fiction than John Updike. Not only has Updike written several novels with themes and characters adapted from Hawthorne's work, but he has also turned his literary criticism to the religious doubts faced by Hawthorne. Updike's address to the American Academy and Institute of Arts and Letters opens with the question, "What did Hawthorne believe?" (*Hugging the Shore,* 73). The answer is a compromise that might describe either writer. Updike does find that Hawthorne's prose is haunted by a "vivid ghost of Christianity" (76), but he still concludes that Hawthorne offers "a psychological rather than a religious truth" (80).

While trying to answer the "question of what settled belief or unbelief Hawthorne held," Updike admits that "religious belief is an elusive and volatile part of a man" and that attempts to pin it down may be "impudent" as well as "impossible" (75). Updike also reports, however, that Melville was "one of the few men ever to break through Hawthorne's reserve" (74). Another writer to do so early in our own century was D. H. Lawrence, especially when he tells us to "look through the surface of American art, and see the inner diabolism of the symbolic meaning" (Lawrence, 83). Melville may have been the first to recognize "this great power of blackness" in Hawthorne's work because he shared many of the same religious doubts (Melville, 9:243). Melville, however, was bold enough in his own fiction to have his tragic hero "strike through the mask" at the hidden and vengeful god (6:164), while Hawthorne was apt to be more circumspect about his challenge to religious authority. He did offend some readers with his portrait of a sinful Puritan minister, but for the most part Hawthorne retained his readers and their respect for him as a writer of historical fables and children's tales. Melville in contrast was hard put to describe the public misperception of Hawthorne: "he seems to be deemed a pleasant writer, with a pleasant style, — a sequestered, harmless man, from whom any deep and weighty thing would hardly be anticipated" (9:242).

How could his contemporaries be so "mistaken in this Nathaniel Hawthorne?" (9:243). Melville places much of the blame on contemporary readers for lacking the "time, or patience, or palate, for the spiritual truth" (9:245) that can be found in the depths of tragic drama or fiction. Thus a superficial reading will fail to reach "those deep far-away things in him; those occasional flashings-forth of the intuitive Truth in him; those short, quick probings at the very axis of reality" (9:244). And, sure enough, when a generation of American critics followed Lawrence's advice to "look through the surface of American art" they found what Melville had described as "the hither side of Hawthorne's soul . . . shrouded in a blackness ten times black" (9:243). In this manner such critics as Harry Levin and F. O. Matthiessen were led to reify the "power of blackness" as a prominent feature of the American Renaissance.[1] Thus an implicit standard for evaluating literature was promoted in American schools and universities as John Updike launched his career as a writer.

Throughout his long career Updike has continued to study and respond to the novels of Hawthorne and Melville, but his strategy for dealing with the possible contradiction of faith and fiction has often been to compromise the difference. This strategy allows Updike to retain some Christian identity, while including a few religious doubts in his fiction, but the result is a compromise that fails to engage the deliberate challenge to Christian dogma implicit in the dark side of Hawthorne's symbolic work.

Writing in the middle of the nineteenth century, Hawthorne knew that his audience would not welcome a bold challenge to their common faith. Thus he might confide to his notebook: "My wife went to church in the forenoon, but not so her husband," while his skepticism is kept under wraps in his fiction (*Centenary Edition*, 8:358). For example, when the Puritan community appears to be going to the Devil in "Young Goodman Brown," which Melville praised in "Hawthorne and His Mosses" for being as "deep as Dante" (Melville, 9:251), Hawthorne is careful to end the tale by recasting it in the perspective of a bad dream. Even the "h-ll-fired story" (*Centenary Edition*, 16:312) of *The Scarlet Letter* ends with the conventional moral: "Be true! Be true! Be true!" (9:260). Perhaps the banal repetition comes less from Hawthorne than from the voice of his narrative persona. In any event, D. H. Lawrence had great fun mocking the simple moral instruction: "*Be good! Be good!* warbles Nathaniel" (Lawrence, 84), but given the latent Calvinism among Hawthorne's immediate public, Lawrence also understood that when Hawthorne found "disagreeable things in his inner soul, he was careful to send them out in disguise" (83).

Writing in the second half of the twentieth century, John Updike has faced the opposite problem. His more secular audience hardly expects religious dogma to be taken with full seriousness. Updike can thus make a fine joke out of the Devil in *The Witches of Eastwick*, or dis-

1. See the chapters on Hawthorne and Melville in Harry Levin, *The Power of Blackness*, and F. O. Matthiessen, *American Renaissance: Art and Expression in the Age of Emerson and Whitman*.

guise the Reverend Mr. Dimmesdale as a fake Hindu religious leader in *S.*, and then unmask him to reveal a half-Jewish hippie from Massachusetts. The result is a wild comedy and satire quite different from what Lawrence saw as "the diabolic undertone of *The Scarlet Letter*" (Lawrence, 84). Updike can afford to be more realistic because he does not have to send out dark sentiments in disguise. Hawthorne could not show the act of adultery in the pages of his Puritan romance, and the only sensual moment suggested in *The Scarlet Letter* is the wonderful meeting in the forest when Hester lets her hair down. Updike's characters, on the other hand, are apt to commit adultery again and again to the point of boredom. Thus we are shown repeatedly how the former wives in Eastwick turn adultery into a joke: "Being a divorcee in a small town is a little like playing Monopoly; eventually you land on all the properties" (*Witches of Eastwick,* 25). The hero of the four Rabbit novels even continues a long series of adulterous affairs by having sex with his daughter-in-law. Updike is quite free to entertain his modern audience with the graphic details of sexual encounters; indeed, he is justly famous for devoting much of his fiction to exploring the contours of human desire. "What the New World was to Renaissance cartographers," writes Alfred Kazin, "sex is to Updike. No one has put so many coasts, bays, and rivers where once there was only silence" ("Easy Come," 3).

What is not possible for Updike, however, is to present adultery as a tragic conflict of body and soul in the manner of Hawthorne. The consequences of adultery in Updike's work may include suffering and death, but not the tormented awareness of sin characteristic of Arthur Dimmesdale. Even when Hawthorne was skeptical of religious dogma, however, and despite his courage to allow Hester to claim "a consecration of its own" (*Centenary Edition,* 1:195) for the very act of adultery, some dark power of Calvinism was still available for his imagination. The force of his art thus owes much to the conflict between the faith still held by many of his contemporaries and the religious doubts that Hawthorne sent forth in disguise. Updike's fiction, in contrast, typically lacks such tension or conflict. As noted by Donald Greiner in his study *Adultery in the American Novel: Updike, James, and Hawthorne,* adultery for Updike "is often a social embarrassment but rarely a cause for individual damnation" (57).

Perhaps the tragic vision of Hawthorne and Melville was only possible at the crux of the American Renaissance, when the rules of

Christian faith were challenged by strong rebels like Hester Prynne and Captain Ahab. At that moment the reading public was still held by the conflict between religious law and individual rebellion. When the Puritan community in New England was first challenged in the seventeenth century by a strong woman like Ann Hutchinson, the result was banishment and death for the individual. Two centuries later, however, Hawthorne allowed his fictional heroine to follow in the footsteps of "the sainted Ann Hutchinson" (*Centenary Edition*, 1:48) — the adjective is a measure of Hawthorne's bold revision — and still hold on to her own romantic heart despite the censure of religious law. The very success of Hester and Hawthorne in shifting the meaning of adultery away from sin and guilt — "many people refused to interpret the scarlet A by its original signification. They said that it meant Able; so strong was Hester Prynne, with a woman's strength" (1:161) — may help to explain why Updike is left in the twentieth century without a tragic subject.

Hester Prynne becomes a very different character in the comic novel *S.* where she is transformed by Updike into the rather foolish and pathetic figure of Sarah Worth. She has a daughter named Pearl, a former husband who is a physician, and a mother descended from the Prynne family, but Updike also gives her a dentist, lawyer, and hairdresser. Like Hester, she has an affair with a hypocritical religious leader whose first name is Arthur, but her experience at his fake Arizona commune has more to do with jealousy and seduction than with spiritual enlightenment. At the religious commune Sarah is called by the Hindu name "Kundalini," which Updike translates as "coiled up" or "the serpent of female energy" (*S.*, 272). Not surprisingly, she is the Updike character whom feminist critics most love to hate. Updike repeatedly makes fun of Sarah's search for sensual and spiritual fulfillment. Although the entire novel is told in her voice as represented by various letters and tapes mailed to relatives and friends from a motel near the Arizona commune, she is often the last person to understand how her life is a sad comedy of deceit and betrayal. Not only has Sarah been fooled by the charade of Hindu religion performed by the "guru" who turns out to be Arthur Steinmetz, but she also learns near the end of the novel that the woman who has been receiving her confidential letters is about to marry her former husband. Instead of Hawthorne's portrait of "a woman's strength," Updike sets up his modern version of Hester Prynne for a series of comic pratfalls. Her few achievements include holding on to some inherited silverware and embezzling a large sum of money from the commune's Treasury of Enlightenment. In this way even Sarah Worth's last name is loaded with irony.

Updike's bold use of material from *The Scarlet Letter* invites a comparative judgment, although it may not be fair to Updike to expect his modern fiction to have the power and depth of Hawthorne's novel. In any event, *S.* can be read as a comic tour de force, a technical experiment in epistolary narrative design, and another display of Updike's virtuoso talent as a wordsmith. Such praise, of course, will not satisfy the critics who blame Updike for turning the strong womanhood of Hester Prynne into a travesty of sexual equality and liberation. Nor will it set aside the suspicion that Updike has avoided the hard choice in the conflict between faith and fiction.

Hawthorne may have disguised himself as the mere editor of Surveyor Pue's old manuscript and catered to his contemporary audience with a few conventional moral tags, but surely Melville and Lawrence were right to praise Hawthorne for his doubts about the stern God of the Puritans and for his dark questioning of religious law. Hester is a tragic heroine because she is able to assume "a freedom of speculation" that permits revolutionary thoughts to visit her "such as dared to enter no other dwelling in New England" (*Centenary Edition*, 1:164). Hawthorne is bold enough to give his Christian audience a character who might have been put to death for "attempting to undermine the foundations of the Puritan establishment" (1:165).

Updike, in contrast, is a self-proclaimed Christian who appears to tailor his writing for a skeptical public. Thus he turns the sinful Arthur Dimmesdale into the charlatan, Arthur Steinmetz, who then stands as an easy target for mockery and satire. Is there a hint of anti-Semitism in this transformation? Not to mention a casual disrespect for the language and faith of Hinduism? Why doesn't Updike question his own beliefs rather than set up a fake guru to ridicule? Does he want to protect his own religious position by making fun of others? The novel raises too many suspicions about the author's motivations because Updike has substituted a compromise for the hard choice that allowed Hawthorne to create Hester as a tragic character for the American Renaissance.

Another way to look at Updike's position as a writer in the late twentieth century would be to argue that he has little or no choice in such matters. Hawthorne could present Hester's challenge to the moral law of the Puritans because so many of his readers were still involved in the debate. They had been educated in schools and colleges that for the most part still followed the pattern of Christian teaching established in the early Puritan colonies. As a student at Bowdoin, Hawthorne had been required to attend morning and evening chapel on weekdays and three religious services on Sunday. Such rules, of course, were never much to his liking, and he was often disciplined at college for breaking them. Hawthorne's inclination is clear in a letter written to his mother even before entering Bowdoin. He is debating "what profession I should have," and sharply rejects the career path of religion: "The being a minister is of course out of the question. I should not think that even you could desire me to choose so dull a way of life" (*Centenary Edition,* 15:138). Hawthorne is hesitant and fearful, however, about a possible future as a writer. "What do you think of my becoming an author," he asks his mother, "and relying for support upon my pen?" This question is followed by a display of mock despair and bravado: "But authors are always poor devils, and therefore may Satan take them." Not many statements in the history of American letters have proved to be so prophetic.

Hawthorne took decades to reach the point in his writing career when he was ready to create *The Scarlet Letter.* The roots of his rebellion against Christian authority are evident in his childhood and college years, but only in mid century when his public was beginning to hear a new challenge to religious experience from Emerson, and new questions about the status of women from Margaret Fuller, was Hawthorne able to present Hester Prynne as a transcendental heroine who rebels against her Puritan culture by following her heartfelt, natural impulses.

A century later John Updike could leave home in Pennsylvania without any resistance to the idea of his becoming a writer. Indeed, such a career might fulfill his mother's lifelong ambition. The education he received at Harvard, the first college founded by Puritans to teach Calvin's theology in the New World, was beyond anything that Hawthorne, not to mention Increase or Cotton Mather, could have imagined. There were many classes in American literature and culture for an aspiring writer and artist to select from, choices that had not been possible in earlier centuries. And by the 1950s the basic tenets of Calvinism were no longer central to the liberal arts curriculum.

Hawthorne's worry about writers being "poor devils" could also be discounted. A job at *The New Yorker* gave the young Updike a fast entry into the world of authors, and popular success was soon to follow. Updike was thus able to skip the decades of obscurity and doubt when Hawthorne was making his craft ready to challenge the religious establishment. Updike's early success also enabled him to avoid the distractions of economic worry and the kind of work that Hawthorne found necessary to support his family. Only when he lost his position at the Customs-House in Salem did Hawthorne find the opportunity to write *The Scarlet Letter,* and the autobiographical introduction is informed by the resentment of a "Decapitated Surveyor" (1:43). In contrast, Updike's career has been a fairly serene example of continued economic and critical success.

Most important of all, Updike has hardly allowed himself to imagine what Hawthorne foresaw when he said about authors: "and therefore may Satan take them." For the tragic writers of the American Renaissance, Hawthorne and Melville in particular, their profession was a kind of Faustian pact with the Devil. In return for the pleasure, knowledge, and power displayed in characters like Hester Prynne and Captain Ahab, the soul of the author could be in thrall to the "great power of blackness." There is little evidence, however, to suggest that Updike has ever felt the weight of such a tragic situation, and if he were to approach his public with such concerns, Updike knows that most of the readers who share his education would not be likely to have any interest in or sympathy for the ghosts of Calvinism.

In his memoir, *Self-Consciousness,* Updike spends less time concerned with the state of his soul than with the condition of his skin. If any writer could raise his anxiety about psoriasis to the level of a spiritual test, perhaps Updike is the one, but the truth is more apt to be that he writes realistic novels about adultery and material success — *Rabbit Is Rich* — because the human comedy that he shares with his late-twentieth-century audience is more or less skin deep.

Updike may also be limited to the surface of things by his realistic style, which is well suited to record the details of physical experience but not to explore the hidden depths of religious faith or doubt. Thus he shows us the sexual comedy of Harry Angstrom making love on a bed full of gold coins, but the realistic details accumulate for more than a thousand pages in the *Rabbit Angstrom* tetralogy without much evidence that Rabbit ever thinks of himself as having a soul that might be in any danger. Nostalgia for his moments of grace playing basketball or golf may be as close as Rabbit gets to religious experience. His lost paradise is only a pleasant memory of youth, and his repeated fall through decades of adultery ends with no thought of redemption. Updike's realistic style is able to show us the hospital where the condition of Rabbit's heart is measured by charts and machines, but the realism of medical science leaves no room in Updike's fiction for the word *heart* to register its older, symbolic meanings.

Hawthorne and Melville, however, share the advantage of being able to write with symbols that most often move the narrative from physical description to metaphysical concerns. In the first chapter of *The Scarlet Letter,* for example, Hawthorne describes a rose as a token of the pity and kindness in "the deep heart of Nature" (1:48). As well as suggesting human qualities for the natural world, Hawthorne also associates the rose with the history of Ann Hutchinson and the color of the rose with the main symbol and title of the novel. The sign of adultery, of course, should be the same color as the blood and passion of nature's heart. How ironic, then, for Hawthorne's narrator to pluck a rose from this bush "and present it to the reader" as a symbol of "some sweet moral bloom" (1:48). The same rich ambiguity of meaning is suggested again with the "fine red cloth" of the scarlet letter that Hester has decorated with "flourishes of gold thread" (1:53). Shame, pride, sin, triumph? What aspects of her natural heart does Hester mean to reveal or hide with the embroidered letter?

Updike likes to portray the realistic details of nature — so many plants are named and described in his latest novel, *Toward the End of Time,* that it reads like a botanical guide — but the natural descriptions seldom resonate with psychological or religious meaning. Does the limitation derive from the unwillingness of a twentieth-century writer to make an old-fashioned attribution of human qualities to nature? Probably not. Updike might shy away from referring to the "deep heart of Nature," and no doubt he has to avoid the capital letter, but the romantic metaphors of nature are still available for writers. Despite the famous tautology from Gertrude Stein — "A rose is a rose is a rose is a rose" — and the strong currents of anti-symbolism that have moved through modern arts and letters, Updike's contemporary, Umberto Eco, is still able to create rich levels of symbolism in *The Name of the Rose.*

Could the limits of his realistic style be a consequence of Updike's early training in the graphic arts and his continued fascination with the craft of representation on a flat surface? Updike admits to being a "highly pictorial writer" (*Picked-Up Pieces,* 509), and his success has been compared by James Plath to the brilliantly detailed canvases of Jan Vermeer: "Love of detail and compositional harmony are what Updike and his fictional characters strive for most and admire" (Plath, "Verbal Vermeer," 213). Plath is very helpful in explaining how Updike and Vermeer cast light on their characters or subjects. The comparison with Vermeer, however, may reveal Updike's limit as well as his strength. Vermeer, after all, is famous for the light that falls on the detailed surface of his still-life subjects, but where are the dark shadows and psychological depth of a Rembrandt? Updike's understanding of and appreciation for realistic painting is most likely a symptom of his sensibility, and neither a consequence of his early education nor a result of his continued study and writing on painters and their work. Updike has much to say about the pleasures of visual art in his collection of essays *Just Looking,* but even the title suggests a witness who remains fairly detached. Thus he writes about the light in artists from Vermeer to Wyeth but tends to avoid any "power of blackness."

If the two best novels of the American Renaissance both have symbolic titles, *The Scarlet Letter* and *Moby-Dick,* what can a realistic author, who remains fascinated by Hawthorne and Melville, write for a late-twentieth-century audience? What happens when the author himself claims to have a Christian sensibility that his readers may not share? The situation is that of Hawthorne and Melville in reverse, and the best example of how Updike succeeds or fails in dealing with it may be his 1996 novel *In the Beauty of the Lilies.* Even the title includes a religious symbol with connections to American history and the natural world. Julia Ward Howe brings together an Easter symbol with the birth of Jesus in the famous lines from "The Battle-Hymn of the Republic": "In the beauty of the lilies / Christ was born across the sea." Updike thus includes a reference to Christ in the title of the novel, but he does so to lament the current absence in American culture of the deity borne across the sea by the ancestors of Hawthorne and Melville. The novel unfolds in Updike's familiar realistic style to show a decline of religious experience through four American generations.

The chronicle begins in 1910 with two coincidental events in Patterson, New Jersey. Just when young Mary Pickford happens to faint on the set of a D. W. Griffith film, Updike reports that the Reverend Clarence Arthur Wilmot "felt the last particles of his faith leave him" (*In the Beauty of the Lilies*, 5). Only the middle name is Arthur, and now at least it is not followed by Steinmetz. Nor does Updike offer another parody of the hypocritical Arthur Dimmesdale as a fake Hindu leader in Arizona. This time the Reverend Clarence Arthur Wilmot has the courage of a nonbeliever and abandons the ministry of his Presbyterian church after he loses his faith.

Starting his modern chronicle of America's religious decline in Patterson may be Updike's nod to William Carlos Williams, the poet who was most responsible for putting the city on the literary map. Updike also appears to recall the passage in Williams's *Autobiography* where a Reverend is described as "an ex-Presbyterian" who had declined to an "almost non-Christian faith" before he "finally went nearly mad over Blake's revolving spheres" (*Autobiography*, 62-63). Updike's minister ironically loses his faith after reading Robert Ingersoll's *Some Mistakes of Moses* in the vain hope of refuting its atheism. When the Reverend Wilmot reaches the conclusion, *"There is no God"* (*In the Beauty of the Lilies*, 6), he abandons his church for a job selling encyclopedias. Nor could William Carlos Williams find any truth in religion. "Heaven," he declared in a letter, "seems frankly impossible" (*Selected Letters*, 147). After rejecting the supernatural, Williams devoted himself to the practice of medicine and the writing of poetry.

The dislike Williams often expressed for symbolist poetry, especially the Dantean echoes of "multifoliate rose" in Eliot's work, may also have registered with Updike. Eliot used such symbols in "The Hollow Men" and *The Waste Land* to show vestiges of Christianity in the modern world of unbelievers. Williams, however, scornfully dismissed *The Waste Land* as "the great catastrophe to our letters" (*Autobiography*, 146). Updike is mindful of the debate when he uses a very realistic style, despite the symbolic title, for his chronicle of religious decline.

What happens to the drama of religious loss when it is presented by Updike in pages of realistic detail? There are some fine touches of irony and coincidence. The simultaneous focus on the film set where Mary Pickford faints and the minister's study where his faith disappears not only suggests some parity of these two events but also introduces the move from religion to cinema that future generations follow in this chronicle. Updike also sets up a double focus on the minister's study with its forty-four volumes of Calvin's Commentaries and the kitchen where his wife and servant are preparing a sweet ham dinner for the Church Building Committee. Later that evening the idea of building a new "Sunday-school and church-social wing" (*In the Beauty of the Lilies,* 36) is opposed in the minister's mind to his new conviction of "God's non-being" (25). The anxious and depressing thoughts of Reverend Wilmot are thus set off against the material world of church buildings and baked ham dinners.

Not all readers have been pleased by such realistic detail. Gore Vidal, for example, makes fun of "the weeds of description" that he finds growing helter-skelter in Updike's novel (Vidal, 5). Vidal objects to the "thousands of little facts" that are presented "to no purpose" (6). While it may not be fair to dismiss *In the Beauty of the Lilies* as a list "of random objects," the relentless piling up of details through four generations does tend to overwhelm the drama of religious decline.

Realism itself is not so much the problem as Updike's reluctance or inability to draw the pieces together into a convincing and dynamic narrative of religious challenge. Melville, after all, piled thousands of facts about the whaling industry into *Moby-Dick,* but the great hunt for the white whale still remains a symbolic quest for the inscrutable face of God. Captain Ahab does not know if the whale is "agent" or "principal" (Melville, 6:164), but he is determined nonetheless to "strike through the mask." Any fact of nature may thus be used by Melville as a symbol of some power behind the surface reality, and given Ahab's ability to pile "upon the whale's white hump the sum of all the general rage and hate felt by his whole race from Adam down" (6:184), the result is a tragic narrative with unprecedented scope and power. Updike's novel, on the other hand, remains close to the surface and does not concentrate its meaning on a central symbol. Ahab's hunt for Moby Dick thus retains its tragic force, while the loss of Wilmot's faith seems mildly comic in the mundane world of his wife at home baking a sweet ham.

Melville, however, shared the same advantage as Hawthorne, the ability to shock and challenge the religious beliefs of his Christian readers. Ahab's determination to harpoon "the glorified White Whale as he so divinely swam" could be presented as a Faustian challenge to the authority and power of God. The only survivor of the tragic quest is Ishmael, who is left floating on the milky surface of the ocean — "a colorless, all-color of atheism" (6:195). Where does that leave Updike and his late-twentieth-century audience? The crew of the Pequod includes a range of beliefs from Starbuck, the obedient Christian, to Fedallah, the fire-worshiping Parsee. After the sinking of the Pequod with its assembled crew of different religious types, what is left but the ripples on the surface of the water, or what Lawrence called "post-mortem effects" (Lawrence, 161)? After the "centre cannot hold," as Yeats predicted, "anarchy is loosed upon the world" (*Collected Poems*, 184). Updike's saga of religious decline in the twentieth century follows the image of widening circles or gyres through four generations until the great-grandson of the faithless minister comes face to face with a rough beast slouching toward Waco to die.

Melville could dramatize his doubts about the existence of God with great intensity because his readers might still feel his challenge to their living faith. Even a friendly review of *Moby-Dick* by Evert Duyckinck in 1851 includes censure of Melville's "piratical running down of creeds" and complaints about "the most sacred associations of life" that the reviewer feels are being "violated and defaced" ("Review," 403-4). Just the opposite is heard in reviews of *In the Beauty of the Lilies.* Assuming that Reverend Wilmot ought to have left his faith behind long ago, Gore Vidal mocks it as something "most boys had pretty much wrapped up before the onset of puberty" (Vidal, 6). Vidal is even amused that "Christianity seems always to have been a fact for Updike . . . as an outward and visible sign of niceness and belongingness" (3). Vidal's satire has its own particular wit and venom, but Updike's mildly comic portrait of Reverend Wilmot is apt to inspire such cynicism.

Once again, however, Updike may be limited to a realistic tour of the human comedy because so many of his readers are beyond any tragic concern or need to aim another harpoon at the image of a hidden God, and Updike may protect his own pleasant vestige of religious faith by not identifying himself with the rather pedantic and foolish minister. The result is a novel with enough historical realism to fill almost five hundred pages, details that range from the making of a silent film in Patterson to a retelling of the confrontation in Waco, but the long chronicle amounts to less than the sum of its parts. *In the Beauty of the Lilies* is a narrative of religious decline that does not fully engage either its author or his audience. If the symbolic novels of Hawthorne and Melville challenge the Christian faith by saying "No! in thunder," the recent fiction of John Updike implies some nostalgia for the American past, for the Christ invoked by Julia Ward Howe, but his tacit support for such religion is a muted applause, merely the sound and fury of one hand clapping. If the question is faith or fiction, the answer for Updike is not another American Renaissance.

Giving the Devil His Due

Leeching and Edification of Spirit in *The Scarlet Letter* and *The Witches of Eastwick*

JAMES PLATH

> When the subconscious soul of woman recoils from its creative union with man, it becomes a destructive force. . . . She doesn't know it. She can't even help it. But she does it. The devil is in her. The very women who are most busy saving the bodies of men . . . they are all, from the inside, sending out waves of destructive malevolence which can eat out the inner life of a man, like a cancer.
>
> D. H. Lawrence (*Studies in Classic American Literature*, 92-93)

Reading Lawrence's remarks about Hawthorne's *Scarlet Letter,* one can't help but think of the way in which cancer, a "sore of guilt," is used as a central motif in *The Witches of Eastwick* (280); or how the witches felt that "healing belonged to their nature," that it was "womanly to want to heal — to apply the poultice of acquiescent flesh to the wound of a man's desire, to give his closeted spirit the exaltation of seeing a witch slip out of her clothes and go skyclad in a room of tawdry motel furniture" (67); or how Alexandra, called "the head witch" by Updike (Plath, ed., 266), had taken to "healing" several lovers and watched as her "cuckolded husband shrank to the dimensions and dryness of a doll" (*Witches,* 7), even thinking at one point that "the devil was getting into her" (48). One also recalls Updike's own declaration that "*The Scarlet Letter* is not merely a piece of fiction, it is a myth by now, and it was an updating of the myth, the triangle redefined by D. H. Lawrence, that interested me" (Schiff, *Updike's Version,* 132).

If Updike in his *Scarlet Letter* trilogy explored the "myth" of an adulterous triangle between a man of science, a man of religion, and a woman of nature as redefined by Lawrence, then by his own careful choice of the novel's very last word (*Witches,* 307), Updike reminds readers that in *The Witches of Eastwick* he explores "legend" — and legend is secular, not mythic. The difference between the two is not insignificant and legitimates an important critical application. According to Mircea Eliade, "sacred history is recounted in the myths. . . . In so far as he imitates his gods, religious man lives in the *time of origin,* the time of the myths . . . eternity" (72). *The Scarlet Letter* takes place in mythic time and space — what Eliade calls "the sphere of the sacred" — in a New England town where "religion and law were almost identical" (Hawthorne, *Centenary Edition,* 1:50). *The Witches of Eastwick* occupies secular space and time, in which religion has shifted from the fore to the background, and each of the witches, acting "without a mythical model, belongs to the sphere of the profane" (Eliade, 96). "The myth operates whenever passion is dreamed of as an ideal instead of being feared like a malignant fever," Denis de Rougemont writes, "whenever its fatal character is welcomed, or invoked as a magnificent and desirable disaster instead of simply a disaster" (24). As Updike explained in a review of *Love Declared,* "de Rougemont is dreadfully right in asserting that love in the Western world has by some means acquired a force far out of proportion to its presumed procreative aim. Do we need a heresy, or even a myth, to explain it?" (*Assorted Prose,* 299).

Hawthorne suggests through wordplay the depth of mythic influence and heretical straying to be found in Hester's Boston, insomuch as his young Reverend Dimmesdale is himself an ironic, self-contained scriptural homily — "Yea, though I walk through the valley of the shadow of death, I fear no evil" (Psalm 23:4). His "dim" faith and fear both of Chillingworth and of having his sin discovered from the valley of his own heart cause the minister's health to deteriorate rapidly. In naming his own Reverend Ed *Parsley,* however, Updike suggests, through the same sort of wordplay, that religion had lost even more of its efficacy and had become little more than a garnish by the time of Lyndon Johnson's presidency. In *The Scarlet Letter* an alchemist enters society and begins to work his dark magic, but in *Witches* the church has already drifted toward a broad receptivity: "In this hazy late age of declining doctrine its interior was decorated here and there with crosses anyway, and the social parlor bore on one wall a large felt banner, concocted by the Sunday school, of the Egyptian tau cross . . . surrounded by the four triangular alchemic signs for the elements" (*Witches,* 35).

In the hyper-religious society of *The Scarlet Letter* witches are treated as ghosts, kept largely offstage as voices "often heard to pass over the settlements or lonely cottages, as they rode with Satan through the air" (Hawthorne, *Centenary Edition,* 1:149), with repeated implications that any townsperson who goes into the forest, into nature, must consort with "the black man" and is therefore a witch or Mephistophelean. Aside from what readers can infer would have been deemed witchcraft had the full circumstances of Hester's sex triangle been revealed, the witches are otherwise present only through the characters of Mistress Hibbins and her friend, who were to be hanged after the main action of the novel (1:49, 1:221), and young Pearl, who is linked to evil primarily because of her mischief (1:154). Satan, meanwhile, is ambiguously embodied in Chillingworth, "a potent necromancer" (1:258) who does the "Devil's work on earth" (1:260).

In *Witches,* divorcees — equated throughout the novel with magic and witchcraft — are so prevalent that there are "hundreds of divorcees running around" mischievously competing for the married men in Eastwick (239); "Being a divorcee in a small town is a little like playing Monopoly; eventually you land on all the properties" (25). Instead of a single adulterous martyr "stigmatized by the scarlet letter" and isolated in a "lonesome cottage by the seashore" (*Centenary Edition,* 1:159), Updike offers a society of martyrs considerably less marginalized: "martyrs too of a sort were the men and women hastening to adulterous trysts, risking disgrace and divorce for their fix of motel love — all sacrificing the outer world to the inner, proclaiming with this priority that everything solid seeming and substantial is in fact a dream" (*Witches,* 201). Updike's language here clearly echoes Hawthorne's fascination with interiors and exteriors and with Plato's allegory of the cave — as well as the debates between what is "real" and substantial versus what is ideal or illusory that dominate both the symbolism and the dialectics of *The Scarlet Letter.* Updike has also multiplied the problem Dimmesdale faced, with his three temptations, where "his inner man" and "interior kingdom" incited him "to do some strange, wild, wicked thing or other, with a sense that it would be at once involuntary and intentional" (*Centenary Edition,* 1:217). Instead, Updike offers an entire town full of people who have given in to their natural impulses in order to commit mischiefs small and large, including infidelity. As Elizabeth Tallent reminds us, "These ancient alternatives — fidelity and adultery — parallel the choices once offered in Eden" (Tallent, 11). If, as Donald Greiner suggests, "adultery is a bridge between the garden and the world" (*Adultery,* 23), then in *Witches* Updike depicts a society so changed from the time of Hester's New England that the witches have moved from the periphery of social intercourse to its very center, and adultery is no longer the aberration — it is endemic. Where once, as Tallent observes, the conflict between flesh and spirit was resolved in Updike's fiction by having his "heroes turn the women they sleep with into wives" (4), the husbands in *Witches* who are "let stray by the women who owned them" (6) indulge in no such purifying fantasies.

Considering Hawthorne's affinities for the Gothic, Updike has concluded that "The haunted is a degenerate form of the sacred" (*Picked-Up Pieces,* 78). A succession of critics has viewed the witchcraft present in Hawthorne's masterpiece akin to what David Van Leer has most recently termed "a disastrous conflation of the material and the spiritual . . . equating as it does verbal formulas and physical recipes with demonic influences." Thus Chillingworth was portrayed as a man of science whose "natural learning" was a substitute for "religious zeal," resulting in "a debased model of the soul" (Van Leer, 77). Yet, in *Witches,* witchcraft is less the debasement that it was during the time period of *The Scarlet Letter* — or the alternative pop-culture religion that it became during the love-beaded, tie-dyed era in which *Witches* was set — than it is a means of challenging authority and trying to tap into the "guiltless energy men have" (56). Or, as Updike has observed, "Witchcraft is a venture, one could generally say, of women into the realm of power" (*Hugging the Shore,* 855).

Perhaps this is why *The Witches of Eastwick,* despite being written after *A Month of Sundays* but before *Roger's Version* and *S.,* hasn't been pointedly connected to Updike's rewriting of the novel he termed "our first American masterpiece" (Plath, ed., 129) and "one of the few 19th-century novels that actually deals with men and women" (207). James Schiff, the critic who has studied Updike's *Scarlet Letter* trilogy most extensively, acknowledges that

> In many ways, *The Witches of Eastwick* is Updike's most Hawthorn-esque work, more so than even the novels of the *Scarlet Letter* trilogy. . . . *The Witches of Eastwick feels* like Hawthorne. . . . Furthermore, through its consideration of evil, witchcraft, telepathy, adultery, art and artists, male-female relations, the scientist's effort to overcome nature, and the relationship between matter and spirit, *The Witches of Eastwick* may represent the point at which Updike's sensibility moves closest to Hawthorne's. (*John Updike Revisited*, 79)

Schiff also perceptively observes that "Hawthorne depicts a world not quite real, not quite believably alive, a world that is nearly other-worldly," and he acknowledges that Updike's world — even in the trilogy — is, for the most part, "a more realistic, trivial, everyday world" (*Updike's Version*, 123). He notes that Updike "experimented with such [otherworldly] worlds in *The Witches of Eastwick*" (123), yet his own discussion stops short of directly linking the novel to *The Scarlet Letter.* "New England carries with it a whole set of associations. I mean, you're in Hawthorne's territory," Updike told one interviewer (Plath, ed., 120). And if one looks closely, *The Witches of Eastwick* is more than just "Hawthornesque." If Updike gives voice in his trilogy to a modern-day Dimmesdale, Chillingworth, and Hester, I would argue that in *Witches* he gives voice to characters relegated to the background in Hawthorne's novel — the witches, the townspeople, and the "black man" himself.

Updike wrote of *Witches* that, in part, he wanted "to give gossip a body and to conjure up human voices as they hungrily feed on the lives of others" (*Hugging the Shore*, 856). Such language is again reminiscent of *The Scarlet Letter,* when Hester is first brought from the prison into the "too vivid light of day" (*Centenary Edition*, 1:52). The first voices to pass judgment on her for adultery and to pronounce the magistrates' punishment "merciful overmuch" are a group of "Goodwives" who stand "in a knot together" as they bemoan the sentence: "It would be greatly for the public behoof, if we women, being of mature age and church members in good repute, should have the handling of such malefactresses as this Hester Prynne," one "hard-featured dame of fifty" remarks. "What think ye, gossips? If the hussy stood up for judgment before us five, that are now here in a knot together, would she come off with such a sentence as the worshipful magistrates have awarded?" (1:51). Forget communal standards; the "goodwives" were more likely agitated because the father of Hester's child, whose identity was yet to be revealed, could have been any one of their own husbands.

In *The Witches of Eastwick,* "It was such unverifiable impressions that spread among us in Eastwick the rumor of witchcraft," the narrator remarks (18), "and if the world not merely accused but burned them alive in the tongues of indignant opinion, that was the price" the witches knew they must pay (67). In giving gossip a body, Updike explores an alternative locus of guilt or blame to those considered by Hawthorne and Lawrence, or to those he explored in his own trilogy. Moreover, Updike not only poses a situation where, as with Hawthorne's novel, adulteresses are regarded as consorts with the devil and judged more harshly by the "good wives" than by their husbands. He also considers the central themes of Hawthorne's novel in the context of a society in which patriarchal religiosity is no longer an oppressive factor. In Eastwick, where the air "empowered women" (8) and the Word of God has been replaced by the *Word* of Man — a local newspaper that prints a "scurrilous column" of gossip just to be "sexy" (294) — Updike explores adultery and male-female relations within a secular state. In Eastwick, divorced women experience sexual power after being freed not only from the constraints of matrimony but also from the constraints of religion that regards marriage as holy. "Female yearning was in all the papers and magazines now; the sexual equation had become reversed" (11).

In considering Hawthorne's adulterous triangle (seducer, adulterer, and cuckold) and the resultant spiritual triangle (sin, guilt, and redemption) within a society in which "Puritanism faded into Unitarianism and then into stoic agnosticism" (*Hugging the Shore,* 66), Updike forces readers to confront the enormous (and not altogether uncomfortable) gap between the spiritual and secular spheres of the two novels. "I don't feel much affinity with the New England Puritan ethos insofar as it still persists," Updike told Jeff Campbell. "I would call myself a Lutheran by upbringing, and my work contains some of the ambiguities of the Lutheran position. . . . Luther's feelings about the devil and the world are quite interesting to me. He seems to greatly admire, to adore, the devil" (Plath, ed., 94). So, apparently, does Updike, for in *Witches,* Updike gives the devil his due: "The book is meant to be about a coven, and the hero of a coven is surely the person who puts on the devil costume" (Plath, ed., 263).

Like *The Scarlet Letter,* which depends upon the three scaffold scenes at beginning, middle, and end for its structure, *Witches* is also organized into three sections: The Coven, Malefica, and Guilt. Both novels revolve around relationship triangles as well, with Updike's triangle a bit more intricate than Hawthorne's, or even Lawrence's reading of Hawthorne's. Only Pearl, the Elf-Child, complicates Hawthorne's threesome of lover, cuckolded husband, and faithless wife, with Hester the martyr and Pearl a petri dish sort of experiment to objectify the debate over natural sin. In a morality tale worthy of Chaucer, Hawthorne invites readers, in effect, to decide which of the two men is the bigger louse — although from the earliest reviews most readers felt that it was no contest. They saw what Evert Duyckinck first observed: that Chillingworth was a "Mephistophilean" who "devotes his life to . . . a fiendish revenge," a "devilish purpose" ("Great Feeling," 323). For Lawrence, who reaches back into Christian mythos to compare Hester to Eve, Hester is the center of the maelstrom, more villain than victim:

> Oh, Hester, you are a demon. A man *must* be pure, just so that you can seduce him to a fall. Because the greatest thrill in life is to bring down the Sacred Saint with a flop into the mud. . . . And then go home and dance a witch's jig of triumph. (Lawrence, 89)

While it appears that Updike found inspiration in Lawrence's comparison of sexual seduction and witchery, the implied natural bond in both Hawthorne's and Lawrence's love triangle is *two,* with the third party a disruption. In *Witches* — and this is most telling — the adulterous triangle is redefined so that *three,* not two, is the natural bond, with a fourth party causing that bond to break down. The three witches find themselves unable to "erect a cone of power" once they begin thinking about the new stranger in town, and they finally realize the reason: that "they were themselves under a spell, of a greater" (*Witches,* 33-34). Also disrupted by Van Horne are the marital triangles in which each witch was involved, and later, once their coven is reestablished with the Satan-figure as their head, their threesome is violated again by Jenny Gabriel. In this manner, Updike has redefined the myth of the adulterous triangle not just by shifting the locus of blame or guilt, as Lawrence did, but by suggesting as well that the adulterous triangle is every bit as natural as the bond of two people entered into marriage, and infidelity as natural as fidelity: "Things fall into threes. And magic occurs all around us as nature seeks and finds the inevitable forms . . . the equilateral triangle being the mother of structure" (5).

As divorcees competing with other divorcees in a small town of married couples, Alexandra, Jane, and Sukie "depended on the infrangible triangle, the cone of power" (57) — with an emphasis on females and sisterhood reinforced by Updike's repeated references to "triangle power" and the female pudenda as a "demure triangular bush" (77). Like Hester, Alex and the other witches are women "infinitely fallen" from social graces, "from the world of decent and dreary amusements" that comprised the evenings of married couples who socialized together (48). But married life was no paradise. On the contrary, the divorced witches discover in their newfound freedom to copulate and in their sisterly cone of power a blissful state that they pronounce "paradise," with Jane urging, "We mustn't ever leave Eastwick" (191-92).

In a way, Updike had been building toward this fictional moment of sexual freedom, where adultery — an act he has said more than once that he felt was natural — could exist without guilt. Only in a secular society would that be remotely possible. Some fifteen years earlier, in *Couples,* Piet takes the burning of the church as a sign that he is removed from guilt. In *Witches,* set in Rhode Island — "Refuge of Quakers and antinomians, those final distillates of Puritanism" (9) — the reverend, not the church, is destroyed, and guilt is never much more than a few fleeting thoughts of how the witches' actions may or may not have been related to the deaths in the novel or to nature.

The eminent literary historian Alfred Kazin has noted that "Just as the structure of [*The Scarlet Letter*] climaxes in a sermon, so the Puritan tradition of reading sermons *to an audience that always knew what to expect*" is reflected in Hawthorne's novel (*God and the American Writer,* 33). But Dimmesdale's stirring sermon and confession have a doubly ironic counterpart in *Witches.* Churchgoers and readers are surprised first by the end-of-novel sermon delivered by Brenda Parsley, the minister's wife, who confesses on behalf of the wives in the congregation that "we have been guilty . . . of overlooking evil brewing in these very homes of Eastwick, our tranquil, solid-appearing homes" (*Witches,* 270) — and then are horrified as moths and butterflies emerge from her mouth, gagging her (272). Even more ironic, the reverend who slept with his parishioners had run away with a radical flower-child and was blown up trying to make anti-establishment bombs; as a result, the very last sermon in the novel comes neither from the minister nor from his wife. The last word from the pulpit comes from Darryl Van Horne, the satanic figure, who, as a guest lecturer, delivers a radical "secular sermon" (294) on the horrors of creation and ends by asking the congregation to "vote for me next time, O.K.? Amen" (293).

In both Hawthorne's and Updike's novels, a Satanic agent ironically acts as the *deus ex machina,* with both men thinking and speaking in terms of "bonds." A physician, Chillingworth talks of being connected to "a woman, a man, a child" by "the closest ligaments" (*Centenary Edition,* 1:76), while Van Horne, an inventor, seeks the "Big Interface" between solar energy and electrical energy (*Witches,* 46) and uses the language of a chemist to discuss male-female relations throughout the novel. Chillingworth tells Hester that drawing on his "old studies in alchemy," including the alchemic search for a universal solvent and elixir, have made him "a better physician" (*Centenary Edition,* 1:71). "I shall seek [the identity of Hester's lover], as I have sought truth in books; as I have sought gold in alchemy" (1:75), Chillingworth vows. Consistent with other reversals in *Witches,* Van Horne's theories all have something to do with selenium, and "Selenic acid can dissolve gold" (*Witches,* 172), not create it through the process of alchemy.

In *The Scarlet Letter,* Dimmesdale was already experiencing severe deterioration before Chillingworth came upon the scene (*Centenary Edition,* 1:120); the minister "tortured, but could not purify, himself" (1:145). Chillingworth works on him like an alchemist mining: "Let us dig a little further in the direction of this vein!" (1:130) until "at some inevitable moment will the soul of the sufferer be dissolved, and flow forth in a dark but transparent stream, bringing all its mysteries into the daylight" (1:124). In a manner befitting the title Hawthorne conferred upon him, Chillingworth tries to "leech" from him the cleansing confession that the author would have readers believe was necessary not only for the cuckold's revenge but also for the minister's salvation. Though Chillingworth experiences a Satanic ecstasy when he sees evidence of the inner disease finally leeched to the surface of the minister's chest (1:138), and though the minister finally perceives himself as a victim, the Leech's growing diabolization pushes the minister toward the confession that releases him from torment (1:252-53).

Leeching in *Witches* is about performance and power. Updike's witches have no real guilt, because, as Alex explains, a "natural principle" is that "we must lighten ourselves to survive" (*Witches*, 97-98), and that includes throwing off blame or guilt. But they are in danger of growing stagnant, and Van Horne serves as the witches' "redeemer from Eastwick *ennui*" (297). In addition to transforming their dull lives via the coven and what Harold Bloom termed "hot tub orgies" (Bloom, 4), he also tries to draw from each witch greater creative triumphs. And the witches are most receptive. Van Horne, looking at Alex's tiny folk-sculptures, tells her to "Think bigger" (*Witches*, 51), and he observes that Alex "could have mated with an elephant, thinking of becoming the next Niki de Saint-Phalle" (208). He tries to coax a novel out of a third-rate gossip columnist and more spirited performances from a second-rate cellist. "Jane came faithfully for her sessions," while Sukie "began to trip back and forth with notes for her novel" and "Alexandra timidly invited Van Horne to come view the large, weightless, enameled statues of floating women she had patted together" (207). Through flattery and discussions about gender and gender relations more frank and honest than any of the witches had ever experienced before, Van Horne makes each witch feel more comfortable about her imperfect body: "Splashing, they emerged cumbersomely: silver born in a chemical tumult from lead" (190) — another echo of Hester, whose "leaden infliction which it was her doom to endure" became "transfigured" by the golden thread used to make the A (*Centenary Edition*, 1:53-54, 57). Van Horne excites each witch by the possibility of attaining something greater, and while using them up physically and ultimately manipulating them into getting rid of Jenny, he nonetheless lifts their spirits in the process. Prior to Van Horne's arrival, the witches leeched strength from the men they slept with, and later grew "strong on Jenny's death, pulling strength from it as from a man's body" (*Witches*, 265). By the same token, Alex thinks how Van Horne "was a bundle of needs; he was a chasm that sucked her heart out of her chest" (47) — perhaps the most pointed allusion to Hawthorne's leech.

As if to distinguish between Satan and satanic agent, both men are summoned to begin their leeching endeavors, rather than acting on their own. "After her return to the prison, Hester Prynne was found to be in a state of nervous excitement that demanded constant watchfulness, lest she perpetrate violence on herself, or do some half-frenzied mischief to the poor babe," and so the jailer thinks to summon a physician "likewise familiar with whatever the savage people could teach" (*Centenary Edition,* 1:70). But Updike's witches are in need of stirring up, not calming down, and Updike has said that Van Horne "stirs them up in ways that the other men in the book don't" (Plath, ed., 263). Sukie, the gossip columnist, makes the first visit to Van Horne, urges Jane to follow, and the two of them cast a spell (242) to bring Alex, the strongest witch, to the "dark man" (*Witches,* 34).

Like Chillingworth, Van Horne begins with a modicum of good intentions and a scientist's curiosity. In the case of the former, however, readers quickly see any medical curiosity give way to Chillingworth's personal agenda: to leech out a confession from Dimmesdale no matter what it does to the minister physically, emotionally, or spiritually. He uses Hester in order to exact his revenge, coaxing a promise from her not to reveal his identity or purpose. Likewise, Van Horne's scientific curiosity and his desire to "leech" the boredom out of the witches' lives and to leech out of them bigger and better artistic accomplishments give way, ultimately, to his own agenda. He uses them to get rid of Jenny Gabriel so that he can run away with her brother, Chris. Updike once observed that this is "one of nature's jokes" — namely, that the witches would compete with each other for the affections of a man who ultimately turns out to be gay (Plath, ed., 265). And yet Updike by no means envisioned his devil as one-sidedly satanic. "*My* devil, Darryl Van Horne, is a weaker figure — no monster," he told one interviewer. "I had the idea to create him as a kind of experimenter, where it would be possible for him, through some short-cut in the physical theory of thermodynamics, to forever solve the energy problems on earth" (261). In this respect, Updike shares Lawrence's belief in Chillingworth as "a magician on the verge of modern science" (Lawrence, 98).

Roy Male is one of few critics to see something positive in Chillingworth, who, despite being a "leech, draining his patient of nerve, will, and physical energy . . . is also the healer. Only by knowing him, confronting him face to face, is moral growth possible" (Male, 96). Inexplicably, Male numbers among the questions that typical readings of the text fail to answer, "Why does Chillingworth wither and die soon after Dimmesdale confesses?" (93). If one extends the leech analogy and notes that as late as 1905 the classic nursing text by I. A.

Hampton included a section on using leeches to purify the blood, certainly Hawthorne was aware that leeching was not just a common but a respected medical practice of drawing out poisons, of purification. It makes more sense, then, to conclude that Chillingworth "leeches" the confession out of Dimmesdale, which, Hawthorne implies, saves the latter's soul.

While Male posits that Chillingworth "gradually shrivels as Hester and Dimmesdale come closer to full recognition of him" (96-97), it seems more consistent with Hawthorne's use of the Leech image to consider that Chillingworth, like a true leech, drops from the host once he has been sated. Hawthorne's leech, though satisfying his own thirst for blood-revenge, is still used by God, Dimmesdale knows: "By giving me this burning torture to bear upon my breast! By sending yonder dark and terrible old man to keep the torture always at red-heat. . . . Had either of these agonies been wanting, I had been lost forever! Praised be his name! His will be done! Farewell!" (*Centenary Edition,* 1:239). Indeed, readers are told that this "diabolical agent had the Divine permission, for a season, to burrow into the clergyman's intimacy and plot against his soul" (1:128), and the house the two men share has a tapestry of David, Bathsheba, and the prophet Nathan (1:126), which reinforces the notion of the Leech as a positive force, and not just "a treasure seeker in a dark cavern" (1:124). Once Hawthorne's Leech is able to extract the "sickness" of spirit that lodged within Dimmesdale's frail body (1:137), once the poisonous sin and guilt had been extracted, the fact that he shrivels and dies is most likely a reflection of the common belief that enough poisons ingested could in fact kill the parasite.

Not coincidentally, Van Horne's final sermon in *Witches* concentrates on nature, but after citing the example of a "predaceous arthropod," he relies almost exclusively on examples of parasites similar to leeches in order to illustrate that "THIS IS A TERRIBLE CREATION" (*Witches,* 287-93). "I've always been fascinated by parasites," he tells the congregation, using a dictionary rather than a Bible (290). Van Horne, like Chillingworth, is associated with both wildness and civilization. The reader's first glimpse of Chillingworth sees him standing next to an Indian and clad in "a strange disarray of civilized and savage costume" (*Centenary Edition,* 1:60), which reflects his practice of both "civilized" medicine, old school alchemy, and American Indian herbal cures. Updike's head witch, meanwhile, forms a first impression of Van Horne that also links him to American Indians: "she had brought with her from the West a regrettable trace of the regional prejudice against Indians and Chicanos, and to her eyes Darryl Van Horne didn't look *washed*" (*Witches,* 36). Sukie thinks he's a "wild man" (135), though when Jenny later says of Van Horne's tennis, "He's quite wild," Jane snaps, "Darryl Van Horne is quite the most civilized person I know" (179).

Like Chillingworth, Van Horne is also slightly deformed both by genetics and according to his indulgences. Chillingworth, who was "misshapen" from birth (*Centenary Edition,* 1:74) and spends more time stooped in study than he does in matters of the heart, has one shoulder higher than the other (1:60). Van Horne, a "dark man" (*Witches,* 34) whose hands were "eerily white-skinned beneath the hair, like tight surgical gloves" (43), strikes Alex as "a monster" at first (94). His penis resembles "one of those vanilla plastic vibrators" (107), imagery that is in keeping with Van Horne's and other males' association with artificiality and science, rather than things natural, and that also alludes to the mechanical way he made love to each witch. Both men also come replete with snake imagery. Across Chillingworth's face a "writhing horror twisted itself across his features, like a snake" (*Centenary Edition,* 1:61), and Van Horne's "vestigial male nipples" were "tiny warts surrounded by wet black snakes" (*Witches,* 110-11). Both men operate under aliases: "Under the appellation of Roger Chillingworth . . . was hidden another name" (*Centenary Edition,* 1:118, 127); "Lawyers now think that Darryl Van Horne was an assumed name" (*Witches,* 307). Just as Chillingworth's touch burns (*Centenary Edition,* 1:73), so does Van Horne's (*Witches,* 93-94, 96) — another *Scarlet Letter* trope.

Other textual echoes and parallels abound. Just as Hawthorne's novel is introduced by a local historian and related years later by an eyewitness, Updike's tale of witchcraft is told retrospectively by a current resident of Eastwick. In addition to a shared language of inner/outer motifs (*Centenary Edition,* 1:57-58, 61; *Witches,* 14, 164), both novels set the mood by offering a condensed local history and introducing themes of societal decay early in the narrative (*Centenary Edition,* 1:21, 50, 58; *Witches,* 9-10, 14, 23). Like Hawthorne, Updike also refers to a pronounced "stain" (*Witches,* 9, 23). Hawthorne's novel begins with Hester enduring the taunts of the townspeople, while Updike's has Alex enduring the name-calling of teenagers on the beach (13). As Hester must walk past Dimmesdale to get to Chillingworth in the novel's opening scenes, Alex must cross a Marsh Field (a playful allusion to Updike's Dimmesdale character from *A Month of Sundays*) in order to get to Van Horne the first time she visits. Both novels invoke the name of early feminist and anti-Puritan Ann(e) Hutchinson in the opening chapter and once again later in the narrative (*Centenary Edition,* 1:48, 165; *Witches,* 9, 269), and both refer to a single old woman suspected of being a witch — Mistress Hibbins (*Centenary Edition,* 1:49, 116, 149) and Abigail Lenox (*Witches,* 10). And in language that echoes Pearl's pebble-throwing incidents, where "Pearl would grow positively terrible in her puny wrath, snatching up stones to fling at [the children who tormented her], with shrill, incoherent exclamations that made her mother tremble because they had so much the sound of a witch's anathemas" (*Centenary Edition,* 1:94), Updike's old widow "went about the lanes muttering and cringing from the pebbles thrown at her by children who, called to account by the local constable, claimed they were defending themselves against her evil eye" (*Witches,* 10). Hawthorne's minister is so tormented by guilt and by his own weakness that he wields a "bloody scourge" against himself (*Centenary Edition,* 1:144, 148). An echo of that self-flagellation can be found in Updike's minister, who also dreams of a freer life, but reminds himself of his limitations: "As if to torment himself he wore a clergyman's collar" (*Witches,* 42).

Like Hester, who taught herself to become a seamstress so extraordinary that her skill transformed — transmuted, one might say — the stigma of the letter A into fine golden embroidery desired in imitation by others in society, the witches are self-taught artisans. While Hester is an adulteress who is publicly condemned and ridiculed from the start of the novel, the witches' public condemnation comes at the end of the novel during the course of Brenda Parsley's sermon. But just as Felicia Gabriel's private denouncement of the witches as "Whores and neurotics and a disgrace to the community" was muffled by feathers and straw coming out of her mouth (127-28), Parsley's condemnation is instantly choked off by moths and butterflies (272). In Hawthorne's novel, Hester endures "every variety of insult" and taunt (*Centenary Edition,* 1:57), and "Dames of elevated rank" tormented Hester "through that alchemy of quiet malice, by which women can concoct a subtile poison from ordinary trifles, and sometimes, also, by a coarser expression, that fell upon the sufferer's defenceless breast like a rough blow upon an ulcerated wound" (1:85).

Moreover, if Hester "entered a church, trusting to share the Sabbath smile of the Universal Father, it was often her mishap to find herself in the text of the discourse" (1:85). In *Witches,* the Other Women not only silence the gossips and rivals, but they are so removed from the gossip that they are not even in attendance to hear themselves slandered: "Sukie, everybody knew, would be in bed with that sly Arthur Hallybread while his wife was at church. . . . Jane Smart had gone all the way up to Warwick to play the Hammond organ for a cell of Moonies starting up. . . . Alexandra would be making her bubbies or weeding her mums" (*Witches,* 273). No public scaffold for any of them. If Hester fashioned an A that "had the effect of a spell" and "seemed to express the attitude of her spirit" — which was to face her accusers with "a haughty smile, and a glance that would not be abashed" (*Centenary Edition,* 1:53-54), then the witches' reaction to town gossips is equally defiant: "I just don't let gossip get to me, frankly," Sukie tells Alex. "Hold your head up and keep thinking, *Fuck you:* that's how I get down Dock Street every day" (*Witches,* 65).

For all their internal strength and spirited individualism, Hester and the witches aren't exactly mother-of-the-year candidates. When Hester "pressed her infant to her bosom with so convulsive a force that the poor babe uttered another cry of pain . . . the mother did not seem to hear it" (*Centenary Edition,* 1:60-61). Alex, afraid she might be stranded at the Lenox Mansion, is worried not about her "kids" but about her dog (*Witches,* 93); Sukie refers to hers as "brats" (78); and Jane admits she's "a dreadful mother" (237). In their preoccupation with Van Horne they begin to neglect their married men as much as their children. Such neglect, as much as anything, would have been enough to cause the wildness in Pearl that mystified Hester, Hawthorne, and readers. Therein lies more intertextuality: just as Pearl constructed "puppets . . . of witchcraft" from "the unlikeliest materials" (*Centenary Edition,* 1:95), Updike's three witches construct voodoo dolls to conjure up "husbands" and to do away with young Jenny Gabriel, who had married the man they had set their sights on.

Hawthorne's tale of adultery offers only the tantalizing promise of coupling, because Hester is able neither to run away to a new land with her lover nor to become reconciled with her legal husband — and she is most emphatically denied the chance of meeting someone else and experiencing passion again. The only "coupling" that occurs happens ironically when Chillingworth moves in with Dimmesdale. In

Hawthorne's purgatorial world, where souls find themselves caught between the laws of Nature and the laws of science and religion, social laws win out in the end. In Updike's Eastwick, where religion has all but lost its efficacy, the witches, who fantasize about marrying Van Horne, are also denied the object of their passion, who, just as Chillingworth "coupled" with Dimmesdale, attaches himself to a male — Jenny's brother, Chris.

In Salem in 1692, nineteen women were hanged because of suspected witchcraft; in Hawthorne's Boston, two witches — Mistress Hibbins and her friend, Ann Turner — are hanged offstage, the latter for the murder of a man (1:221); but in Updike's Eastwick, the only hanging is the suicide of *Word* editor Clyde Gabriel, yet another reversal in Updike's secular feminist version and a herald, perhaps, of things to come in the world of male-female relations. The dramatic question raised in *The Scarlet Letter* centers on women: "is there no virtue in woman, save what springs from a wholesome fear of the gallows?" (1:52); in *Witches,* the question, like so many other elements, is reversed: "Men aren't the answer, isn't that what we've decided?" Alexandra says, while Jane responds, "They're not the answer. But maybe they're the question" (*Witches,* 32).

In considering "the whole race of womanhood," Hester reasons that "the whole system of society is to be torn down and built up anew" and "the very nature of the opposite sex . . . is to be essentially modified before woman can be allowed to assume what seems a fair and suitable position" (*Centenary Edition,* 1:165). Such thoughts bring Hester to the edge of her own "insurmountable precipice," and for a time she wonders "whether it were not better to send Pearl at once to heaven, and go herself to such futurity as Eternal Justice should provide" (1:166). In Updike's fictional world, where the witches *do* have power, they not only contemplate but actually commit murder. "I was trying to explore, on the realistic level, the whole question of power in women," Updike has said. "Would it become less murderous in female hands? And, of course, my thought was, it wouldn't" (Plath, ed., 264).

In suggesting that language "*is* the curse, that took us out of Eden" (*Witches,* 146), Updike goes beyond Hawthorne's exploration of the stigma of a single letter to consider the ramifications that language — especially negative language, such as gossip — may have on a society. For those to whom Hester ministered, the letter A was a beacon that seemed to signify "Able": "Elsewhere the token of sin, it was the taper of the sick-chamber. It had even thrown its gleam, in the sufferer's hard extremity, across the verge of time. It had shown him where to set his foot, while the light of earth was fast becoming dim" (*Centenary Edition,* 1:161). Likewise, a meteor shaped like an A is taken to mean "Angel," since the phenomenon occurred on the night of the Governor's death (1:154-55, 158). And in having Pearl decorate herself with a green version of her mother's badge of shame (1:178), Hawthorne invites the reader to consider, not just the nature of sin, but the nature of signs and symbols as well.

"How short life is, how quickly its signs exhaust their meaning," Alex thinks (*Witches,* 236). In *Witches,* rather than a letter-shaped meteor, Updike provides readers with a longer airborne linguistic unit when, considering what to do about their rival, Jenny, the witches speak the vengefully magic word *hex:* "The word, like a shooting star suddenly making its scratch on the sky, commanded silence" (264). Leaving their own sisterly paradise, the witches experiment with a new "language" with Van Horne, "using the parts of his body as a vocabulary with which to speak to one another" (119). When Van Horne, in his devilish arrogance, asks to have his buttocks kissed squarely in the middle after a tennis game, "The smell seemed to be a message he must deliver, a word brought from afar" (183). "Words are just words" Jane argues at one point, Sukie disagreeing (160). But the central discussion of language occurs, fittingly, near the center of the novel within the point of view of *Word* editor Clyde Gabriel, who thinks, "Marriage is like two people locked up with one lesson to read, over and over, until the words become madness" (149). The right words can flatter and woo; the wrong words can insult, or kill, or, as happens, incite the Gabriels' murder-suicide, which ends with Clyde's skull filled with redness, "followed by blackness, giving way with the change of a single letter, to blankness" (156). A single word is capable of much. When Van Horne calls females "the superior mechanism," Alex thinks of all the routines in her life and concludes that she is "a robot cruelly conscious of every chronic motion" (68). A single, irritating word alters her mood and perspective, and "irritation, psychic as well as physical, was the source of cancer" (24) — Updike's argument for gossip being a real malignancy.

In "Emersonianism," Updike wrote that Hawthorne "remained at heart loyal to the Puritan sense of guilt and intrinsic limitation which Emerson so exultantly wished to banish" (*Odd Jobs,* 151). While

Updike all but banishes guilt in the secular state of Eastwick, in rewriting *The Scarlet Letter* from the perspective of Satan and the witches Updike sends typically mixed signals. While he suggests that Lawrence's revisionist view of Hester as an evil force may be interesting, he also seems to believe what Hawthorne is too timid to state outright: that Nature ultimately absolves everyone of blame or guilt. If nature was for Hester a sympathetic refuge (*Centenary Edition,* 1:203), Updike paints a less symbolic and one-dimensional portrait. The witches are used by Nature for birth, when "you're just a channel for this effort that comes from beyond" (*Witches,* 108), and for death, when "at worst [they] were the conduit" used to bring about Jenny's death (267). Nature, not the Satanic figure, remains the most ominous presence in *The Witches of Eastwick.* "Nature is always waiting, watching for you to lose faith so she can insert her fatal stitch," Alex thinks (24). And when Jenny tries to defend her marriage to Van Horne, Jane remarks, "Naturally nature took its nasty natural course" (231). "What's nature for if it's not adaptable?" one of the witches asks, while another responds, "It's adaptable to a point. Then it gets hurt feelings" (52). "There must also be sacrifice," Alex thinks as she crushes crabs to death on the beach. "It was one of nature's rules" (16).

Updike even endeavors to use nature to explain Clyde and Felicia's argument, which spirals out of control. There was "no reasoning with Felicia when her indignation started to flow, it was like a chemical, a kind of chemical reaction" (127-28). Felicia speaks with "a chemical viciousness that had become independent of her body, a possession controlling her mouth" (147), and as the "chemical and mechanical action that had replaced her soul surged on" and she continued to shout at her husband, Clyde found that his "own chemicals took over; he hit her head with the poker again and again" (148). Likewise, "We're not hurting Jenny," Sukie argues. "DNA is hurting Jenny," Jane says (268). But in *Witches* nature is also forgiving, taking at least as much pity as nature does in Hawthorne's novel. "Nature absorbs all," Alex thinks, recalling a time when as a young girl she urinated on the ground and saw a "dark splotch" on the "dry earth" (8). Nature absorbs all and absolves all. Hawthorne's Leech assures Hester, "Think not that I shall interfere with Heaven's own method of retribution, or, to my own loss, betray him to the gripe of human law" (*Centenary Edition,* 1:75). In other words, Chillingworth will go against neither God nor religion. He will let nature take its course — his own, and Dimmesdale's as well.

While Updike seems to build a meticulous case for Nature winning out, with Van Horne a necessary evil needed to "redeem" the witches briefly from their boredom, their redemption is short-lived. Each of the witches marries again, leaving their sisterly paradise and leaving behind any power they enjoyed as divorced women. Whereas Hester, in her isolation, "roamed as freely as the wild Indian in his woods" (*Centenary Edition*, 1:199), Alex marries her ceramics instructor, and he "took her and his stepchildren back west, where the air was ecstatically thin and all the witchcraft belonged to the Hopi and Navajo shamans" (*Witches*, 303-4). If Updike thinks the adulterous triangle a natural state, it is not, apparently, a permanent one.

In personifying gossip, Updike may "give gossip a body," but he does not give gossip much of a voice. The two women who would speak out against the witches — Felicia Gabriel and Brenda Parsley — are silenced with spells of feathers and butterflies, symbols of flight, trademarks of witches, and, one might speculate, a reflection of *human* nature. In giving gossip a body in a novel about sex, Updike also poses a Freudian alternative to Hawthorne's dilemma regarding the spirit and the flesh: that guilt is an internalized projection of external values transmitted, among other ways, through language. Alex's lover, Joe, is a strict Roman Catholic, and therefore "adultery had been a step toward damnation for him, and he was honoring one more obligation [in sleeping with her with the same weekly loyalty devoted to sports teams], a Satanic one" (59). Likewise, Sukie thinks about "the storms of [Ed Parsley's] guilt she would have to endure once he was sexually satisfied" (80). In *Witches*, only those who carry the vestiges of religion are bothered by guilt, and as Schiff observes, anyone who would condemn the divorcees/witches, such as a "highly judgmental moralist" like Felicia Gabriel or Brenda Parsley, is quickly silenced (*John Updike Revisited*, 83).

Though Updike claims he's "not a good Barthian" (Plath, ed., 103), he nonetheless accepts Karl Barth's views of nothingness as "that which God does not will. . . . Thus the devil — to give nothingness his name — thrives in proportion, never falls hopelessly behind, is always ready to enrich the rich man with ruin, the wise man with folly, the beautiful woman with degradation, the kind average man with debauches of savagery" (*Picked-Up Pieces*, 90). "Barth's formulas fit," he wrote in his introduction to *Soundings in Satanism:* "man is a battlefield, and Satan at best is 'behind one'" (*Picked-Up Pieces*, 90). In giving the devil his due, Updike, whether consciously or subconsciously, apparently tries to even the score, or at least underscores the primacy of a moral and ethical dialectic for balance or variety. "The heart *prefers* to move against the grain of circumstance; perversity is the soul's very life," Updike has written (*Assorted Prose,* 299). In the end, evil — whether it takes the form of mischief or malice, Nature or Satan — is more than just a welcome diversion from the boredom and routine of everyday goodness. It's edifying. As Alex senses, in "vileness there was something to push against and give her spirit exercise" (*Witches,* 71). Hawthorne ends his novel by having the narrator wonder if Pearl's "wild, rich nature had been softened and subdued, and made capable of a woman's gentle happiness" (*Centenary Edition,* 1:262), or if the "demon offspring" (1:261) and little witch (1:95) "might have mingled her wild blood with the lineage of the devoutest Puritan" (1:261). In *The Witches of Eastwick,* perhaps Updike suggests an answer.

Guru Industries, Ltd.

Red-Letter Religion in Updike's *S.*

JUDIE NEWMAN

In *Karma Cola,* her account of the mutual self-deception of East-West cultural encounters, Gita Mehta tells the tale of an Indian boy who gave his guru his faulty watch, only to have it returned, accurate once more, indicating the correct date, recording different time zones, and with an additional meter for measuring the depth of water.

> The devotee was staggered.
> "How did you do that?" he asked the guru.
> "You really want to know?" said his Master.
> "Yes, yes, Swami, I do," exclaimed the boy.
> "Look at the inscription on the back," counseled the Master.
> The boy turned the watch over and found engraved on his changed and wonderful timepiece the following words: Guru Industries, Ltd. (Mehta, 8)

In its image of the technological-corporate guru, the anecdote offers an appropriate point of entry to *S.*, Updike's third rewriting of *The Scarlet Letter. S.* situates its Hawthornian heroine in an American ashram, loosely based upon that of Rajneeshpuram in Oregon, demystifying and demythologizing the legend of Hawthorne's heroic Hester and drawing heavy critical fire in the process. Recent reconsiderations of *The Scarlet Letter* have tended to emphasize the Puritan background, with slavery, Native Americans, and witchcraft high on the agenda, whether in critical accounts or recent adaptations. Consider, for example, the slave girl's story of Maryse Condé's *I Tituba* and the Puritan origins in Britain of Christopher Bigsby's *Hester* and *Pearl*. And then there is the namesake 1995 film in which, irrespective of the original, the screen is knee-deep in Native Americans to whom Dimmesdale is pastor. Further, a well-endowed female slave features prominently (but redundantly) in a bath, and Demi Moore, as a convicted witch, is rescued from the scaffold by Dimmesdale on a charger. Updike is not, however, the first to draw an Indian connection. Bharati Mukherjee's *The Holder of the World* excavates links between pre-colonial Mughal India and seventeenth-century Massachusetts as the heroine moves from Salem to the Coromandel Coast and the court of Aurangzebe, focusing closely on the trade with the Indies that was the economic mainstay of mercantile New England.[1]

As Luther S. Luedtke has amply demonstrated, between the 1780s and 1830s Hawthorne's native town of Salem was a major international port for the East Indies and China trade, dealing especially in pepper, for which it had a virtual monopoly. So extensive were Salem's Eastern contacts that some traders actually believed that Salem (not America) was a sovereign nation. It was probably the richest American city per capita by 1790. In "Old News" Hawthorne himself noted the luxury of the New England merchants' houses, their silks, damasks, ivory, china, and cashmere, all dependent upon a process of quasi-colonial looting of Eastern others. In *S.* Updike makes much of Sarah Worth's Puritan ancestors, from whom she inherits a quantity of plate, a sea chest that "accompanied Daddy's great-granddaddy back and forth to China countless times" (*S.*, 264), and antique pepper shakers — invoking both the profits and the raw material of the trade on which Hawthorne's family fortunes were founded. To those same ancestors she also owes her glossy hair and swarthy complexion, which recall Hawthorne's famous description of his heroine as having "a rich, voluptuous, Oriental characteristic" (*Scarlet Letter*, 83).

Where Hawthorne chose to emphasize Puritan religious history, glossing over the mercantile and imperialist enterprise in the empty space between the contemporary decline of "The Custom-house" and

1. See Newman, "Spaces in Between," for details of recent adaptations.

the scene of origins in the 1640s, Updike turns the tables. He displays an Indian religious community, transplanted to America, where its leaders pursue their own "errand into the wilderness," found their own "city on a hill," and face considerable hostility from the prior inhabitants. Just as the Puritan settlement exhibited its goods as evidence of divine favor, with material goods an index of spiritual good, so Updike's ashram, dedicated to technological and capitalist triumphalism, masks global exploitation and profiteering — though in this case the direction of trade is reversed. Updike therefore offers an instructive account of the imperialist purposes to which apparently "alternative" religion may be put, exploring the new market in alterity and considering the relation between American idealism and its material embodiments.

While the novel engages with issues concerning a woman setting herself free from patriarchal power, as suggestive readings by Schiff and Bower, among others, attest, it is the economic revenge of the previously exploited that occupies center stage. Critical readings of *S.* have tended to focus upon Sarah-as-Hester, rather than on the Indian-as-Other, perhaps because the Arhat, Updike's guru, is revealed in the closing pages to be Art Steinmetz, a Jewish-Armenian-American from Watertown, Massachusetts. The impersonation brings into sharp relief the major focus of the novel, the commercial uses to which the "Other" can be put and the advantages of exotic identity for religious marketing purposes. In his portrayal of the ashram, Updike's focus is relentlessly economic, as Sarah eventually rises through the corporate hierarchy to become the Chief Accountant of what is effectively less a religious cult than a transnational corporation. Sarah writes the Arhat's begging letters, plus letters of thanks for donations, and is responsible for correspondence over unpaid bills. She is also embroiled in her own financial entanglements following the end of her marriage, her mother's investments, her dentist's and psychiatrists's accounts (both seen as excessive given their poor results), and the bills for her hired car and her personal banking arrangements — which include accounts into which a considerable proportion of the Arhat's donations are diverted.

For all the manifold connections that commentators have drawn between Puritanism and capitalism, this heroine is a far cry from the one depicted in *The Scarlet Letter.* Do readers ever imagine Hester Prynne walking off with the contents of the collection plate? Yet this is essentially what Sarah does. By looting, in her turn, the fortunes of the cult Sarah reenacts her ancestors' predations and casts contemporary

American materialism into sharp relief. In the epistolary form of the novel Sarah's letters therefore offer an alternative, proliferated reading of *The Scarlet Letter,* recalling less the red letter marking calendrical holy days, religious inscriptions, and moral corrections than the red ink of old-fashioned accountancy. Sarah contributes, quite literally, to getting the ashram "in the red."[2] Because the ashram polices its mail, opening letters and keeping its inhabitants under a surveillance as strict as that of the Puritans, Sarah's letters fall into two categories. The first is those for public consumption — accounts of her religious experiences, innocuous family communications, and form letters adapted to order at the Arhat's behest. The second is those dispatched secretly from a nearby motel, which bleed out the ashram's funds to Sarah's own Swiss and Bahaman bank accounts, transfer other funds from marital to individual accounts, and — in an image that in the light of events in the White House in the late 1990s has become evocative of a culture in which personal relationships are convertible into hard cash — convey for safe keeping into the hands of her brother in Latin America a tape of a sexual encounter, for purposes of future blackmail.

In targeting the economic and exploitative purposes of letters, therefore, Updike's satire targets both American and Indian materialisms and also scores a hit at contemporary cultural economics. Sarah's letters to her daughter, a student successively at Yale and at Oxford, make sly sideswipes at Bloom and other academics, deconstruction, and the flourishing career of that contradiction in terms, a Marxist professor in an Oxford college. The combined result is to induce Pearl to abandon the study of letters altogether in favor of a return to the Old World in the arms of a Dutch count, a "Red Letter" man — a Roman Catholic in British parlance, one who regularly observes the calendar's red-lettered holy days.

Up to this point it may appear that Updike's portrayal is entirely satiric at the expense of Eastern religion and of American materialism. There is, however, a sting in the tale. The ashram is not quite as easily discounted as it first seems. Two intertexts are available to the reader — Hawthorne's *The Scarlet Letter* and the Neo-Sannyas International Movement (popularly known as the Rajneeshees) led by their Bhagwan, which forms Updike's other major source.

2. The phrase is itself the product of imperialism. The British were the first to use red ink for deficits and the practice spread throughout the British Empire.

Of the two, the references to Hawthorne are unlikely to be missed by any reader with a high school education. The novel's two epigraphs are taken from *The Scarlet Letter.* In Hawthorne's novel, set in Puritan New England, Hester Prynne is condemned to wear a scarlet letter A on her chest as a badge of shame. In the absence of her physician husband, Roger (aka Roger Chillingworth), Hester yields to erotic temptation with Arthur Dimmesdale, the local pastor, to whom she bears a daughter, Pearl, a child who is almost removed from her by the elders of the community. Social ostracism sets Hester free to some extent from the narrow constraints of Puritan ideology, and she transmogrifies into a freethinker and emblem of passion and rebellion. In the novel's outcome Chillingworth succeeds in defeating Hester's escape plans, Dimmesdale confesses and dies, Pearl returns to the Old World, and Hester ends her days in gloomy Boston, still something of a walking sandwich board against sin.

Updike's Sarah, a descendent of the Prynnes (*S.*, 26), is the wife of Charles Worth (a physician repeatedly described as of a chilly nature), falls in love with her Arthur (Art/Arhat), and follows his religious leadership to the extent of decamping to his ashram in Arizona, there to indulge her own passions fairly comprehensively in a sexualized neo-Tantric theocracy. Passing through the Hawthorne area of Los Angeles to put pursuers off her track, she drives to the ashram via the Babbling Brook Motor Lodge in Forrest, Arizona, a parodic reminder of Hawthorne's crucial "forest scene" between Hester and Dimmesdale. She settles down in an "A-frame" whence she writes letters to her mother, repeatedly singing the praises of vitamin A; to her "elf-child" (90) daughter Pearl, who imitates the fate of her original; and to her brother, who stores her tape away, much as Hester's story was hidden. When Pearl announces her intention to marry, Sarah sees herself as consigned to the role of ancestor, "a sad old story, buried amidst the rubbish in the custom-house attic" (206), though pragmatically she advises her pregnant daughter to wear a concealing A-line wedding dress. The letter A unpacks and proliferates to include her decidedly non-phallic Lesbian lover, Alinga ("Dearest A" in lovenotes), the Arhat, the ashram, accounting, and Arizona. Updike transfers events to the region of Phoenix, in homage to the personal symbol of that most perspicacious critic of Hawthorne, D. H. Lawrence.

Like her original, Sarah's hair is gleaming (21), and her complexion also dark, though Updike invokes a different Indian resonance —

"like a squaw" (7). Where Hester embroidered the scarlet letter, Sarah describes her letters (her wiggles) as embroidery (158). Previously she had attempted to embroider a series of place mats with the letter W (for Worth), but gave up. Hawthorne embroidered his original name, Hathorne, with a W, to separate himself from his ancestors. Since Sarah tapes some of her letters clandestinely with the recorder secreted between her breasts, the novel also re-creates the spatial position of Hester's letter. Hester was imprisoned for her crimes and retained a sympathy for other outcasts; Sarah describes marriage as a jail (166), with her husband as warden, and writes sympathetically to a prisoner, her hairdresser's delinquent son. Sarah is well aware of the implications of her Puritan heritage. She describes "earthly prosperity as a sign of divine election" (66) and laments her repressed upbringing in "atrophied Puritan theocracy" (103). Even her worries about the real estate left behind in Massachusetts are of a piece with Hawthorne's anxieties over the skyrocketing real estate values of his day, a motive force (according to Walter Benn Michaels) in his choice of the romance genre. The plot also involves medical terrorism reminiscent of Chillingworth's torture of Dimmesdale (assorted poisonings with mind-altering drugs).

In one respect, however, Updike breaks with his original. Sarah makes good her escape to the Bahamas. Charles is left to marry Midge Hibbens, the witchy Mistress Hibbens of Hawthorne's tale, while Sarah is free from patriarchal shaming. In Hawthorne's novel, the scarlet letter, a piece of red cloth signaling a woman's shame, has biological implications that hardly need to be spelled out, invoking Eve's female wound and her punishment. Updike translates A into S, the first letter of *The Scarlet Letter*'s title, which also means Sarah, sex, $, and serpent. Sarah is renamed Kundalini, little serpent, by the Arhat, a name that revalidates female sexual energy and its various expressive "wiggles." Critics, however, while generally amused by Updike's ludic play with his original, and often perceiving a general appropriateness in his adaptation of the novel that he himself described as "the one classic from the lusty youth of American literature which deals with society in its actual heterosexual weave" (*Odd Jobs*, 858), have been puzzled by the specifics of the literary reference. As one reviewer put it,

> What he has not provided is any convincing reason to consider Sarah a modern equivalent of Hester Prynne, of *The Scarlet Letter,* although

he certainly wishes her to be seen in that character. Now, why should Updike cling to Hawthorne's coat-tails? (Adams, 78)

The answer is to be found in the other intertext, the Indian material. In the first place the Rajneeshee sect offers almost too good an opportunity to translate Hester physically into a twentieth-century image. Like the Rajneeshees, Sarah and her fellow disciples are clad in "sunset colors" — red, scarlet, pink, purple — the uniform of the movement. They are embodied red letters, physical representations of a religious message. Just as Sarah's own letters are irremediably concerned with the physical (bodily functions, sex, dentistry, and hair dye, as Bower notes), so the sexual and physical emphasis of the cult is proclaimed in its sumptuary laws. Quite apart from the sunset colors, Bhagwan also believed in the separation of mother and child — "all the damage that is done to a child is done by the mother," he said (Milne, 283), and one reason the local people were alienated was the Rajneeshee takeover of the local school.

Most importantly, the Arhat leads a religion that is a mirror image of Puritan self-denial — a religion of indulgence. Updike acknowledges the Rajneeshees and their Oregon settlement as his source in his "Author's Note," though with the usual disclaimer underlining the novel's entire fictionality. Readers who have yet to encounter the Rajneeshees will find an abundant secondary literature at their disposal, though the stories elaborate almost as many conflicting meanings as Hawthorne's A. In one version, the Rajneeshees, led by their Bhagwan, settle peacefully on poor land in a remote area of Oregon, building an ecologically friendly agricultural commune and pursuing their own ideals of love and peace. Friendly commentators emphasized the productive nature of the community, the importance of women in its governing hierarchy, a general emphasis on gender equality, a high proportion middle-class population profile of "drop-ups" rather than dropouts, well-educated disciples — many with doctoral degrees — the interest in new irrigation and farming techniques, and the classically American Utopian mission.

Although in the end the community collapsed, that failure is ascribed to local hostility, with the native Oregonians variously described as bigots, rednecks, right-wing fundamentalists, or the pawns of the land-use lobby. The ashram fell apart largely as a result of a ruling that its main settlement, Rajneeshpuram, violated the federal church-state separation — in short, that it was a theocracy. As liberal commentators argued, however, the Utopian religious community has a long history in America. The Shakers, Mormons, Oneida community, Twenties, Amines, and even the Transits were variously invoked as successful examples of American tolerance for communities at variance with the public political norm. The image of a religious group, ostensibly fleeing persecution in its original location to find religious freedom in America and then falling afoul of the original inhabitants, struck a resonant historical chord.

The question of what constitutes a religion, and what immunities are not granted to religions by secular societies, remains a delicate and still to some extent an open issue in American law. The Rajneeshees' vigorous defense of their way of life, construed by many Oregonians as overaggressive, was also linked to the large number of Jewish disciples (see Murphy), a group who had continually in their mind the example of the dangers of not resisting the original threat sufficiently forcefully. (Updike's Arhat embodies two histories of genocide, Armenian as well as Jewish.) A disturbing insight into the American psyche was provided by the many letters to local papers, often invoking the Rajneeshees garments and the slogan "better dead than red." Even setting aside the usual complement of fanatics (accusations of Satanism and human sacrifice were commonplace), many U.S. citizens clearly did not extend religious toleration beyond the various forms of Christianity. A writer to the *Madras Pioneer,* March 3, 1983, simply argued that the religious freedom of the American pioneers excluded "the pagan religion or 'isms' of the Eastern world" (Bromley et al., 148). In realizing their aim of creating an alternative model of society for humankind, the Rajneeshees had a long way to go before they could earn much credit with their neighbors, to whom the red-letter side of the spiritual and social ledger was a great deal more obvious. Among the accusations leveled at the sect were sexual orgies (the film *Ashram,* with its images of naked Westerners engaged in a variety of group sex acts, often violent, was widely shown in Oregon cinemas), mind control, racketeering, drug smuggling, and prostitution.

Hugh Milne, a British ex-sannyassin (the term for disciple), describes the central belief system of the movement as Tantric. Members indulge themselves (in sexual or material terms) in order to transcend indulgence. All energy is understood as fundamentally sexual, finding its origin in the base of the spine, imaged as Kundalini, the little coiled serpent. When properly freed, it will travel up the spine to the brain, uniting with the mind and spiritual heart in an embrace of love and consciousness. Though the process is portrayed in sexual terms and in ancient images, it is with the understanding that the Tantric energies are harnessed to a discipline of awareness (Milne, 137). Tantric followers therefore believe that it is through fulfillment rather than austerity that true enlightenment is reached. Bhagwan's beliefs come essentially from the Advaita tradition of Hinduism, a view of the universe in which there is no separation between the spiritual and the material, or between God and humankind. All aspects of life are coexistent as manifestations of the universal "One." In India, Bhagwan had married the essentials of Tantrism with a whole shopping basket full of Western "human potential" practices — Rolfing,[3] primal screaming, EST,[4] dynamic meditation, bio-energetics, and gestalt — stirred into a potent cocktail, with an eclectic blending of Freud, Jung, Nietzsche, Maslow, Tao, Sufi, and Zen thrown in to boot. As a result the movement was able to access an extensive preexistent network of Western "seekers." In contrast, the reception in India cooled rapidly. Open displays of sexual behavior did not find favor with the inhabitants of Poona. The Bhagwan's cheerful instruction to couples to "Let the whole neighborhood know when you are making love" was not advice likely to endear the sannyassin to their Hindu neighbors. Bhagwan became known as the "guru of the vagina." He gave long lectures on the female orgasm and the function of the clitoris. The sexual side of the movement was, however, a clear expression of a belief that enlightenment depended upon the transcendence not only of repression (and the social institutions that supposedly cripple self-realization) but also of indulgence.

As a "mall religion," however, it was the financial aspect of the movement that was most striking. Bhagwan's first modest apartment had been paid for by the A1 biscuit factory in Bombay. By the time he left India, enmeshed in complex financial disputes over taxes, the movement had spread across five continents in two decades, with secondary ashrams, massage parlors, discotheques, "Zorba the Buddha" restaurants, and radical therapy centers. Milne estimates (295) that by

3. "Rolfing" is a technique of deep muscular massage aimed at releasing emotional energy presumed to be lodged in the muscles.

4. EST is an acronym that stands for Erhard Seminar Training, now re-named The Forum, a strict form of self-help therapy.

1985 the movement had twenty-eight bank accounts in five countries plus America, with twenty-four corporations, foundations, institutes, and "universities" worldwide, and assets estimated in 1983 at $30.8 million. Unlike the popular image of the ascetic guru, Bhagwan espoused capitalism with a vengeance, arguing that "whenever a country becomes very rich it becomes religious" (Price, 38), since it is only when basic needs for food and shelter have been met that human beings can occupy themselves with spiritual matters rather than the daily battle for survival. Bhagwan had no time for Gandhian socialism, and he saw the salvation of his fellow Indians as vested in technology. Eventually he had four web sites; digitalized videos of his lectures were available, and the ashram boasted extremely up-to-date bugging techniques. One of the ashram's souvenir stickers read, "Moses Invests, Jesus Saves, Bhagwan Spends." The prominent display of wealth included a fleet of Rolls Royces. As an esoteric religion, defined by practices rather than codified beliefs, and without a defined ideological system, Rajneeshism could be swiftly tailored to different markets. More concretely, the ashram included its own mall, which followed the same financial principles as Disneyland: everything the visitor or resident could want was under one roof. No money could escape into the surrounding community. Products included Bhagwan beer steins, pillowcases, videocassettes, audiocassettes, and T-shirts.

When harassment began in Oregon, Bhagwan hired a former troubleshooter for a multinational company whose advice was trenchant. In his view, Bhagwan's mistake was to have tried to set up a non-profit-making company with several "front" corporations, when he was clearly making money: "The best thing you can do is come clean. Abolish them all and form one honest, profit-making company. If you pay tax in America, no-one will bother you" (Milne, 225). This advice was disregarded, and grand juries, immigration and tax authorities, and state investigators eventually closed in, with evidence presented suggesting that Bhagwan was in America under false pretences, had lied to the INS (Immigration and Naturalization Service), arranged bogus marriages for immigration purposes, and, contrary to the U.S. statute that enjoins the separation of church and state, had used his religious standing to influence county elections. Bhagwan attempted to leave for Bermuda or the Bahamas, was held in custody, and eventually was given a ten-year suspended sentence, five years probation, a fine of $400,000, and five days to leave the country.

Supporters nonetheless continued to see Bhagwan as more sinned against than sinning. Control of the ashram had been taken over, according to some accounts, by a group of women. Paradise had once more found its traitorous Eve. Milne paints a darker picture of bugging, wire-tapping, surveillance, poisoning, an armed security force, false AIDS tests, mind-altering drugs in the canteen food, salmonella sprinkled on the salad bars of The Dalles (to reduce the voting electorate for a crucial election), Bhagwan's addiction to nitrous oxide or dentist's laughing gas (hence his sibilant speech), and a variety of other abuses. Bhagwan's main female associate was rumored to have a large collection of cassette tapes, secretly recording Bhagwan's instructions to her on how to run the commune — and preserved to be used in her defense. In Milne's view,

> [Bhagwan] knew as much as the head of any large multi-national corporation knows what is going on in his organisation. He chose all his top executives, manipulated and controlled their public and private lives, and used a peculiar form of economic blackmail to keep them in harness. He allowed them to amass enormous personal fortunes, then used greed as a lever to obtain precisely what he wanted, including 43 Rolls Royces. (307)

In the end, thirty-four Rajneeshees were charged with twelve kinds of state or federal offenses — attempted murder, first- and second-degree assault, first-degree arson, burglary, racketeering, harboring a fugitive, immigration conspiracies, lying to the U.S. authorities, and criminal conspiracy. It seemed a very far remove from the Mormons or the Trappists.

Which of the different stories does Updike espouse? The parallels between Updike's Arhat and the historical Bhagwan and his movement are very close. Updike shifts the scene to Arizona, but specific events common to Bhagwan and Arhat include the following: daily limousine wave-by (*S.*, 30), the use of sunset colors (33), the description of work as worship (32), the construction of an enormous community hall (officially a greenhouse), construction work, A-frames, a shopping mall, the absence of children, the origins of the ashram in India (34), local redneck opposition (35), a central fountain surrounded by rainbow jets (36), armed guards (37), compulsory V.D. checks (40), continual surveillance (40), dynamic meditation involving violence and rape attempts (43), the combination of Tantric yoga with encounter therapy (47), the educated "yuppie" population, the guru's dental chair (74) and his limousines and wristwatches, the suggestion of doctored food (115), charges of drug smuggling and prostitution by group members (described in the same context as "to gather sweets," 124), problems over land-use laws (142) and taxes (146), immigration problems (174), a flurry of lawsuits (190), controversy over control of local children's education, financial decline following over-zealous centralization policies, the evolution of a female-dominated hierarchy, blackmail tapes, and the Bahaman escape.

Ostensibly the closeness of the parallels inclines the reader to an unfavorable reading of the activities of the ashram, suggesting that Updike takes a satirical view of the hybrid blend of Eastern and Western beliefs. Yet in one respect at least Sarah acts upon Eastern beliefs. In *The Scarlet Letter* Hester Prynne is marked by her silence, keeping the secrets of her love affair and of Pearl's paternity, both biological and — in the person of her disguised husband — legal. The letter A keeps its meaning. Hawthorne never tells us that it stands for adultery (see Calinescu), and Angel, America, Art, alpha, alphabet, Able, Abolition, and apocalypse are only a few of the alternative meanings offered. In contrast, Sarah is nothing if not voluble, babbling, disclosing, filling every last inch of recording tape — almost embarrassing her reader with an unedited flood of tapes, letters, and notes to her family and friends, her hairdresser and *her* family, her dentist and psychoanalyst, and her husband — discussing, *inter alia,* lawn care, vitamin supplements, hair dyes, and sexual encounters in minutely specific detail. In short, we are informed about everything from her domestic plumbing to the state of her back teeth. Significantly, she has never worked out how to erase. The reader's experience is further complicated by the frequent use of Sanskrit words and phrases, helpfully glossed by Updike but, as Sarah admits, susceptible to various interpretations. Every Sanskrit word contains "a whole lotus of meanings" (98).

On the one hand, the very elaboration and proliferation of the letters reveals her own deceptions (of self and others). In rapid succession, for example, the reader notes a letter decrying materialism (95) followed in two days time by another depositing $18,000 in her personal account. Fulsome letters seeking a donation for the ashram from Mrs. Blithedale (the name recalling the similarly naive Utopians of Hawthorne's *The Blithedale Romance*) are followed by grateful acknowledgment of $500,000 on December 1, and by two deposits each of $100,000 in her personal accounts on December 3. As "read" letters, letters that we read as the omniscient readers, as opposed to the variously deceived recipients, Sarah's outpourings betray her even more comprehensively than Hester's scarlet letter. Like the scarlet letter, however, elaboration alters the meaning, if not from adulteress to angel, at least away from straightforward condemnation. Elaboration is itself in tune with the creed of finding oneself through indulgence.

At one point Sarah encloses a tape of the Arhat as a present for Midge, a recording of a long and over-detailed yarn spun by the guru in one of his public audiences concerning the ascent of Kundalini. At the close, however, the Arhat erases the tale:

> Did you believe the story of her journey? . . . All a lie. . . . The story of her journey is a very detailed lie, like the horrible cosmology of the Jains or the Heaven and Hell of Dante. (82)

He closes with the moral — that immersion in such detailed accounts is nonetheless the way to enlightenment.

> That is why I have told you the fairy story of Kundalini, the little snake that lives at the bottom of our spine. While you were hearing it, no other garbage was in your hearts or heads or stomachs; little Kundalini burned it all away. (83)

The story of *S.* is also, of course, the story of Kundalini-Sarah, as told by Updike, whose witty defense of his elaborate fiction depends also upon the notion of using "foolishness to drive out foolishness" (83), fiction to gain access to truth. Sarah purifies the ashram of its "garbage" by spiriting much of it away. Sarah's story is Kundalini's, full of deceit, foolishness, redundant details, and deceptions; but her story also immerses the reader in an exaggerated version of the American mission gone wrong, of materialism, plunder, and sexual indulgence, with the aim of clearing the ground for a fresh start. Where Hester's story is an untold story, undercutting its society by its secret content (see Calinescu), Sarah's story is a "read" story, a retelling of a story with which we are already familiar. As a "read" letter the story reaches toward truth through over-elaboration, embroidery, over-indulgence, redundancy — exactly the *modus operandi* of the Arhat and his original, the Bhagwan. Where Hester herself disappeared behind the embroidered letter, her secret both advertised and kept hidden, Sarah's wiggles (the letters she now does "instead of embroidery," 158) turn elaboration into revelation. At various points Sarah signs her letters Sarah, S, Mother, Sarah Worth, Sarah Worth (Mrs. Charles), Sally Worth, Sare, Sarah P. Worth, Sis, Sara née Price, #4723-9001-7469-8666, Ma Prem Kundalini, and Arhat. Her letters are, in the serpentine imagery of Kundalini, a form of "skin-shedding" in the service of the emergence of a new self.

In the final analysis, therefore, Updike's novel owes as much to its Indian materials as Hawthorne's did to his. *S.*'s critique of materialism and deception depends for its method upon an Indian model. It also looks ahead to the future. If on one level *S.* offers the cautionary spectacle of the West depending on its formerly exploited "others" for self-definition, it also highlights the new imperialism of transnational corporatism. The Bhagwan's enterprise was not just a cult but a non-located capitalist enclave with a marketable alterity. Like any giant company, the Rajneeshees transferred capital, raw materials, labor, and sales outlets across national boundaries, with loyalty owed to a corporate rather than a national identity. Updike commented on Hawthorne that "it needs no Max Weber to connect Puritanism with the dark forces of material enterprise" (*Hugging the Shore,* 76), clearly identifying the devil in Massachusetts with an emergent mercantile capitalism. In *S.*, American idealism takes something of a fall, but the economic impulses embedded within it survive and flourish. It is not for nothing that the novel ends with an alternative image of American beginnings. Sarah ends the novel in "a little paradise" (*S.*, 240), the spot where Columbus reputedly first landed, the alpha point for American meanings. Updike's rival tale of origins locates its newly liberated heroine, not on the shores of a new England, as a noble spiritual pilgrim seeking an immaterial good, but in the Bahaman tax haven where Columbus landed, intent on discovering the spices of the Indies, which were to become the economic foundation of New England.

Chaos and Society

Religion and the Idea of Civil Order in Updike's *Memories of the Ford Administration*

GEORGE S. DIAMOND

It was not a dark and stormy night. It was a crisp and clear Friday, March 13, 1982, the ideal transition between winter and spring, and it was the day I had the privilege of driving John Updike to his mother's home in Shillington, Pennsylvania, a rural enclave near Reading. Updike had just completed a day at Moravian College in Bethlehem, meeting informally with groups of students, and — to a packed and enthusiastic house — reading from his work and answering questions about the art and craft of writing. There is an especially warm feeling for Updike at Moravian College. When our new library was dedicated in October 1967, we gave him an honorary degree, for a career in progress. Over the years we watched as his career blossomed and he matured as an artist. Now, fifteen years later, he had returned for a very successful visit, and as we drove west on PA Route 22 we left a campus cheered and enriched by his presence.

Updike was visibly tired after a busy day at the college, but we had a chance to talk in the hour and a half it took to drive out to Shillington. The conversation was mostly about current affairs and politics, and in the course of our dialogue I was struck by Updike's belief in and affection for both this country and the democratic experiment. He also expressed confidence in and concern and admiration for the men who had been elected its presidents. There was none of the sarcasm, bitterness, and acrimony that had been poured upon the nation and its leaders by many in the community of letters during the turbulent historical period that had taken place in America between Updike's two visits to the college.

In his later memoirs, *Self-Consciousness,* Updike alludes to this acrimony, which he found disturbing and disquieting. In that work he had declared himself a registered Democrat who was interested in the successful operation of the political process. In fact, he had played an active role in Jimmy Carter's successful run for the presidency, but despite his political orientation he had no rancor toward the Republican Party and even expressed good will toward Ronald Reagan, then in office fourteen months. About the protests during the Vietnam era he said: "But I — I whose stock and trade as an American author included an intuition into the mass consciousness and an identification with our national fortunes — thought it sad that our patriotic myth of invincible virtue was crashing, and shocking that so many Americans were gleeful at the crash" (*Self-Consciousness,* 124).

There seemed a moderate and a temperate quality in his political views, reminiscent of the civil and civilized attitude of Saul Bellow, that provided a refreshing alternative to the angry noise that had washed across the land for almost a decade and a half. One did not need to be an old-fashioned patriot, waving the flag — or the bloody shirt — to understand that there is a point at which national self-hatred becomes a dead end, a philosophical black hole from which no light can emerge. As he has since demonstrated, Updike clearly possesses an admirable grasp of history and its ramifications, including a historian's perspective. He seems to have developed the awareness and the wisdom to comprehend that people and events must be understood within the context of the time in which they have lived and acted. In examining Updike's political preferences, one might conclude that, instead of demanding immediate reform and redress, instead of damning the process and its executors, he knows that matters must be kept in perspective, that circumstances change, crises pass, and, more often than not, those elected to public office — in spite of their weaknesses and their flaws, in spite of a necessarily limited perspective — do the best they can. Political leaders generally try to ignore the criticism of the present and leave history to judge the results of their actions.

The surprisingly moderate tone of Updike's political point of view that he expressed to me personally on that drive to Shillington is evident in an examination of his writings. Something more than the objectivity of a novelist *cum* historian seems to be at work there, something that runs very deep in his psyche. This may offer a clue as to why, of all the historical figures Updike might have chosen to celebrate, it was Pennsylvania's own, President James Buchanan. It is Buchanan who appears in two of Updike's works: a play, *Buchanan Dying,* and the novel *Memories of the Ford Administration.*

Alas, poor Buchanan! Our fifteenth president has never enjoyed a high standing with historians. They have tended to denigrate Buchanan's contributions to the presidency and the nation — even in relation to the other well-meaning bunglers who occupied the presidency before the Civil War. His status as the only bachelor president (according to Updike also the only virgin president) is apparently as noteworthy as anything he attempted or accomplished during his term of office. Updike critic James Schiff, referencing Henry Steele Commager and other historians, describes Buchanan as "among America's least memorable presidents," if not in fact the worst (*John Updike Revisited,* 128). So why then Buchanan? Is there something in Updike himself, in his Shillington upbringing, his education, and his religious rearing, that has enabled him to cast a benign eye on Buchanan and his presidency? And does this benign eye tell us something deeper about Updike's belief in the importance of civility, in civil government, and the sources from whence it comes? The answers may be found in an examination of the novel *Memories of the Ford Administration,* supplemented by the novelist's candid description of his own life and times in *Self-Consciousness.*

First of all, *Memories of the Ford Administration* is something of a misnomer, since there is precious little history of the Ford administration in the novel. The narrator there describes the unfolding of events fifteen years after they have occurred, from a perspective in the early nineties. His thumbnail sketch of the Ford administration, which he relates with some admiration, tells us something of his political and philosophical viewpoint, but more importantly it affirms his acceptance of the idea that human action is always limited in its influence, even when the actor is the most politically powerful individual on earth. As the narrator of this story, Alfred Landon Clayton, professor of history, relates the major events of the Ford administration, we can hear the echo of Updike approving the fundamental decency and the actions of his subject — a very, very accidental president:

> As far as I could tell, Ford was doing everything right — he got the *Mayaguez* back from the Cambodians, evacuated from Vietnam our embassy staff and hangers-on (literally: there were pictures of people clinging to the helicopter skids in the newsmagazines in my dentist's office), went to Helsinki to meet Brezhnev and sign some peaceable accords, slowly won out over inflation and recession, restored confidence in the Presidency, and pardoned Nixon, which saved the nation a mess of recrimination and legal expense. As far as I know, he was perfect, which can be said of no other President since James Monroe. Further, he was the only President to preside with a name completely different from the one he was given at birth — Leslie King, Jr. "President King" would have been an awkward oxymoron. (*Memories,* 354)

Such a quality of appreciation serves as a parallel to the events that unfold during the Buchanan administration. Although there may be a shade of irony in this quotation, particularly the idea of a "perfect" presidency, it may be genuinely reflective of what the narrator and his creator, author Updike, believe it is possible for the chief executive — any chief executive — to accomplish, given the political restraints of the office and the officeholder's own human limitations.

In its own way, *Memories of the Ford Administration* is a strange history. Although it purports to present memories of Gerald Ford's administration and to provide a history of James Buchanan and his administration, it is incomplete, supplanted by the narrator's own disordered history. What the narrator perceives about the exciting and salacious events of his own life are more attractive to his memory than the dull but efficient workings of the Ford administration and the machinations of President Buchanan as he desperately attempted to hold the Union together and avoid civil war. The narrator of the novel, and its protagonist, is one Alfred Landon Clayton, named for Franklin Delano Roosevelt's defeated opponent in the election of 1936. He is a history professor at Wayward Junior College for Women in southern New Hampshire. The institution, whose name may be a shade too obvious, and Clayton justify that name in the full flush of the indulgent 1970s. Its professors are seducing each other's wives, its students, and its students' mothers. Clayton has been asked to record his "memories and impressions" of the Ford administration for the academic journal of his regional historical association. His perception of the time is complex, filtered through his personal experiences and his view of the abandon — general and sexual — of that period:

> We had worn love beads and smoked dope, we had danced nude and shat on the flag, we had bombed Hanoi and landed on the moon, and still the sky remained unimpressed. History turned another page, the Union limped on, the dead were plowed under, the illegitimate babies were suckled and given the names of wildflowers and Buddhist religious states, the bad LSD trips were being paid for by the rich parents who covered the bills from the mental institutions. Young American men and women, sons and daughters of corporation lawyers, had sinned against the Holy Ghost and got up the next morning to take a piss and look in the mirror, to see if there was a difference. There didn't seem to be. Everything was out of the closet, every tabu broken, and still God kept His back turned, refusing to set limits. (247-48)

Interspersed almost seamlessly with these impressions of the time is Clayton's *magnum opus,* his historical text — which it becomes clear is really his apologia for the Buchanan administration and even for Buchanan's life, neither of which is perceived to have been very successful. After all, Buchanan's beloved fiancée broke her engagement to him following a totally absurd misunderstanding and died shortly thereafter, perhaps by suicide. And despite Buchanan's best efforts, his beloved nation drifted headlong into disunion and into that ultimate oxymoron, civil war — the ultimate incivility. Schiff has identified the essence of the life of Clayton and of the novel:

> *Memories [of the Ford Administration]* weaves together three periods of American history: the historical past of Buchanan's life (1791-1868), the remembered past of the Ford Administration (1974-77), and the present in which Clayton is writing (the early 1990s). What generates the plot and thematically holds the three periods together is the ongoing conflict between union and separation. . . . Staying together and breaking apart is the quintessential dilemma for nations, tribes, marriages, and households. (*John Updike Revisited,* 136-37)

To understand the personal and social dilemmas of Clayton, Ford, and Buchanan unfolded in the novel is to understand Updike's attitude toward his country and its leaders. Clayton is the protagonist of the novel, its narrator and interpreter. He is a historian attempting to write the history of his own era, the history of the Ford administration, and the history of the Buchanan administration — and he never finishes any of them. A man of inadequacy and disarray, Clayton slowly comes to realize the meaning of his personal chaos — its effect on his life and its relation to the life and work of Buchanan:

> Clayton's analysis of Buchanan's domestic (national affairs) dilemma cannot be extricated from Clayton's own current domestic (household affairs) dilemma, in which he is caught between wife and mistress. Separated from wife, Norma, the Queen of Disorder, and their three children, Clayton desires a divorce that would lead to union with his mistress, Genevieve Mueller, the Perfect Wife, currently married to his deconstructionist colleague. However, simultaneously he wishes to return to his wife and family. Like Buchanan, Clayton is in limbo, unable to commit fully to either mistress or wife. Interestingly, his professional life parallels his personal affairs in that he is also unable to commit fully to his Buchanan manuscript, which stands as a hodgepodge of narrative, facts, and gaps. (Schiff, *John Updike Revisited,* 138)

It is through this "hodgepodge of narrative, facts, and gaps" that Clayton's and Updike's regard for the hapless Buchanan emerges and that we come to sense Updike's respect for the man trying to do his best in this sacred office. Perhaps Buchanan was too cautious by half in attempting to prevent the great Civil War catastrophe from coming to fruition. Even in his early years, with an apparent life of love, accomplishment, and success before him, Buchanan recognized that the cost attached to public service might be too high a price to pay. Before the stark events of his life transpire, Buchanan muses, "'Thank God in His Providence . . . that with my second term in the Assembly I am forever finished with public office; my [future] wife will never be exposed, dearest Ann, to the humiliations and manifold thanklessness of politics'" (*Memories,* 44). The reader cannot help being struck by the heavy irony and the poignancy of this sentiment. Buchanan's ability to foresee and manage the future was severely limited, and that, it is made clear to us, is the true nature of the human condition.

To begin with, due to an absurd series of events, Buchanan is to lose his love and never marry since "dearest Ann" is to make an early and unexpected exit. However, as noted above, Buchanan's musing asks a larger question. Is it worth it to sacrifice the privacy of one's personal life, bow to ambition, and achieve the highest office in the land, only to be burdened with compounded miseries and the possibility, heroic efforts notwithstanding, of being labeled the worst chief executive of them all? Surely, this is a concern — however quickly put aside — that must afflict every person who has contemplated running for the presidency. In 1650 Henry Vaughn wrote "The World," a metaphysical composition contrasting the debasement of this earth with the joys of life eternal. Vaughn's description of the politician, the "darksome statesman," may have been aimed at those who held power in his own time, but its bitter truth seems to describe those who hold political power in any age. Certainly, it appears to reflect accurately the life of Buchanan in his becoming a prisoner of the very awesome responsibility that he held:

> The darksome statesman hung with weights and woe
> Like a thick midnight fog moved so slow
>   He did nor stay nor go;
> Condemning thoughts, like sad eclipses, scowl
>   Upon his soul,
> And clouds of crying witnesses without
>   Pursued him with one shout.
> Yet digged the mole, and, lest his ways be found,
>   Worked underground,
> Where he did clutch his prey. But one did see
>   That policy:
> Churches and altars fed him; perjuries
>   Were gnats and flies;
> It rained about him blood and tears, but he
>   Drank them as free. (Vaughn, 1408)

If it did not exactly rain "blood and tears" during Buchanan's administration, it surely did, despite his best efforts, during that of his successor. Buchanan, it seems, "was destined to have a tragic part in history because in a time of national convulsion his appeal was always to reason, to law, to tradition, to custom, and to safety" (Kazin, "The Middle Way," 45). Throughout the course of his term in office, Buchanan desperately tried to knit the country back together, a country that was increasingly fractious and fracturing. In Kazin's words, Clayton portrays Buchanan ultimately

> as a battered figure helplessly appealing for time as he is caught between the pro-Union Pennsylvanians in his cabinet, and the secessionists formerly in it now representing the independent State of South Carolina. The Pennsylvanians supported the presence of a Federal garrison on Fort Sumter in Charleston harbor. The secessionists insisted that Buchanan had given them his word not to allow Major Anderson to occupy the fort. (45)

Using the utmost of his narrative power, Updike brilliantly and seamlessly interweaves the history of Clayton's own life and escapades with the ups and downs of Buchanan's personal life and political career, which began in the state legislature and moved on to the national scene. Tragically, however, the harder Buchanan tries, the more he sees the country sliding toward disintegration and events spiraling out of control. At a critical moment, a Southern favor-seeker has the following exchange with Buchanan, which sums up the human and political transformation that has taken place in his life. In this exchange, the president refers to himself in the third person and pronounces himself "dead" as an individual. He sees himself as the personification of the nation, and this suggests his sacrifice, a selfless and admirable sacrifice, of individual identity and personhood for a greater cause:

> "'Buchanan, don't be an imbecile. Your interest has always lain south, and still lies there.'
>
> '*Mr.* James Buchanan, as a seeker of his own interest, is dead. There remains only the President of the United States. He has many duties to perform. Sir, you are excused.'" (*Memories,* 319)

For Clayton the joining of man, office, and nation is significant because it demonstrates the sincerity of Buchanan and the depth of his struggle for the Union, vain though that struggle was destined to be. For Updike, however, Buchanan's assertion that he is dead "as a seeker of his own interest" signifies the subverting of his own identity to that of the Republic's, a sacrifice virtually religious in nature. This kind of sacrifice, Updike seems to believe, has characterized many of those individuals who have achieved the highest office in the land. And that kind of sacrifice should be honored and not scorned, no matter what the eventual outcome.

Before he became president, Buchanan had told a friend: "'The

Union . . . is as dear to me as my heart's blood. I would,' he ringingly avowed, 'peril life, character, and every earthly hope, to maintain it'" (240). At his noblest, Buchanan fulfilled that intention. As president, however, he made serious errors of judgment and understanding, one of which involved the question of slavery. When he described slavery as "'not a question of general morality, affecting the consciences of men, but . . . a question of constitutional law'" (240), he seriously undermined his own moral authority and his ability to see the crisis through to a successful resolution. And that is almost certainly why in the final analysis Clayton, the fictional historian — and all historians, in fact — came to conclude that Buchanan for all his effort was a poor leader. It may also be why he has been thought of and dismissed as a "fussy . . . pro-Southern strict constitutionalist whose timorous legalisms were all to be swept away by a bloodbath and Lincoln's larger, less scrupulous perceptions of the rights and duties of the high office to which he succeeded" (242-43).

In the end, rather tragically, Buchanan was accused of treason by many in the North and in the South. Toward the end of his life he was ignored and even scorned, being left with only a few close friends and "Cabinet loyalists" who visited him in his Pennsylvania home, Wheatland. But Clayton and Updike have affection for him, maintaining that he did the best he could do under impossible circumstances, trying to avoid a brutal, bitter, destructive Civil War that he understood would leave chaos in its wake.

In assessing Buchanan, his administration, and the historical period in which he operated, Updike has suggested that despite our best efforts it is ultimately impossible to recover the past in all its contradictions: "The path . . . toward historical truth is unusually complex and multilayered" (Schiff, *John Updike Revisited,* 141). Updike accepts Buchanan's best efforts as he accepts the man. But what about Clayton? He never quite finishes his narrative, but he does bring some tranquility to his own disordered life. Rejected by his mistress, the Perfect Wife, because of a one night's stand with a student's mother, he returns to the Queen of Disorder, his own wife, and intently contemplates the past, cryptically telling us in the end, "The more I think about the Ford Administration, the more it seems I remember nothing" (*Memories,* 369). This can hardly be Updike's final judgment about the meaning of our social experience and our personal histories. He described his social attitudes and his political beliefs in *Self-*

Consciousness long before he created Clayton and wrote about Buchanan and Ford. The sources of these beliefs, it becomes clear there, are to be found in his small-town rearing, his education, and his religious tradition.

Self-Consciousness is a compilation of six essays in which Updike purports to tell us about his life, his work, and his beliefs. The six chapters and a foreword form not a cohesive autobiography but rather a collection of memories told to us through and within the author's consciousness and self-understanding, as far as that can be done even by an accomplished and brilliant writer. Two of these fascinating chapters get to the very nub of the author's philosophy and attitude toward government and its leaders: "On Not Being a Dove" (chapter 4) and "On Being a Self Forever" (chapter 6). It is especially in these chapters that we come to understand in some detail what has motivated the author, how he came to believe as he does, and what during the Vietnam era engendered his unusual public position in a time of national clamor and protest.

Even when Updike is attempting to be totally accurate and entirely serious about his life and the manner in which its events unfolded, there is something vaguely ironic in the way he tells his story. In "On Being a Self Forever," Updike explains that he was born into the Lutheran Church and that Christianity and Lutheranism were not simply abstract religious designations taken as surface tokens but were essential elements in his personal identity, an expression of the fabric of his self-understanding. And, although he found unbelief around him in these traditions, he persevered until he discovered his own unique identity as a person of faith. It was not exactly an easy or comfortable search:

> During . . . adolescence, I reluctantly perceived of the Christian religion I had been born into that almost no one believed it, believed it really — not its ministers, nor its pillars like my father and his father before him. Though signs of belief (churches, public prayers, mottos on coins) existed everywhere, when you moved toward Christianity it disappeared, as fog solidly opaque in the distance thins to transparency when you walk into it. I decided I nevertheless *would* believe. I found a few authors, a very few — Chesterton, Eliot, Unamuno, Kierkegaard, Karl Barth — who helped me believe. (*Self-Consciousness,* 230)

In a resolute reaction to the apostasy that Updike saw around him, his personal faith became stubborn, leading him to conclude that even if no one else took the Christian faith seriously, he was going to give it unapologetic commitment. It is this religious commitment, then, which provides the foundation for his unflinching justification of the need for social order in the face of cultural chaos — the kind that broke out in the Vietnam protests. His response was religiously principled.

Recognizing his heritage as an American Protestant, he adds, "I was . . . a Christian, and Christ said, 'Render unto Caesar those things which are Caesar's.' I was, by upbringing, a Lutheran, and Luther had told the 'murdering and thieving hordes' . . . of rebellious peasants to cease their radical turmoil and submit to their Christian princes" (130). Citing Lutheran theologian Paul Tillich, Updike attempts to explain Luther's "positivistic authoritarianism." He explains that Lutheranism and revolution are theologically incompatible. The reason for this has to do with the state's power, God's love, and the state's need to suppress the "aggression of the evil man, of those who are against love; the strange work of love is to destroy what is against love. . . . Thus, Luther was 'unambiguously' against revolution" (130) — that is, social revolution through public chaos — though clearly he was a religious revolutionary himself. Although Updike does not categorically reject the idea of revolution or the right of an oppressed people to engage in revolution and cast off the shackles of an oppressive government, he has a tendency to be skeptical of the mob, revolution, and revolutionary movements. This deeply ingrained skepticism was no doubt the stimulus that led the author to honor the hapless James Buchanan, a leader who perceived the coming of a murderous conflict and who tried to thwart that conflict with all the effort he could muster. It was this very skepticism that caused Updike to reject some of the more extreme attitudes of some of his countrymen during the Vietnam war.

Updike cannot help recognizing that his personal identity and his background are inextricable, and so he asks himself this question: "Was I conservative? I hadn't thought so, but I did come from what I could begin to see was a conservative part of the country. Conservative in dress, in mores, in attitudes. The Germans of Berks County didn't move on, like the typical Scots-Irish frontier-seeking Americans" (129). What Updike asks and answers is the question about how culture intertwines with religion. His culture and his religion form an essential part of his background, his identity. His preoccupation with and linkage to Pennsylvania, to Reading, to Shillington is evident in many of his works. Despite his decades-long residence in Massachusetts and the exotic settings of his New England works, he regularly returns to his native soil. And he sees himself akin to the Germans of Berks County, to whom he feels a special bond: "They stayed put, farming the same valleys and being buried in the same graveyards, one generation after another" (129). And the Germans had not been the only Pennsylvanians who had found an enticing mother earth and sunk their identities into it. There were also the Quakers who had sought religious freedom and found it in William Penn's colony. Once there, they became "conservative, thrifty, accumulative, suspicious of all but inner revolutions. The cautious spirit of Ben Franklin's maxims still lived in the air" (129). This conservative skepticism has led Updike to beliefs that made him no friends during the Vietnam war and might even be seen as something of a political dead end:

> Faith alone, faith without any false support of works, justified the Lutheran believer and distinguished him from the Catholic and Calvinist believer. In all varieties of Christian faith resides a certain contempt for the world and for attempts to locate salvation and perfection here. The world is fallen, and in a fallen world animals, men, and nations make space for themselves through a willingness to fight. Christ beat up the money-changers in the temple, and came not to bring peace, He distinctly said, but a sword. (130)

Such a set of beliefs led Updike to certain attitudes about his native land that he seems to confirm in *Memories of the Ford Administration,* beliefs he expressed to me in our drive together to his mother's farm homestead in Shillington. This set of beliefs and accompanying political attitudes did not endear him to a variety of readers and critics during the Vietnam era who, no doubt, expected from him a much more severe and trenchant inquiry into the violent actions of his own country — especially since he was considered one of its leading writers. After all, as we saw earlier, Updike described himself as an author "whose stock in trade . . . included an intuition into the mass consciousness and an identification with our national fortunes" (124). Updike, instead, thought it sad that our patriotic myth of invincible virtue was in the process of disappearing. Some were deeply shocked by his assertion that "Peace depends upon the threat of violence. The threat cannot always be idle. Privately and in the aggregate, we walk through life with chips on our shoulder, and when the chip is knocked off, we must fight" (130). Such an attitude may seem to be in stark contrast to Updike's gentlemanly and even pacific demeanor and the quiet life he has led. However, his attitude makes sense when understood within the context of his cultural background and his religious beliefs.

Nor was this philosophy developed intuitively. As a man of faith and a church-goer Updike has thought long and hard about the church and his Lutheran faith: "I had learned from Kierkegaard and Barth to say the worst about our earthly condition, which was hopeless without a scandalous supernatural redemption" (149). Despite his membership in an intellectual elite, however accidental or reluctant, he has continuously wrestled with profound questions of being and non-being, heaven and hell, and has come to the conclusion that

> Evidence of God's being lies with that of our own; it is on our side of the total disparity that God lives. In the light, we disown Him, embarrassedly; in the dark, He is our only guarantor, our only shield against death. The impalpable self cries out to Him and wonders if it detects an answer. Like the inner of the two bonded strips of metal in a thermostat, the self curls against Him and presses. (229)

After a long, philosophical consideration of the case, Updike concludes that "[God's] answers come in the long run, as the large facts of our lives, strung on that thread running through all things. Religion includes, as its enemies say, fatalism, an acceptance and consecration of what is" (229). Perhaps this is the key to Updike's understanding and acceptance of history's ambiguity so evident in *Memories of the Ford Administration,* his lack of bitter criticism toward his nation, his good will toward its leaders, and also his surprising and accepting attitude toward Lyndon Johnson and the Vietnam war, a view that left many of his readers and admirers bitterly disappointed.

Linked to Updike's description of God as "a dark sphere enclosing the pinpoint of our selves, an adamant bubble enclosing us, protecting us, enabling us to let go, to ride the waves of what is" (229), is the Lutheran acceptance of the authority of the state. Add to that his own Pennsylvania tradition of "staying put" and it is perhaps no wonder that

Updike was not one to hurl anger and hatred at those who were creating and implementing foreign policy. He also candidly admits that there is the possibility, aside from his "authority-worshipping Germanness" and a "delusional filial attachment to Lyndon Baines Johnson" (134), that to a degree he may have been reacting against the Unitarian pacifism of his then wife. Ultimately, however, in his own mind, he could never genuinely challenge the power of authority. In countless arguments, he could not be still. During the period of hostilities, he responded to the protests and the opposition of almost everyone he knew with a vehemence and an anger that bordered on the obnoxious: "I wanted to keep quiet, but could not. Something about it all made me very sore. I spoke up, blushing and hating my disruption of a post-liberal socio-economic-cultural harmony I was pleased to be a part of" (126). Almost driven to take positions he hardly thought he would ever have to support, he became obliged to defend the likes of "Johnson and Rusk and Rostow, and then Nixon and Kissinger." He described his face during these debates becoming "hot, my voice high and tense, and wildly stuttery; I could feel my heart race in a kind of panic whenever the subject came up, and my excitement threaten to suffocate me" (124).

In the end, he chose to take his family to London during 1968 and 1969. In flight from the contention and bitterness around him, foreign climes were a better alternative to an "interfering" peace movement. Remembering the Vietnam era was to remember

> a sticky, strident, conflicting time, a time with a bloody televised background of shame. Hawk, dove, soldier, draft evader, and even middle-class householder were caught in a superheated mire as an empire tried to carry out an ugly border action under the full glare of television. The soap opera of the nightly news and the clamor of a college generation that had not been raised to be cannon fodder . . . permitted no one to look away. (146)

Updike does not so much regret his own political position during this painful national period, but rather sees it as a time when the aggregate beliefs of his own background led him into an area of issues he did not expect. He now thinks such a confrontation of issues was inevitable for him. In the final analysis, he is ready to admit that

> Of my own case, looked at coldly, it might be said that, having been given a Protestant, Lutheran, rather antinomian Christianity as part of

> my sociological make-up, I was too timid to discard it. My era was too ideologically feeble to wrest it from me, and Christianity gave me something to write about, and a semblance of a backbone, and a place to go Sunday mornings, when the post offices were closed. (234)

Though he ends his apologia with a half-hearted joke, the point is clear enough. History moves on, past James Buchanan, past Lyndon Johnson, past Richard Nixon, past Gerald Ford. New events and new crises replace the old ones. Three decades after the fall of Saigon, Updike's support for — or, more accurately, lack of condemnation of — government policy may still disappoint and mystify some. From the perspective of more than thirty years, however, the shrill, bitter, self-hating verbal overkill of other leading citizens and opinion makers equally disappoints and mystifies many others. In the final analysis, John Updike *is* a civil and a civilized man. He argues for social order and against public chaos. Because of his religion and heritage, and perhaps in spite of them, he realizes that in a democratic society our leaders are merely extensions of ourselves, and, like us, they are summoned to do their best amid trying and confounding situations. And as we would want others to treat us, Updike proposes, we also ought to offer them our good will, our good wishes, and, most of all, our understanding.

The World as Host

John Updike and the Cultural Affirmation of Faith

DONALD J. GREINER

In 1987 John Updike published a collection of short stories titled *Trust Me.* Perusing these tales of domestic tension and thwarted hope, the reader understands that the title is largely ironic. Trust in these stories is honestly offered and earnestly sought, but it is rarely confirmed. Updike has long considered the interface between trust and faith to be an accurate indicator of cultural health, of a society's ability to confront discord and still affirm the future. The delicacy of affirmation — the sheer effort involved in trying to shore up hope — is a particular emphasis in his short stories and essays that will be the focus of this chapter. Although Updike has been much honored for his understanding of the border between theology and domesticity, his tales and nonfiction prose suggest that his career-long discourse on faith extends beyond the merely religious.

A case in point is "Made in Heaven." Collected in *Trust Me,* this short story probes an irony of faith: one person's faith is another's disillusion. On the surface "Made in Heaven" traces the life of a marriage from youthful courtship to the death of the wife in old age, but Updike is more concerned with the paradoxes of faith and with the relationship between personal hope and cultural health. Initially attracted to the arcane mysteries of the Christian worship service, the wife finally repudiates the solace of Holy Communion on her deathbed because the husband has inadvertently crowded her sanctuary. He joins her in church where she once worshiped alone, but she comes to resent the masculine invasion of "a fragile feminine space" (*Trust Me,* 193). The irony is that the non-believing husband's faith waxes as the wife's wanes. He has "believed" in her for a lifetime.

Faith in this story is pointedly defined as "the worn path to the Crucifixion and the bafflement beyond" (194). Noting, however, the symbiosis between domestic tension and societal turmoil, Updike suggests a broader view of faith as cultural affirmation. Late in the story, for example, he remarks on the "misfortunes" that sear the country while the wife loses confidence in traditional religion. Bafflement reigns when a nation declines to believe. The title "Made in Heaven" echoes the proud label "made in America," an echo that resounds through Updike's short stories and essays as he points to the 1960s to date the crisis of belief that has challenged American affirmation in the second half of the twentieth century.

In the summer of 1960, before President Kennedy's assassination, before the civil rights movement, and before Vietnam, he published a short essay titled "Why Robert Frost Should Receive the Nobel Prize," later included in *Assorted Prose.* Initially taken in by the directness of the title, the reader soon realizes that Updike's remarks are ironic. In the less tarnished atmosphere of the early 1960s, one could still poke fun at those who resisted the literary modernity of existentialism and eccentricity in favor of the comforting rhymes of Robert Frost. Updike most certainly misjudged Frost, but he did not misinterpret the conservative backlash against a literature that matters.

Rereading Updike's essay today, one understands a further irony. For while Updike once smiled in his relative youth at the life's work of a major poet, he has now achieved in his late middle age the stature of a major writer. Those who read only his best-selling novels may perceive him as primarily the sensitive chronicler of the hidden bedroom and corner church, but such perceptions are clouded. The sharper vision peers through the publicity to the extraordinary accomplishment: not only a career that has spanned more than four decades and that has produced more than fifty books, but a canon that has a distinctive signature expressed through his ruminations on belief.

Consider the achievement. It is not that he has won the National

Book Award, the National Book Critics Circle Award, the American Book Award, and the Pulitzer Prize for volumes as different as *The Centaur* (1963), *Rabbit Is Rich* (1981), *Hugging the Shore* (1983), and *Rabbit at Rest* (1990); his real achievement is that he has detailed the decline of the social structure since he began writing for *The New Yorker* in 1954 and yet has never given up on faith. Despite the stunning flourishes of his intricate style, Updike refuses to allow his concern with language to interfere with his analysis of the social dilemma. What is lacking in the community, he understands, is the surety of faith — not simply religious faith, though that is an issue too, but the more general faith in society that is necessary to get things done.

Some readers continue to judge Updike as relatively controversial because of his bold depiction of contemporary sexuality, but they should note that, more than a sensationalist of suburban adultery, he is a commentator on personal hope despite social faltering. How, he asks, can a person pursue the promise of tomorrow when stuck in the disintegration of today? Rabbit Angstrom is not the only Updike character who watches his dreams recede faster than he can run after them. John Hook, for example, embraces the perspective of old age when the order he helped craft slips from belief to "busyness" *(The Poorhouse Fair)*. Hook's commitment to mundane details, to the intricate workings of what Updike calls "middleness," has no chance when faced with the bureaucracy of the welfare system. George Caldwell laments the loss of civility and learning as he trudges through the snow to the high school for the sake of his son's future *(The Centaur)*. And Henry Bech confronts the cheapening of art in his own silence and in the gaudy tackiness of the New York elite *(Bech Is Back)*. Craftsmanship, faith, knowledge, and art — the traditional supports of an advancing civilization — all seem threatened by crassness and despair.

It was not always that way. As a child of the Great Depression and the Second World War, Updike is aware of the contrast between the social unity that commits a people to a cause and the shoddiness that condemns a society to decline. In 1971 he published a short story — in truth, a lyrical meditation about the 1950s — titled "When Everyone Was Pregnant." Having survived the catastrophes of the 1960s, the narrator looks back to the previous decade when he did not have time for apocalypse. An absolute enemy may have mobilized across the ocean, and Korea, Communism, and the specter of the bomb may have threatened the horizon, but the narrator knows that social guiltlessness neutralized personal despair. The promise of tomorrow was personified in the pregnancies of the day, and uncertainty was overwhelmed in a continuing expression of belief. Yet Updike and the narrator realize that such faith is no longer the case: "The world's skin of fear shivered but held. . . . Viewed the world through two lenses since discarded: fear and gratitude. Young people now are many things but they aren't afraid, and aren't grateful" (*Museums and Women*, 93). Guilt surfaces with the turn of the decade, and America suffers another of its falls from grace. At that moment Updike matured as a writer. By the early 1960s, he knew that the country was never guiltless.

His little-known nonfiction pieces, particularly those collected in *Assorted Prose*, directly chronicle the combination of decline and faith that his fiction indirectly dramatizes. Such evocation of a lost moment is one of the glories of his art. As he explained in a 1973 interview, "I think our lives really are solipsistic, self-centered. And perhaps, in part, because of a new sensibility about such things, the particular swing to life that we knew in the 'fifties is really not around anymore. The difference between the heroes elevated by the early 'fifties and those of 1970 reflects this" (Gado, 89).

The decline of traditional heroism is a cultural indicator, a sure sign that a society has drifted from faith to uncertainty. Updike marks this transition as occurring during the unhappy decade between 1957 and 1967. Although his first book, *The Carpentered Hen*, was published in 1958, he had been writing for *The New Yorker* since 1954, primarily for the "Talk of the Town" column. In his several occasional pieces about the then-fledgling space program, for example, written between November 1957 and August 1964 (see *Assorted Prose*), Updike details the diminishment of mystery when television comedians and hawkers of cereal exploit space exploration for profit. The lack of poetry in technological advances is obvious enough, but with his wider view of a burgeoning social dilemma he sees in this lack a metaphor for the slipping of a culture. The ingenious but impersonal space probes — the new symbol of "made in America" — fail to generate a fresh sense of heroism, and the explorations that prove the absence of life on other planets not only diminish the collective imagination but also exacerbate the frightening sense of cosmic loneliness.

The slide from the guiltlessness "when everyone was pregnant" underwrites the shabbiness of cultural morality that Updike saw in the early 1960s. His glance over his shoulder is not only nostalgia for a small town boyhood but also astonishment at the pervasive sullying of a society. Before the assassinations of the 1960s, the debacle of the Vietnam war, and the corruption of Richard Nixon's presidency, he was asking a difficult question: Whatever happened to the "simplicity of good faith?" ("Morality Play," *Assorted Prose,* 86). Eight years prior to the disgrace of the 1968 Democratic National Convention in Chicago, he pondered the stability of a political process that must confront the amorality of a television screen. Deploring the "smirks, rudeness, and cynicism" of the network reporters, Updike wondered what would happen to the rational discussion of social issues when news commentators who clamor to be media heroes goad a nation's leaders into platitudes and lies in front of the camera. What will result, he asked, when technocrats are exempt "from mundane considerations like courtesy" ("Obfuscating Coverage," *Assorted Prose,* 91)?

A society that once held firm to its faith in moral action now stumbles to make way for a jaded successor. Aspiration is exchanged for functionalism. Courtesy is swapped for a news scoop. Even the artistic expression of the society suffers when the young are no longer afraid, no longer grateful. Examining the architecture of tall buildings, for example, those astonishing constructions that should unify a culture to appreciate the glory of the Gothic cathedral on the one hand and the soaring of the space probes on the other, Updike detects nothing but diminishment and loss. What is lacking, he notes, is faith: "What we miss, perhaps, is hopefulness. These new skyscrapers do not aspire to scrape the sky; at the point of exhaustion, where the old skyscrapers used to taper, gather their dwindling energy, and lunge upward with a heart-stopping spire, these glass boxes suffer the architectural embarrassment of having to house the air-conditioning apparatus, and slatted veiling snuffs out their ascent" ("Mostly Glass," *Assorted Prose,* 109). For "skyscraper" one may read "nation." Guiltlessness fades when a culture no longer aspires to scrape the sky.

The same dispiriting absence of aspiration infects the literary establishment. As Updike observed in 1963,

> A fever of self-importance is upon American writing. Popular expectations of what literature should provide have risen so high that failure is the only possible success, and pained incapacity the only acceptable proof of sincerity. When ever in prose has slovenliness been so esteemed, ineptitude so cherished? In the present apocalyptic at-

> mosphere, the loudest sinner is most likely to be saved. . . . The study of literature threatens to become a kind of paleontology of failure, and criticism a supercilious psychoanalysis of authors. ("No Use Talking," *Assorted Prose*, 264)

Updike's own character Henry Bech lives this dilemma, but Updike also has in mind such an author as Salinger, whose retreat into silence is his guarantee of perpetual devotion. The apocalyptic atmosphere in the arts reflects the national deterioration of the culture.

Two deaths in the 1960s best illustrate the decline. The assassination of President Kennedy in 1963 and the death of T. S. Eliot in 1965 signaled for Updike the shrinking of the political, cultural, and religious presence necessary to the moral health of a society. With the murder of the president, the country lost the last leader who embodied the aspiration that once urged the populace beyond the complacency of mediocrity. The violent loss, writes Updike, was more than a political disaster; it was a symbol of a "deep unease" ("The Assassination," *Assorted Prose*, 119). The memorial mass celebrated after the president's death indicated the need for a reacquaintance with artistic and religious sureties, a need that was reaffirmed with the death of Eliot: "As long as he was alive our literature seemed in some sense restrained from the apocalyptic formlessness and obscenity that it seeks" ("T. S. Eliot," *Assorted Prose*, 122).

The point is that today Updike's art offers a similar restraint, not as noticeably as Eliot's perhaps, and not as dramatically, but offers it nonetheless. If all he provided were the catalogue of failings noted above, no matter how urgently expressed or stylishly described, he would be little more than yet another exquisite nay-sayer, another fashionable cynic of social illness. But like Faulkner, who also witnessed a cycle of decline, Updike refuses to accept "the end of man." Acknowledging what Faulkner called the author's "duty" to write about humanity's "spirit capable of compassion and sacrifice and endurance," Updike avoids the flashily dramatic to feature the drably mundane, the little moments — the grace notes, as it were — that frame faith in an era of disquiet. The religious aura that shapes his canon, the acceptance of Karl Barth's rigorous theology, which insists that humanity must profess the first tenet of the Apostles' Creed, is more than the consistent asserting of a personal faith; it is the unblinking commitment to a universal hope.

"What is a hero?" Updike asks in *The Centaur,* and his answer is not a faceless astronaut or an inept president but a befuddled father who sacrifices his dreams for his son's future (298). The possibility of reversing the cultural faltering that Updike first noted in 1954 is the celebration that marks the affirmation of his art. In *The Poorhouse Fair,* the possibility is found in belief; in *The Centaur,* sacrifice; in *A Month of Sundays,* faith; in *Marry Me,* love; in *Roger's Version,* once again belief; and in *In the Beauty of the Lilies,* the children. Some of his characters may stumble and some of them may run, but they rarely give up on hope.

Only the shoring up of little lives will slow the slide, and it is for this reason that Updike writes of "middleness." It is not that he foresees a return to the time when everyone was pregnant but that he refuses to belittle the likelihood of the moment when everyone finds grace. Not merely religious grace, though that is important too, but also graceful movement, the fluidity of motion through a life that can counter the hardness of the heart.

This is why Updike turns so often to the past. His backward glance is more than a sentimental attachment to an era receding with the years; it is an acknowledgment of history that, like the backward looks of Faulkner and García Márquez, points up the contrast between then and now as well as the celebration of what may be. His small towns are Faulkner's hamlets and García Márquez's villages, places where courtesy and compassion and faith continue to direct meaningful lives. Graceful motion through life is impossible without assimilation of where one has been. What Updike understands, what makes him a spokesman for a culture, is that most people move through the realm of the middle. Neither saints nor villains, they live the life he himself has witnessed.

He expressed this understanding early in his career in an autobiographical memoir titled "The Dogwood Tree: A Boyhood," published in 1962. From the perspective of maturity, Updike recalls his childhood years and specifies the solidity of middleness as an anchor in a sliding world:

> [T]here is . . . a quiet but tireless goodness that things at rest, like a brick wall or a small stone, seem to affirm. A wordless reassurance these things are pressing to give. An hallucination? To transcribe middleness with all its grits, bumps, and anonymities, in its fullness

> of satisfaction and mystery: is it possible or, in view of the suffering that violently colors the periphery and that at all moments threatens to move into the center, worth doing? Possibly not; but the horse-chestnut trees, the telephone poles, the porches, the green hedges recede to a calm point that in my subjective geography is still the center of the world. (Martin Levin, 196)

Suffering and violence are recognized for what they are, as inimical forces that crowd the periphery of common life and menace the center, but the still point of middleness holds firm when acknowledged as the foundation of experience. Updike is our acknowledger, for he knows that the decay of culture is halted by individual stubbornness and personal belief. What one needs — for one's own sake as well as society's — is a center firmly grounded in middleness.

The loss of cultural aspiration and the emergence of apocalypse in the arts are thus countered by common things — by, in Updike's metaphor, horse-chestnut trees and telephone poles. Kennedy's murder and Eliot's death grab the headlines, but the green hedges are always there. As Updike writes in the foreword to *Olinger Stories*: "*We are rewarded unexpectedly.* The muddled and inconsequent surface of things now and then parts to yield us a gift" (vii). That gift is the persistence of the middle whose firmness finds its shape in the past. When faith in its stability threatens to fade, social deterioration gains momentum. This is why Updike argues that similar losses damage both individuals and societies. He notes in "In Football Season," a short story of mutability and time, that "as children we had lived in a tight world of ticking clocks and punctual bells, where every minute was an admonition to thrift and where tardiness, to a child running late down a street with his panicked stomach burning, seemed the most mysterious and awful of sins. Now, turning the corner into adulthood, we found time to be instead a black immensity endlessly supplied, like the wind" (*Music School*, 7). The "air of permission" that he felt as a child has fled as he walks as a man. Updike knows that his duty, especially his duty as a writer, is to retrieve the air of permission.

This he does in perhaps his finest story, "The Music School," a tale that offers a coda drawing on a metaphor of faith, the communion wafer: "The world is the host; it must be chewed" (*Music School*, 190). Right and proper action is to live in the face of loss. To have such strength, however, one must submit to the past, to history, to what

Updike suggests is the archeology of a culture and a life. The narrator of "The Music School" understands not only that he exists "in time" but also that "in the end each life wears its events with a geological inevitability" (184). In this complex story of domestic strife and ensuing guilt, Updike urges the rekindling of aspiration that finds a harmony beyond the artificial order of numbers and computers.

Updike locates that harmony in the realms of music and faith, disciplines that offer harmonious strains whose essence, unlike computer mathematics, is immaterial yet felt. Sitting in the music school housed in the basement of a church, the narrator senses the unity of art, belief, and human action as he listens to the stumbling sounds of the apprentice musicians: "hints of another world, a world where angels fumble, pause, and begin again" (186). Hope is defined as beginning again. Updike's point is the positive relation of the aspiring individual to the discordant world. Both musical score and computer mathematics rely on arcane notations, but the former leads to vision, to that affirmative quality created by the combination of faith and action that Updike finds absent in the general cultural malaise. Social heroes — for example, President Kennedy and T. S. Eliot — narrow the distance between vision and act: "How great looms the gap between the first gropings of vision and the first stammerings of percussion! Vision, timidly, becomes percussion, percussion becomes music, music becomes emotion, emotion becomes — vision. Few of us have the heart to follow this circle to its end" (186-87).

Those who do complete the circle, those who try to reverse the cultural fall, understand that life, like the communion wafer described in the tale, must be chewed — that is, it must be actively pursued and rigorously lived. Passive acceptance and translucent belief are not enough in a coarse world. Life itself is a sacrament made fully valid not by transubstantiation but by ingestion of the secular. Defining faith as more collective societal outlook than received doctrine, Updike broadens the meaning of redemption. Thus, at the conclusion of "The Music School," he personifies the affirmative movement that he calls for in the guise of a woman who, embarrassed at finding a priest at a party just after she has returned from consulting a divorce lawyer, takes two steps forward to counter the one taken backward, and thereby "completes the circle." Like the neophytes in the music class, she stumbles, pauses, and begins again. Her faith is Updike's coda not only for the story but also for society: "The world is the host; it must be chewed."

This nameless woman, with her mundane life and her acceptance of her past, exemplifies Updike's sense of what is needed to slow the social slide he has witnessed since the late 1950s. Using the solidity of small town America and the "middleness" of little things, he has created a canon that addresses the broad, human issues which touch the daily lives of his readers. He may agree with Walt Kelly's perceptive comment about the disastrous 1960s, that "we have met the enemy and he is us," but he also insists that the enemy can be transformed. John Updike deserves our notice for one significant reason: He prompts us to remember what we fear we have lost.

Bibliography of Citation Sources and Updike Criticism

Updike Citation Sources

Books

Assorted Prose. New York: Knopf, 1965.

Bech: A Book. New York: Knopf, 1970.

Bech at Bay: A Quasi-Novel. New York: Knopf, 1998.

Bech Is Back. New York: Knopf, 1982.

Brazil. New York: Knopf, 1994.

Buchanan Dying. New York: Knopf, 1974.

The Carpentered Hen and Other Tame Creatures. New York: Harper & Brothers, 1958.

The Centaur. New York: Knopf, 1963.

Collected Poems 1953-1993. New York: Knopf, 1993.

Couples. New York: Knopf, 1968.

Hugging the Shore. New York: Knopf, 1983.

In the Beauty of the Lilies. New York: Knopf, 1996.

Just Looking: Essays on Art. New York: Knopf, 1989.

Marry Me: A Romance. New York: Knopf, 1976.

Memories of the Ford Administration. New York: Knopf, 1992.

Midpoint and Other Poems. New York: Knopf, 1969.

A Month of Sundays. New York: Knopf, 1975.

More Matter: Essays and Criticism. New York: Knopf, 1999.
Museums and Women and Other Stories. New York: Knopf, 1972.
The Music School: Short Stories. New York: Knopf, 1966.
Odd Jobs: Essays and Criticism. New York: Knopf, 1991.
Of the Farm. New York: Knopf, 1965.
Olinger Stories: A Selection. New York: Vintage, 1964.
Picked-Up Pieces: Essays and Criticism. New York: Knopf, 1975.
Pigeon Feathers and Other Stories. New York: Knopf, 1962.
The Poorhouse Fair. New York: Knopf, 1959.
Problems and Other Stories. New York: Knopf, 1979.
The Poorhouse Fair — Rabbit, Run. The Modern Library. New York: Random House, 1965.
Rabbit Angstrom: A Tetralogy. New York: Knopf, 1995.
Rabbit at Rest. New York: Knopf, 1990.
Rabbit Is Rich. New York: Knopf, 1981.
Rabbit Redux. New York: Knopf, 1971.
Rabbit, Run. New York: Knopf, 1960.
Roger's Version. New York: Knopf, 1986.
S. New York: Knopf, 1988.
The Same Door: Short Stories. New York: Knopf, 1959.
Self-Consciousness: Memoirs. New York: Knopf, 1989.
Toward the End of Time. New York: Knopf, 1997.
Trust Me: Short Stories. New York: Knopf, 1987.
The Witches of Eastwick. New York: Knopf, 1984.

Articles, Essays, Messages

"The Persistence of Evil." *The New Yorker,* 22 July 1996, pp. 62-65.
"Remarks on Religion and Contemporary American Literature." *New Letters* 60, 4 (Fall 1994): 77-80.
"A Special Message for the First Edition." In *Brazil.* Franklin Center, PA: Franklin Library, 1994.
"A Special Message for the First Edition." In *In the Beauty of the Lilies.* Franklin Center, PA: Franklin Library, 1996.
"The State of Letters." Interview with Sanford Pinsker. *Sewanee Review* 104 (Summer 1996): 423-33.

Secondary Citation Sources (with additional sources for Updike Criticism)

Adams, Phoebe-Lou. Review of *S. The Atlantic* 261 (April 1988): 78.

Arendt, Hannah. *The Human Condition.* Chicago: University of Chicago Press, 1958.

Atwood, Margaret. "Memento Mori — but First, Carpe Diem." *New York Times Book Review,* 12 October 1997, pp. 9-10.

"The Augsburg Confession." In *The Book of Concord: The Confessions of the Evangelical Lutheran Church.* Philadelphia: Fortress Press, 1959.

Augustine. *The Basic Writings of Saint Augustine.* Edited, with an introduction and notes, by Whitney J. Oates. 2 vols. New York: Random House, 1948.

Augusto, Sergio. "American Writer Comes in March to São Paulo." *Folha de São Paulo,* 10 December 1991, p. 5,1.

Baker, Nicholson. *U and I: A True Story.* New York: Random House, 1991.

Barth, Karl. *Anselm: Fides Quaerens Intellectum.* Translated by Ian W. Robertson. New York: World, 1962.

———. *Church Dogmatics.* Translated by G. W. Bromiley and T. F. Torrance. 4 vols. (13 books.) Edinburgh: T. & T. Clark, 1956-75.

———. *Dogmatics in Outline.* Translated by G. T. Thomson. New York: Harper & Row, 1959.

———. *Epistle to the Romans.* Translated by Edwyn C. Hoskyns. Oxford: Oxford University Press, 1968.

———. *The Humanity of God.* Translated by John Newton Thomas and Thomas Wieser. Atlanta: John Knox Press, 1960.

———. *Karl Barth, Letters, 1961-1968.* Edited by Jürgen Frangmeier and Hinrich Stoevesandt. Translated by Geoffrey W. Bromiley. Grand Rapids: Eerdmans, 1981.

———. *Wolfgang Amadeus Mozart.* Translated by Clarence K. Pott. Foreword by John Updike. Grand Rapids: Eerdmans, 1986.

———. *The Word of God and the Word of Man.* Translated by Douglas Horton. New York: Harper Torchbooks, 1957.

Bédier, Joseph. *The Romance of Tristan and Iseult.* Translated by Hilaire Belloc and Paul Rosenfeld. New York: Vintage Books, 1994.

Birkerts, Sven. "The Shape of Things to Come." *Washington Post,* 2 November 1997, "Book World": 5.

Bloom, Harold, ed. *Modern Critical Views: John Updike.* New York: Chelsea House, 1987.

Booth, Wayne C. *Modern Dogma and the Rhetoric of Assent.* Notre Dame, IN: Notre Dame University Press, 1974.

Bower, Anne. *Epistolary Responses. The Letter in Twentieth Century American Fiction and Criticism.* Tuscaloosa, AL: University of Alabama Press, 1977.

Braun, Kirk. *Rajneeshpuram, The Unwelcome Society: Cultures Collide in a Quest for Utopia.* West Linn, OR: Scout Creek Press, 1984.

Broer, Lawrence R., ed. *Rabbit Tales: Poetry and Politics in John Updike's Rabbit Novels.* Tuscaloosa, AL: University of Alabama Press, 1998.

Bromley, David G., Mary Jo Neitz, and Marion S. Godlman. *Sex, Lies and Sanctity: Religion and Deviance in Contemporary North America.* Greenwich, CT: JAI Press, 1995.

Burchard, Rachel C. *John Updike: Yea Sayings.* Carbondale, IL: Southern Illinois University Press, 1971.

Busch, Eberhard. *Karl Barth: His Life from Letters and Autobiographical Texts.* Translated by John Bowden. Philadelphia: Fortress Press, 1976.

Calinescu, Matei. "Secrecy in Fiction: Textual and Intertextual Secrets in Hawthorne and Updike." *Poetics Today* 15, 3 (1994): 444-65.

Callister, Scotta. *For Love and Money: The Rajneeshees, From India to Oregon.* Portland: The Oregonian, 1985. First published in *The Oregonian,* 30 June–19 July 1985.

Calvin, John. *Institutes of the Christian Religion.* Edited by John T. McNeill. 2 vols. Philadelphia: Westminster Press, 1960.

Campbell, John H. *Updike's Novels: Thorns Spell a Word.* Wichita Falls, TX: Midwestern State University Press, 1987.

Card, Orson Scott. *How to Write Science Fiction and Fantasy.* Cincinnati: Writer's Digest Books, 1990.

Carter, Lewis F. *Charisma and Control in Rajneeshpuram: The Role of Shared Values in the Creation of a Community.* Cambridge: Cambridge University Press, 1990.

Chiu, Hanping. "Sex, Literature and Law: John Updike's *S.*" *Tamkang Review* 25, 3-4 (1995): 377-405.

Contract with the American Family: A Bold Plan to Strengthen the Family and Restore Common Sense. Distributed by the Christian Coalition, n.p., n.d.

Couto, José Geraldo. "Updike Wants to Bring Literature Closer to Life." *Folha De São Paulo,* 9 March 1992, p. 1,7.

De Bellis, Jack. *John Updike: A Bibliography, 1967-1993.* Foreword by John Updike. Bibliographies and Indexes in American Literature, Number 17. Westport, CT: Greenwood Press, 1994.

de Rougemont, Denis. *Love in the Western World.* New York: Pantheon, 1956.

Democracy's Next Generation: A Study of Youth and Teachers. Washington, DC: People for the American Way, 1989.

Detweiler, Robert. *Breaking the Fall: Religious Readings of Contemporary Fiction.* San Francisco: Harper & Row, 1989.

———. *Four Spiritual Crises in Mid-Century American Fiction.* University of Florida Monographs. Gainesville, FL: University of Florida Press, 1963.

———. *John Updike.* Rev. ed. Boston: Twayne Publishers, 1984.

Dickinson, Emily. *The Complete Poems of Emily Dickinson.* Edited by Thomas H. Johnson. Boston: Little, Brown and Company, 1955.

Duyckinck, Evert A. "Great Feeling and Discrimination." Review of *The Scarlet Letter. Literary World* 6 (30 March 1850): 323-25.

———. "Review of *Moby-Dick,* by Herman Melville." *Literary World,* 22 November 1851, pp. 403-4.

Eco, Umberto. *The Name of the Rose.* Translated from the Italian by William Weaver. San Diego: Harcourt Brace Jovanovich, 1983.

Eichman, Erich. "Magic Is Not Enough." *The New Leader,* 27 December 1993, pp. 28-30.

Eliade, Mircea. *The Sacred and the Profane: The Nature of Religion.* Translated by Willard R. Trask. San Diego: Harcourt Brace Jovanovich, 1959.

Eliot, T. S. *The Complete Poems and Plays.* New York: Harcourt, Brace, 1958.

The Epic of Gilgamesh. Translated by Maureen Gallery Kovacs. Stanford, CA: Stanford University Press, 1989.

Fitzgerald, Frances. *Cities on a Hill: A Journey through Contemporary American Cultures.* New York: Simon and Schuster, 1986.

Freyre, Gilberto. *Casa-Grande & Senzala.* Rio de Janeiro: n.p., 1989.

———. *The Masters and the Slaves: A Study in the Development of Brazilian Civilization.* Translated from the Portuguese of the fourth and definitive Brazilian edition by Samuel Putnam. New York: Knopf, 1956.

Gado, Frank. "Interview with John Updike." In *First Person: Conversations on Writers & Writing*, pp. 80-109. Schenectady, NY: Union College Press, 1973.

Galloway, David. *The Absurd Hero in American Fiction: Updike, Styron, Bellow, Salinger.* 2nd revised edition. Austin, TX: University of Texas Press, 1981.

Gardner, John, and John Maier. *Gilgamesh.* New York: Knopf, 1984.

Gilkey, Langdon. *Reaping the Whirlwind: A Christian Interpretation of History.* New York: Seabury, 1976.

Glendon, Mary Ann. *Rights-Talk.* New York: Macmillan, 1991.

Graves, Robert. *The White Goddess: A Historical Grammar of Poetic Myth.* Amended and enlarged edition. New York: Farrar, Straus and Giroux, 1966.

Gray, J. Glenn. *The Warriors: Reflections on Men in Battle.* New York: Harper & Row, 1967.

Greiner, Donald J. *Adultery in the American Novel: Updike, James, and Hawthorne.* Columbia, SC: University of South Carolina Press, 1985.

———. "John Updike." In *American Novelists Since World War II*, ed. James R. Giles and Wanda H. Giles, 143: 250-76. Dictionary of Literary Biography, Third Series. Detroit: Gale Research, Inc., 1994. Updated 1999 online at the Gale Publishers DLB subscription website: http://www.Galenet.Gale.com.

———. *John Updike's Novels.* Athens, OH: Ohio University Press, 1984.

———. *The Other John Updike: Poems/Short Stories/Prose/Play.* Athens, OH: Ohio University Press, 1981.

———. "Updike on Hawthorne." *Nathaniel Hawthorne Review* 13, 1 (1987): 1-4.

Gullette, Margaret Morganroth. *Safe at Last in the Middle Years; The Invention of the Midlife Progress Novel: Saul Bellow, Margaret Drabble, Anne Tyler, and John Updike.* Berkeley, CA: University of California Press, 1988.

Hamilton, Alice and Kenneth. *The Elements of John Updike.* Grand Rapids: Eerdmans, 1970.

Hamilton, Rosemary. *Hellbent for Enlightenment: Unmasking Sex, Power, and Death with a Notorious Master.* Askland, OR: White Cloud Press, 1998.

Hampton, I. A. *Nursing: Its Principles and Practice.* Cleveland, OH: E. C. Koeckert, 1905.

Harper, Howard M. *Desperate Faith: A Study of Bellow, Salinger, Mailer, Baldwin, and Updike.* Chapel Hill, NC: University of North Carolina Press, 1967.

Hawthorne, Nathaniel. *The Centenary Edition of the Works of Nathaniel Hawthorne.* Edited by William Charvot et al. 20 vols. Columbus, OH: Ohio State University Press, 1962-88.

———. *The Scarlet Letter.* Edited by Brian Harding. Oxford: Oxford University Press, 1990.

Heidegger, Martin. *Being and Time.* New York: Harper & Row, 1962.

Hunt, George W. *John Updike and the Three Great Secret Things: Sex, Religion, and Art.* Grand Rapids: Eerdmans, 1980.

Hutcheon, Linda. *The Politics of Postmodernism.* London: Routledge, 1989.

Inwood, Michael. *Heidegger.* New York: Oxford University Press, 1997.

Kakutani, Michiko. "On Sex, Death and the Self: An Old Man's Sour Grapes." *The New York Times,* 30 September 1997, pp. E1, E8.

Kazin, Alfred. "Easy Come, Easy Go." *New York Review of Books,* 19 November 1981, p. 3.

———. *God and the American Writer.* New York: Knopf, 1997.

———. "The Middle Way: *Memories of the Ford Administration." The New York Review of Books* 17 (2 December 1992): 45.

Kierkegaard, Søren. *Fear and Trembling.* Translated with an introduction by Alastair Hannay. New York: Penguin Books, 1985.

———. *Kierkegaard's Attack on "Christendom," 1854-1855.* Translated by Walter Lowrie. Princeton, NJ: Princeton University Press, 1968.

Kingsolver, Barbara. "Desire Under the Palms." *The New York Times Book Review,* 6 February 1994, pp. 1, 26-27.

Kort, Wesley A. *"Take, Read": Scripture, Textuality and Cultural Practice.* University Park, PA: Pennsylvania State University Press, 1996.

Lawrence, D. H. *Studies in Classic American Literature.* New York: Thomas Seltzer, 1923. Reprint, New York: Viking Press, 1964.

Levin, Harry. *The Power of Blackness.* New York: Knopf, 1958.

Levin, Martin, ed. *Five Boyhoods.* New York: Doubleday, 1962.

Lewis, C. S. *The Pilgrim's Regress.* Grand Rapids: Eerdmans, 1933.

———. *The Problem of Pain.* New York: Macmillan-Collier, 1962.

Luedtke, Luther S. *Nathaniel Hawthorne and the Romance of the Orient.* Bloomington, IN: Indiana University Press, 1989.

Lundin, Roger. *The Culture of Interpretation: Christian Faith and the Postmodern World.* Grand Rapids: Eerdmans, 1993.

Luscher, Robert M. *John Updike: A Study of the Short Fiction.* New York: Twayne, 1993.

Luther, Martin. *Luther's Works* (American Edition). Edited by Jaroslav Pelikan (1-30) and Helmut T. Lehmann (31-54). 55 vols. St. Louis: Concordia Publishing House, and Philadelphia: Muhlenberg Press, 1955-76.

Macnaughton, William R., ed. *Critical Essays on John Updike.* Boston: G. K. Hall, 1982.

Maier, Pauline. *American Scripture: Making the Declaration of Independence.* New York: Knopf, 1997.

Male, Roy R. *Hawthorne's Tragic Vision.* New York: W. W. Norton, 1964.

Markle, Joyce B. *Lovers and Fighters: Theme in the Novels of John Updike.* New York: New York University Press, 1973.

Martin, John Stephen. "Rabbit's Faith: Grace and the Transformation of the Heart." *Pacific Coast Philology* 17, 1-2 (November 1982): 103-11.

Matthiessen, F. O. *American Renaissance: Art and Expression in the Age of Emerson and Whitman.* New York: Oxford University Press, 1941.

Mazurek, Raymond A. "'Bringing the Corners Forward': Ideology and Representation in Updike's Rabbit Trilogy." In *Politics and the Muse: Studies in the Politics of Recent American Literature,* edited by Adam J. Sorkin. Bowling Green, OH: Bowling Green University Popular Press, 1989.

Mehta, Gita. *Karma Cola.* London: Jonathan Cape, 1980.

Melville, Herman. *The Writings of Herman Melville.* Edited by Harrison Hayford et al. 15 vols. Evanston and Chicago: Northwestern University Press, 1968-89.

Michaels, Walter Benn. "Romance and Real Estate." *Raritan* 2 (1983): 66-87.

Milne, Hugh. *Bhagwan: The God That Failed.* London: Caliban Books, 1986.

Modern Fiction Studies 20 (Spring 1974). "John Updike Special Issue," consisting of articles on Updike, reviews of Updike criticism, and a checklist of Updike criticism by Arlin Meyer and Michael Olivas.

Modern Fiction Studies 37 (Spring 1991). "John Updike Special Issue," consisting of articles and extensive checklist of Updike criticism by Jack De Bellis.

Mookerjee, Ajit. *Kundalini: The Arousal of Inner Energy.* London: Thames and Hudson, 1982.

Morey, Ann-Janine. *Religion and Sexuality in American Literature.* Cambridge Studies in American Literature and Culture, 57. Cambridge: Cambridge University Press, 1992.

Morrow, James. "Introduction." *Nebula Awards 27.* New York: Harcourt Brace, 1993.

Murphy, Dell. *The Rajneesh Story: The Bhagwan's Garden.* West Linn, OR: Linwood Press, 1986.

Neal, William R. "The Theology of Karl Barth as an Interpretive Key to the Fiction of John Updike." Ph.D. dissertation. University of Mississippi, 1977.

Neary, John. *Something and Nothingness: The Fiction of John Updike and John Fowles.* Carbondale, IL: Southern Illinois University Press, 1992.

Newman, Judie. *John Updike.* New York: St. Martin's Press, 1988.

———. "Spaces in Between: Hester Prynne as the Salem Bibi in Bharati Mukherjee's *The Holder of the World.*" *Journal of Literary Studies,* Special Issue: Politics and the Novel, 13, 1-2 (June 1997): 62-91.

Oates, Joyce Carol. "Future Tense." *The New Yorker,* 8 December 1997, pp. 116-17.

O'Connell, Mary. *Updike and the Patriarchal Dilemma: Masculinity in the Rabbit Novels.* Carbondale and Edwardsville, IL: Southern Illinois University Press, 1996.

O'Connor, Flannery. *Wise Blood.* 2nd edition. New York: Farrar, Straus and Giroux, 1952.

Olivas, Michael A. *An Annotated Bibliography of John Updike Criticism 1967-1973, and a Checklist of His Works.* New York: Garland, 1975.

Otto, Rudolf. *The Idea of the Holy.* Translated by John W. Harvey. New York: Oxford University Press, 1958.

Ovid. *The Metamorphoses of Ovid.* Translated by Allen Mandlebaum. New York: Harcourt Brace, 1993.

Pasewark, Kyle A. "The Troubles with Harry: Freedom, America and God in John Updike's *Rabbit* Novels." *Religion and American Culture* 6, 1 (Winter 1996): 1-33.

Placher, William C. *Unapologetic Theology.* Philadelphia: Westminster Press, 1989.

Plath, James. "Verbal Vermeer: Updike's Middle-Class Portraiture." In *Rabbit Tales: Poetry and Politics in John Updike's Rabbit Novels,* ed. Lawrence R. Brorer, pp. 207-30. Tuscaloosa, AL: University of Alabama Press, 1998.

Plath, James, ed. *Conversations with John Updike.* Jackson, MS: University Press of Mississippi, 1994.

Price, Marie Daly. *Rajneeshpuram and the American Utopian Tradition.* Discussion Paper Series No. 87. Syracuse, NY: Department of Geography, Syracuse University, 1985.

Pritchard, William H. "A Journey into the Future." *Wall Street Journal,* 8 October 1997, p. A20.

Ristoff, Dilvo I. *John Updike's "Rabbit at Rest": Appropriating History.* Modern American Literature Series, Volume 18. New York: Peter Lang, 1998.

———. *Updike's America: The Presence of Contemporary American History in John Updike's Rabbit Trilogy.* American University Studies, Series 24: American Literature, Volume 2. New York: Peter Lang, 1988.

Rothstein, Mervyn. "The Origin of the Universe, Time and John Updike." *New York Times,* 21 November 1985, p. C21.

Rubin, Merle. "This Brightly Hued, Lushly Lurid Romance." *The Christian Science Monitor,* 14 February 1994, p. 15.

Searles, George. *The Fiction of Philip Roth and John Updike.* Carbondale, IL: Southern Illinois University Press, 1985.

Schiff, James A. *John Updike Revisited.* New York: Twayne, 1998.

———. "Updike's Meditation on Aging, Time, and the Universe." *Cincinnati Enquirer,* 7 October 1997, p. D4.

———. *Updike's Version: Rewriting "The Scarlet Letter."* Columbia, MO: University of Missouri Press, 1992.

Schlesinger, Arthur M., Jr. *The Vital Center: The Politics of Freedom.* Boston: Houghton Mifflin, 1962.

Sheed, Francis Joseph, ed. *Soundings in Satanism: A Collection of Essays.* New York: Sheed and Ward, 1972.

Smith, Kent D. *Faith: Reflections on Experience, Theology, and Fiction.* Lanham, MD: University Press of America, 1983.

Tallent, Elizabeth. *Married Men and Magic Tricks.* Berkeley, CA: Creative Arts Book Co., 1982.

Tanner, Tony. *City of Words: American Fiction 1950-1970.* London: Jonathan Cape, 1971.

Taylor, C. Clarke. *John Updike: A Bibliography* [1949-1967]. Kent, OH: Kent State University Press, 1968.

Taylor, Charles. *Sources of the Self: The Making of Modern Identity.* Cambridge, MA: Harvard University Press, 1989.

Taylor, Larry E. *Pastoral and Anti-Pastoral Patterns in John Updike's Fic-*

tion. Preface by Harry E. Moore. Carbondale, IL: Southern Illinois University Press, 1971.

Thompson, Judith, and Paul Heelas. *The Way of the Heart: The Rajneesh Movement*. San Bernardino, CA: Borgo Press, 1988.

Thorburn, David, and Howard Eiland, eds. *John Updike: A Collection of Critical Essays*. Englewood Cliffs, NJ: Prentice Hall, 1979.

Tillich, Paul. *Systematic Theology*. 3 vols. in 1. Chicago: University of Chicago Press, 1967.

Tolstoy, Leo. *The Death of Ivan Ilych and Other Stories*. Translated by Aylmer Maude. New York: Penguin, 1960.

Trachtenberg, Stanley, ed. *New Essays on "Rabbit, Run."* Cambridge: University of Cambridge Press, 1993.

Turra, Cleusa, and Bustavo Venturini, eds. *Racismo Cordial: a Mais Completa Análise sobre O Preconceito de Cor no Brasil* [Cordial racism: the most complete analysis of color prejudice in Brazil]. São Paula: Editora Atica, 1995.

Unamuno, Miguel de. *The Tragic Sense of Life in Men and Nations*. Translated by Anthony Kerrigan. Princeton, NJ: Princeton University Press, 1972.

Uphaus, Suzanne Henning. *John Updike*. New York: Frederick Ungar, 1980.

Van Leer, David. "Hester's Labyrinth: Transcendental Rhetoric in Puritan Boston." In *New Essays on "The Scarlet Letter,"* edited by Michael J. Colacurcid. Cambridge: Cambridge University Press, 1986.

Vargo, Edward P. *Rainstorms and Fire: Ritual in the Novels of John Updike*. Port Washington, NY: Kennikat, 1973.

Vaughan, Philip H. *John Updike's Images of America*. Reseda, CA: Mojave, 1981.

Vaughn, Henry. "The World." In *The Norton Anthology of English Literature* Sixth Edition, ed. M. H. Abrams, 1:1407-8. New York: W. W. Norton, 1993.

Vickery, John B. *Robert Graves and the White Goddess*. Lincoln, NE: University of Nebraska Press, 1972.

Vidal, Gore. "Rabbit's Own Burrow." *The Times Literary Supplement*, 26 April 1996, pp. 3-7.

Wake, Bob. *Infinite Jest: Reviews, Articles, and Miscellany*. [Online.] Available from www.smallbytes.net/~bobkat/observer2.html.

Wallace, David Foster. "John Updike, Champion Literary Phallocrat,

Drops One; Is This Finally the End for Magnificent Narcissists?" *The New York Observer,* 13 October 1997, p. 1.

Webb, Stephen H. *Re-Figuring Theology: The Rhetoric of Karl Barth.* Albany, NY: SUNY Press, 1991.

Weber, Max. *The Sociology of Religion.* Translated by Ephraim Fischoff. Boston: Beacon Press, 1963.

Williams, William Carlos. *The Autobiography of William Carlos Williams.* New York: New Directions Publishing, 1951.

———. *Selected Letters.* Edited by John C. Thirlwall. New York: McDowell, Obolensky, 1957.

Wingren, Gustaf. *Luther on Vocation.* Translated by Carl C. Rasmussen. Philadelphia: Muhlenberg Press, 1957.

Wolkstein, Diane, and Samuel Noah Kramer. *Inanna: Queen of Heaven and Earth.* New York: Harper & Row, 1983.

Wood, James. *The Broken Estate: Essays on Literature and Belief.* New York: Random House, 1999.

Wood, Ralph C. *The Comedy of Redemption: Christian Faith and Comic Vision in Four American Novelists.* Notre Dame, IN: University of Notre Dame Press, 1988.

———. "Into the Void: Updike's Sloth and America's Religion." *The Christian Century,* 24 April 1996, pp. 452-57.

Yeats, W. B. "The Second Coming." In *Collected Poems of W. B. Yeats.* New York: Macmillan, 1956.

Yerkes, James. "Beyond Time, Death and the Cosmos." *The Christian Century,* 19-26 November 1997, pp. 1079-83.

———. "Time as a Pitiable but Delicious Reprieve." *Theology Today* 54, 4 (January 1998): 529-31.

Internet Websites

"The Centaurian: A Home Page for John Updike Information and Discussion." http://www.users.fast.net/~joyerkes.

"John Updike: Life & Times." *The New York Times* on the Web. http://www.nytimes.com/books/97/04/06/lifetimes/updike.html.

Contributors

Charles Berryman is Professor of English and American Literature at the University of Southern California. His published works include *From Wilderness to Wasteland: The Trial of the Puritan God in the American Imagination* and *Decade of Novels: Fiction of the 1970s.*

Marshall Boswell is Assistant Professor of English at Rhodes College in Memphis, Tennessee. His article "The Black Jesus: Racism and Redemption in John Updike's *Rabbit Redux*" has been published in *Contemporary Literature* (Spring 1998).

George S. Diamond is Professor of English at Moravian College in Bethlehem, Pennsylvania.

Donald J. Greiner holds the Chair of Carolina Distinguished Professor of English at the University of South Carolina in Columbia, South Carolina, where he is Associate Provost and Dean of Undergraduate Affairs. His published works include *The Other John Updike; John Updike's Novels;* and *Adultery in the American Novel: Updike, James, and Hawthorne.*

Avis Hewitt is Visiting Assistant Professor of English at Grand Valley State University in Grand Rapids, MI. Her article "Hasidic Hallowing and Christian Consecration: Awakening to Authenticity in Denise Leverton's 'Matins'" has been published in *Renascence* (1998).

Darrell Jodock is the Drell and Adeline Bernhardson Distinguished Professor of Religion at Gustavus Adolphus College in St. Peter, Minnesota. He has published *The Church's Bible: Its Contemporary Authority; Ritschl in Retrospect: History, Community, and Science;* and *Catholicism Contending with Modernity: Roman Catholic Modernism and Anti-Modernism in Historical Context.*

Wesley A. Kort is Professor of Religion in the Department of Religion and the Graduate Department of Religion at Duke University. His published works include *Moral Fiber: Character and Belief in Recent American Fiction; Modern Fiction and Human Time; Bound to Differ: The Dynamics of Theological Discourses;* and *"Take, Read": Scripture, Textuality, and Cultural Practice.*

David Malone is Assistant Professor of English at Union University in Jackson, Tennessee.

Judie Newman holds the Chair of American Studies at the University of Nottingham, UK, and is a Fellow of the Royal Society of Arts. Her published works include *Saul Bellow and History; John Updike;* and *Dred: A Tale of the Great Dismal Swamp, by Harriet Beecher Stowe.*

Kyle A. Pasewark is currently studying at Yale Law School. He has published *A Theology of Power: Being Beyond Domination* and *The Emphatic Christian Center: Reforming American Political Practice.*

James Plath is Professor of English at Illinois Wesleyan University in Bloomington, Illinois. He has published *Conversations with John Updike* and is coauthor of *Remembering Ernest Hemingway* with Frank Simons.

Dilvo I. Ristoff is Professor of English and American Literature and Provost of Undergraduate Studies at the Federal University of Santa Catarina, Brazil. He has published *Updike's America: The Presence of Contemporary American History in John Updike's Rabbit Trilogy* and *John Updike's Rabbit at Rest: Appropriating History.*

James A. Schiff is Adjunct Assistant Professor of English at the University of Cincinnati. He has published *Updike's Version: Rewriting "The Scarlet Letter"; Understanding Reynolds Price; Critical Essays on Reynolds Price;* and *John Updike Revisited.*

Stephen H. Webb is Associate Professor of Religion and Philosophy at Wabash College in Crawfordsville, Indiana. His published works include *Blessed Excess: Religion and the Hyperbolic Imagination; Re-Figuring Theology: The Rhetoric of Karl Barth;* and *On God and Dogs: A Christian Theology of Compassion for Animals.*

James Yerkes is Professor of Religion and Philosophy at Moravian College in Bethlehem, Pennsylvania. He has published *The Christology of Hegel.*

Index